Counseling Office
2004/2005

KAPLAN®

Other Kaplan Books Relating to College Admissions

SAT* OR ACT*?

TEST YOUR BEST*

Seppy Basili, Maureen Blair, Gordon Drummond
and the Staff of Kaplan Educational Centers

Simon & Schuster

Kaplan Books
Published by Kaplan Educational Centers and Simon & Schuster
1230 Avenue of the Americas
New York, NY 10020

Editor: Doreen Beauregard
Production Editor: Maude Spekes
Cover Designer: Amy McHenry
Desktop Coordinator: Gerard Capistrano
Assistant Managing Editor: Brent Gallenberger
Managing Editor: Kiernan McGuire
Executive Editor: Del Franz

Manufactured in the United States of America
Published simultaneously in Canada

July 1997

Cataloging-in-Publication data on file with the Library of Congress

ISBN 0-684-84162-2

Contents

ABOUT THE AUTHORS

Seppy Basili is the director of precollege programs for Kaplan Educational Centers. He supervises the development of Kaplan's ACT, SAT, PSAT, and college admissions courses, books, videos, software, online services, and private tutoring for the college entrance exams. He is also the editor of the Kaplan/*Newsweek* guide entitled *How to Get Into College.*

Maureen Blair has focused mainly on SAT, PSAT, ACT, and other pre-college curriculum in her four years at Kaplan, and has also taught and tutored students for these exams. She graduated from Wellesley College with a B.A. in English literature, and plans to complete her M.A. in that discipline. Maureen is an avid reader and film watcher, and also enjoys studying the Italian language and culture.

Gordon Drummond has worked in SAT, ACT, LSAT, GMAT, and GRE course development at Kaplan for over six years. He received his M.A. in English literature from University of Edinburgh in Scotland, and is currently taking a B.F.A. in jazz at the New School of Social Research in New York City. When he's not conjuring up fiendish new test questions, he plays the saxophone.

How to Use This Book

For more than 50 years, Kaplan has prepared students to take SATs and ACTs. Our team of teachers and researchers knows more about test preparation than anyone else, and you'll find their accumulated experience and knowledge in this book. As you work your way through each chapter, we'll show you exactly what skills and strategies you need to do your best on the SAT or ACT. You'll discover the most effective way to tackle each type of question, and you'll reinforce that learning with a lot of practice questions and explanations. By recording your results as you go on the "SAT or ACT? Score Comparison Chart" (on page 211), you'll be able to gauge which test you're performing better on—giving you the information you need to organize your study time and decide which test you'll take. At the back of the book, you'll find practice sets for both tests with answer keys and detailed explanations.

Get Ready to Prep

If you're not opening this chapter at the last minute, plan to work through this book bit by bit over the course of a few weeks. Don't fall prey to "the dog ate my homework" syndrome—cramming the week before the test is not a good idea. You can often review material you've *already* learned at the last minute, but it's difficult to absorb much *new* information at that point.

Get the Inside Story

Before you run out and order SAT or ACT registration forms, take some time to familiarize yourself with the admissions process. Chapter 1 provides you with an overview of the admissions process, mapping out the strategic issues that could influence your decision on which test to take. This chapter also introduces you to the question types that appear on the SAT and the ACT, contrasting the skills required for success on each test.

Know the Test Format

If you're new to the SAT or ACT, you should get familiar with the format of each test first. Understanding this overall structure is key to success on standardized tests; you'll perform much better if you know what to expect on each section, understand how to pace yourself, and know when to guess.

For example, did you realize that there are 75 questions on the ACT English section, but you have only 45 minutes to answer them? This means that on the English section you'll have only a minute to scan each passage, and less than 30 seconds to answer each question. But since ACT English tests *commonsense* understanding of grammar, the answers are usually pretty straightforward. In addition, since the test makers realize that you're under time pressure, the conversion scale is weighted accordingly—which means that you can get as many as ten questions wrong and still get a great score!

Chapter 2 focuses on mastery of the SAT and ACT. In that chapter, we'll explain how understanding the format of the SAT and ACT can help you develop a strategic approach on the day of the test. Knowing what to expect can save you a lot of anxiety when you sit down to confront the real thing. In addition, understanding how these tests function can help you decide which test to take.

Learn Skills, Strategies, and Test-Taking Techniques

Once you've got the big picture, it's time to learn some of the problem-solving skills you need for success on the day of the test. In Chapters 3 through 7, we'll cover Kaplan's proven strategies for every question type that appears on the SAT and ACT. You'll learn the step-by-step methods that successful test takers use to answer questions quickly and confidently. We'll guide you through some of the tempting wrong-answer "traps" that appear on each test, showing you how to avoid them. Along the way, you'll complete practice quizzes (with explanations) that will help you assess your strengths and weaknesses, and compare your performance on SAT and ACT questions.

Need More Help?
If you finish this book and decide you need to study more for the SAT or ACT, or that you simply need more practice material, you should definitely consider buying some of Kaplan's other titles to supplement your preparation. For more strategies for SAT and ACT success, and practice material that's just like the real test, look for the following titles at your nearest bookstore:

- *SAT 1998*
- *ACT 1998*
- *SAT Math Workbook*
- *SAT Verbal Workbook*

Hone Your Skills

At the back of the book, you'll find SAT and ACT practice sets subdivided by topic (for example, Analogies, Reading Comprehension, Quantitative Comparisons) that will enable you to *hone* your testing skills. If you're comfortable with the material, work through ten questions at a time, or even an entire practice set in one sitting. If you're not so comfortable, try two or three questions at a time, checking your answers against the explanations at the back of the book.

SAT or ACT? Tracking Your Performance

The best way to find out which test you'll perform better on is to take a whirl through the practice quizzes and practice sets for each test, monitoring your comfort level and success rate as you go. At Kaplan, we call this *taking a test drive.* To track your performance on these practice questions, enter your results in the "SAT or ACT? Score Comparison Chart" on page 211. This will allow you to compare your strengths in each subject area, test to test. For example, you'll find out whether you're more comfortable on ACT English or SAT Analogies; it could influence your decision on which test to take.

Take a Break Before the Day of the Test

If possible, don't study the night before the test. Relax! Read a book or watch a movie. Get a good night's sleep. Eat a light breakfast the morning of the test and quickly review a few questions if you feel like it (just enough to get your mind on the test). Walk into the test center with confidence—you're ready!

A Special Note for International Students

Approximately 500,000 international students pursued academic degrees at the undergraduate, graduate, or professional school level at U.S. universities during the 1995–1996 academic year, according to the Institute of International Education's *Open Doors* report. Almost 50 percent of these students were studying for a bachelor's or first university degree. This trend of pursuing higher education in the United States is expected to continue well into the next century. Business, management, engineering, and the physical and life sciences are particularly popular majors for students coming to the United States from other countries.

If you are not from the United States, but are considering attending a U.S. college or university, here's what you'll need to get started:

- If English is not your first language, start there. You'll probably need to take the Test of English as a Foreign Language (TOEFL) and the Test of Written English (TWE), or show some other evidence that you are fully proficient in English in order to complete an academic degree program. Colleges and universities in the United States will differ on what they consider to be an acceptable TOEFL score. A minimum TOEFL score of 550 or better is often expected by the more prestigious and competitive institutions. Because American undergraduate programs require all students to take a certain number of general education courses, all students, even math and computer science students, need to be able to communicate well in spoken and written English.
- You may also need to take the SAT or the ACT. Many undergraduate institutions in the United States require both the SAT and TOEFL of international students.
- There are over 2,700 accredited colleges and universities in the United States, so selecting the correct undergraduate school can be a confusing task for anyone. You will need to get help from a good advisor or at least a good college guide that explains the different types of programs and gives you some information on how to choose wisely. Since admission to many undergraduate programs is quite competitive, you may also want to select three or four colleges and complete applications for each school.
- You should begin the application process at least a year in advance. An increasing number of schools accept applications year round. In any case, find out the application deadlines and plan accordingly. Although September (the fall semester) is the traditional time to begin university study in the United States, at most schools you can also enter in January (the spring semester).

- Finally, you will need to obtain an I-20 Certificate of Eligibility in order to obtain an F-1 Student Visa to study in the United States. This you will request from the university. The school will send you the I-20 document once you have been accepted.

For details about the admissions requirements, curriculum, and other vital information on top colleges and universities, see Kaplan's *Road to College*.

Access America™

If you need more help with the complex process of undergraduate school admissions and information about the variety of programs available, you may be interested in Kaplan's Access America program.

Kaplan created Access America to assist students and professionals from outside the United States who want to enter the U.S. university system. The program was designed for students who have received the bulk of their primary and secondary education outside the United States in a language other than English. Access America also has programs for obtaining professional certification in the United States. Here's a brief description of some of the help available through Access America.

The TOEFL Plus Program

At the heart of the Access America program is the intensive TOEFL Plus Academic English program. This comprehensive English course prepares students to achieve a high level of proficiency in English in order to successfully complete an academic degree. The TOEFL Plus course combines personalized instruction with guided self-study to help students gain this proficiency in a short time. Certificates of Achievement in English are awarded to certify each student's level of proficiency.

Undergraduate School/SAT or ACT Preparation

If your goal is to complete a bachelor of arts (B.A.) or bachelor of science (B.S.) degree in the United States, Kaplan will help you prepare for the SAT or ACT, while helping you understand the American system of education.

Applying to Access America

To get more information, or to apply for admission to any of Kaplan's programs for international students or professionals, you can write to us at:

Kaplan Educational Centers
International Admissions Department
888 Seventh Avenue, New York, NY 10106

Or call us at 1-800-522-7770 from within the United States, or 01-212-262-4980 outside the United States. Our fax number is 01-212-957-1654. Our E-mail address is world@kaplan.com. You can also get more information or even apply through the Internet at http://www.kaplan.com/intl.

1 SAT or ACT? A Strategic Approach

Often portrayed as "the road to college," the admissions process can sometimes seem more like a maze. Before you even set foot on campus, there are forms to fill out, deadlines to meet, interviews to schedule, visits to make, catalogs to read, letters to write. Students and parents alike are likely to find the whole process bewildering and aggravating, not to mention very, very tense. Add to this the complication of choosing the right admissions test to take—SAT or ACT?—and you've got a headache the whole family can share.

You might wonder why you have to choose between the SAT and the ACT—maybe one of the two is favored by the students in your school. Ten or 20 years ago, choosing which test to take wasn't even an issue. Until recently, the ACT was traditionally required by colleges in the midwest, and the SAT was the test of choice in the northeast and on the east and west coasts. But now an increasing number of students are taking the ACT, and the majority of schools in the United States now accept *both* SAT or ACT test results.

This increased acceptance of the ACT gives today's savvy students a strategic advantage. The SAT and ACT are *significantly* different tests, and in many ways, they measure different skills. So depending on your particular strengths and weaknesses, you may perform much better on one test than the other. As a result, many students embarking on the admissions process are now considering *both* the SAT and ACT—to figure out which test provides a better showcase for their abilities. Here are some of the factors that make the SAT and ACT very different breeds:

- The ACT includes a science reasoning test; the SAT does not.
- The ACT math section includes trigonometry.
- The SAT tests vocabulary much more than the ACT.
- The SAT is not entirely multiple choice.
- The SAT has a guessing penalty; the ACT does not.
- The ACT tests English grammar; the SAT does not.

Confused about which test to take? This book is designed to help you choose the test that's right for you. Every test taker has different strengths, depending on his or her education and background. This book gives you the lowdown on the skills and strategies required for success on each test, showing you which areas you test your best on—and which areas might require a little work! Understanding the format of the test is key to success on standardized tests, so we'll analyze the format of the SAT and ACT to help you develop a strategic approach on guessing, pacing, and avoiding trap answers. Finally, we'll give you sets of practice SAT and ACT questions to drill on, so that you can compare your performance on equivalent sections on each test.

The rest of this book is devoted to helping you understand these tests and improve your performance on them. But before we start honing those SAT and ACT skills into tools of laser-like intensity and surgical precision, let's take a step back and discuss the role of these tests in the admissions process.

The Purpose of Standardized Tests

While the SAT and ACT are very different tests, they both fulfill the same role in the admissions process. The SAT and ACT are designed to provide college admissions officers with two things: a predictor of first-year academic achievement in college, and a common yardstick to use in comparing students from a wide range of educational backgrounds.

The Power of Prediction

Ever wonder why the SAT contains such a weird mix of different types of questions (for example, Analogies, Sentence Completions, Quantitative Comparisons, Grid-ins)? There's method to the madness. In order to figure out whether you're ready for the demands of college, the test makers specifically attempt to put together a test that simulates the challenges of your first year in school: college-level reading, advanced vocabulary, critical thinking, and advanced math. In fact, the College Board regularly conducts a study to make sure that high school GPA and SAT scores combined have a high correlation with freshman GPAs.

The Big School Difference
Bigger schools tend to rely on the SAT and ACT scores more than smaller ones because they have many more applications to sift through. Scores give them a quicker method of comparing students and cut down on their horrendous workload. It ain't pretty, but it's true!

An Inch Is as Good as a Yard

Let's consider the concept of a "common yardstick" for a moment. Colleges place a high priority on standardized test scores because it's the one part of every student's application that's a known quantity. In an ideal world, admissions decisions would be based entirely on your achievements as a high school student (your GPA, teacher recommendations, number of advanced courses taken, etcetera). But since the quality of education and assessment varies so much from one school to the next, admissions folks are forced to rely on SAT and ACT test scores to help them sort out the deluge of candidates.

The Strategic Approach to Admissions

Getting a high score is obviously the most direct way of maximizing your chances of acceptance. But can your choice of test also influence your prospects? Yes and no. Most colleges throughout the United States now accept *both* the SAT and ACT, and use equivalence tables to assess the competitiveness of your score in relation to other students. (See the comparison table on the next page.) So whichever test you ultimately take, admissions officers have the information to give you a fair hearing.

Equipercentile Concordance Table

The following chart is provided for admissions officers by ACT, Inc. (Reprinted with permission)

ACT Composite Score	Concordant SAT Verbal and Math Score	ACT Composite Score	Concordant SAT Verbal and Math Score	ACT Composite Score	Concordant SAT Verbal and Math Score
36	1600	27	1220	18	870
35	1550	26	1180	17	830
34	1520	25	1140	16	790
33	1470	24	1110	15	740
32	1420	23	1070	14	690
31	1380	22	1030	13	640
30	1340	21	990	12	590
29	1300	20	950	11	550
28	1260	19	910		

Better the Test You Know . . .
Even though most colleges now accept both SAT and ACT scores, familiarity is an important factor in the admissions process. If most students in your state take the SAT, for example, and you take the ACT, admission officers may wonder why. Admissions officers may also exercise personal preferences; for example, some prefer the ACT because it yields a wider range of subscores (Science, English, Reading, and Math).

ACT—One Size Fits All

Can you imagine how much time you have spent taking and preparing for tests by the time you've reached junior year? Probably a semester if you were to add it all together. One good reason for considering the ACT is that it may save you from having to take *four* SAT tests. We kid you not! Many competitive colleges now require applicants to take both the SAT I Reasoning Test and up to three SAT II Subject Tests (there are 22 of them—ranging from Chemistry to Japanese Listening). The SAT II Subject Tests are achievement tests designed to measure how much you know about a particular subject.

But here's the exciting part. There are a number of schools—including Bryn Mawr, Boston College, and Duke—that do not require you to take SAT II tests *if you take the ACT.* So taking the ACT might save you hours of testing (and even more hours of preparation), and save you or your parents money. **Note:** Before you get psyched about the one-size-fits-all ACT, keep in mind that these policies vary from school to school. There are a number of schools that require the SAT II regardless of their ACT or SAT I requirements.

Repeat Testing

How many times should you take the test? At Kaplan, we advocate preparing as if you've got only one chance to take the test. This means investing in the study time required to get a higher score—that is, using a thorough study guide (you're holding one right now) or taking a preparation course. But naturally not everyone performs their best the first time around, and the beauty of standardized tests is that you've got a second chance or more if necessary.

Here are the answers to some common student inquiries about repeat testing:

- *If I take the test more than once, will this count against me?*
  Absolutely not. If you improve, you'll improve your chances of acceptance, and many admissions officers regard repeated testing as evidence of your commitment.

The Golden Rule
The golden rule with SAT/ACT admissions is to check with your target schools about their requirements. If you have specific colleges in mind, find out from the schools or your guidance counselor which exam the schools require or prefer. Certain programs and scholarships also require specific tests.

- *Do colleges look at my highest score, or average them out?*

This varies from school to school. Some schools average your scores, and many just take your highest score, taking into consideration how many times you've taken the test.

- *When should I start preparing?*

Prepare early (junior year or before) and test early—in the spring of your junior year. This gives you the chance to retake the test if you need a higher score, without delaying your college application.

- *I have to take SAT IIs too—when should I take these?*

The bottom line for SAT IIs is to take them whenever your related course work is still fresh in your mind. So it's a good idea to take them in June of the year in which you finish the subjects concerned. If you're taking multiple tests, though, make sure you stagger the test dates—taking several tests all at once can be stressful and counterproductive.

The Admissions Process

Although it's easy to obsess about SAT and ACT test scores, they usually aren't the primary factor in admissions decisions. Admissions officers generally state that a student's academic record is the most influential part of his or her application. However, for the reasons we've just discussed, course work and grades are not always a reliable source of information, so to get a more complete picture, colleges consider a *range* of factors in evaluating a candidate:

- **Courses.** Did you take demanding academic courses? Regardless of how well you performed in your favorite classes, high grades in introductory calculus are more highly respected than high grades in batik or hangliding.

- **Grades.** What were your grades, and how competitive is your school? Obviously, earning good grades at Egghead High puts you in a better position than earning good grades at a less competitive school. In particular, admissions officers will consider how good your grades were at the end of junior year, and how consistent your grades were in senior year.
- **Standardized Test Scores.** What was your overall percentile ranking, and what was your performance in each subject area? If you're applying to a school with a strong English or science program, for example, the school may specifically look at your performance in the related areas on the test.
- **Counselor/teacher recommendations**. Competitive colleges, particularly the smaller ones, put a lot of emphasis on these. Teacher recommendations are useful because they provide insight into a student's work rate and behavior in a class setting.
- **Personal statement.** Admissions officers rate these highly. It's their one opportunity to find out about a student's goals and aspirations, and to get a flavor for the applicant's personality.

Food for Thought
If you think *applying* to college is tortuous, imagine the task confronting a college admissions officer every spring: thousands of applications to review, from students of all abilities, each of whom may have something promising to offer.

Maximize Your Test Scores

So the good news is that test scores on the SAT and ACT *aren't* all-important: they're only one of several factors that colleges consider. But that doesn't mean you should put your SAT or ACT preparation on the back burner. Au contraire! Arguably the smartest, most strategic move you can make toward improving your college application is to put some serious time into getting ready for these tests. If you think about it, you work for *years* at school trying to raise your grades, get into better courses, and earn your counselor/teacher recommendations. But as little as ten or 20 hours invested in preparing for the SAT or ACT can bring you a higher score, giving you a better shot at the school of your choice!

Choosing the Best Test

To figure out which test is best for you, you've got to understand the nature of the beasts. Admissions officers and educators often describe the difference between SAT and ACT in these terms: the ACT is a content-based test, whereas the SAT tests critical thinking and problem solving. This perception is one reason why many educators (off the record) express a preference for the ACT—because they believe that the ACT is closer to testing the "core curriculum" taught in most school classrooms. In fact, this contrast isn't exactly watertight. As you'll see in working through this book, many questions on the ACT test critical thinking, and there *is* a predictable range of material that's tested on the SAT. But the SAT and ACT reward different attributes, so performing well on each test can all boil down to what kind of test taker you are.

Let's compare the skills you need for each test, section-by-section.

The Verbal Sections

SAT Analogies and Sentence Completions

Here's a question to ask yourself before you consider taking the SAT. Say you're reading an article, and you come across one or two difficult or unfamiliar words. You have no idea what the words mean, but you have to finish your school report in time to watch the latest episode of *Alien Encounters*. Do you handle the situation with *aplomb*—or does the whole situation throw you into a *paroxysm*?

Verbal Remedies
There are 19 Analogies and 19 Sentence Completions on every SAT. To test your best, you'll want to move quickly through these short questions (aim for about 40 seconds per question) leaving more time for Critical Reading.

One skill that's particularly important on the SAT is the ability to figure out the meaning of unfamiliar words from context. Often regarded as straight tests of vocabulary, Analogies and Sentence Completions on the SAT more often than not test your ability to work your way around tough vocabulary, using your reasoning skills. On Sentence Completions, for example, you're asked to identify the word or pair of words that most logically *completes* a sentence:

1. Despite the government's show of ----, intelligence reports indicated that they were on the verge of agreeing to a truce.

    (A) decrepitude
    (B) mendacity
    (C) altruism
    (D) intransigence
    (E) congeniality

Not Just a Test of Vocabulary
Possessing a good vocabulary is definitely helpful on SAT Sentence Completions and Analogies. But equally important is your ability to *work your way around* tough vocabulary, using your reasoning skills.

If you weren't familiar with tough vocab words such as *mendacity* or *altruism,* a tough Sentence Completion like this one might seem impossible to solve. But Sentence Completions aren't just a test of vocabulary—and this means that you can use your reasoning skills to crack the toughest questions. First of all, you can use structural clues in each sentence to predict the meaning of the missing word. Here, the word *despite* gives you a huge clue that the missing word contrasts with *on the verge of agreeing to a truce.* So you could predict that the missing word means something like "not flexible," "warlike," or "uncompromising." Then you would check the answer choices to see which word matches—and it's choice (D), intransigence, which means "refusal to move."

The ability to work around tough vocabulary to figure out word meanings is equally important on SAT Analogies. The odd-looking SAT Analogy tests your ability to figure out the relationships between pairs of words. At first glance, Analogies also look like a straight vocabulary test—either you know the word, or you don't. But in reality, the toughest Analogies can be solved using your innate reasoning skills and some strategic thinking. For example, here's the kind of tough Analogy you might see on your SAT:

2. RECLUSE : GREGARIOUS ::

 (A) savage : civilized
 (B) editor : painstaking
 (C) zealot : religious
 (D) philanthropist : eccentric
 (E) librarian : reserved

Your task here is to identify the relationship between RECLUSE and GREGARIOUS, picking the answer choice that fits this relationship best. If you didn't know either word, you might have thought it was a hopeless situation. The truth is, though, you know more about these words than you think! For example, you already know their parts of speech. Scanning the words in each column, you can tell that the words in the left are all types of people (nouns), and the words on the right are all descriptive (adjectives). Once you've done your homework (that is, read the rest of this book) you'll know that all stem pairs on the Analogy section (and all correct answers) have *strong bridges*—they are linked by a strong and necessary connection. Using this knowledge, you can figure out that a RECLUSE must either be someone who's *very* GREGARIOUS, or who's by definition *not* GREGARIOUS. Looking at the available answer choices, choice (A), savage : civilized, should pop out as a good answer—a savage is a person who is by definition *not* civilized.

ACT English

Not so good at working your way around knotty vocabulary problems? Then ACT English might be a better challenge for you. The ACT English section tests your understanding of standard written English through a series of sentence- and paragraph-correction questions based on reading passages. If you're a budding writer—or better yet, if you're the kind of reader who can spot a grammatical, punctuation, or stylistic flub when you see one—ACT English might be right up your alley.

Success on ACT English is all about using your ear. The most commonly heard misconception about this section is that you need to remember all the grammar rules you've been taught since fifth grade. Not true. The ACT doesn't test arcane grammar rules; it tests your ability to identify and correct garbled or redundant prose, using your logic and your common sense. There *are* a few hard-and-fast grammar rules you should bone up on before the test, but it's nothing you'd need a Ph.D. to tackle. Here is a sample of the kind of questions you'll encounter on the ACT English section:

It used to be that when people wanted to see a scary movie, they could choose from films such as *Dracula* and *Frankenstein*. But these classic monster movies, with an occasional exception, <u>has been replaced</u> (3) by a new breed of horror <u>film the</u> (4) slasher movie. It is interesting and perhaps somewhat disturbing to examine the implications of such changes in taste.

3. A. NO CHANGE
   B. have been replaced
   C. were being replaced
   D. replaced

4. F. NO CHANGE
   G. film, which is the
   H. film: the
   J. film known, as the

Question 3 involves a subject/verb agreement problem. Even though the word *exception* appears before the verb, the subject is *movies*—so you need a plural verb, as provided in choice (B). But even without knowing the terminology, your ear should tell you that *has* just sounds wrong; *have* sounds like it matches better.

ACT English also tests your punctuation smarts. Question 4 runs together a trend and its definition: a new breed of horror film and the slasher movie. To make a logical connection, you need either punctuation or a connecting phrase. Choices (G) and (J) are too wordy, but (H)'s colon works just fine.

English Spoken Here
ACT English is a 45-minute section that contains 75 questions, based on five passages. To get a good score, you'll need to move quickly through each passage, answering each question in no more than 20–30 seconds.

The Reading Question

In 1993, the College Board revised the format of the SAT to reflect the needs of a changing educational system. Among the changes: straight vocabulary questions (Antonyms) were discarded, new student-entered math question types were introduced (Grid-ins), and the Reading Comprehension section was updated and renamed the Critical Reading section. So what's in a name? Quite a lot, actually. In fact, the term *Critical Reading* is key to illustrating the difference between the reading sections on the SAT and ACT.

The Critical Reading sections on the SAT test what educators call "critical thinking skills." You're given four passages from different subject areas (humanities, social sciences, science, narrative), each written with a strong authorial point of view. Topics from previous SATs, for example, have included passages about threats to animal habitats, the beauty of Navajo art, and the

The Critical Difference
On the SAT, you'll encounter 40 Critical Reading questions, based on four passages. One of these passages will be a "paired passage" consisting of two passages written by two different writers on a similar topic. Three to four paired-passage questions will ask you to compare and contrast both authors' points of view.

early experiences of immigrants. The questions that accompany SAT passages revolve around interpreting the underlying points of words, phrases, or examples, and relating these details to the author's overall argument. Here's an example of such a question:

5. Which of the following would most weaken the author's thesis concerning the wolves' "strong feeling of property" (line 60)?

   (A) Disputes over boundaries are a frequent occurrence.
   (B) Wolf territories are typically around 100 square miles in area.
   (C) Wolf families often wander from place to place to find food.
   (D) Territorial conflicts between wolves and human beings are rare.
   (E) Wolves are generally alert when encountering other animals.

To answer questions like this, you need to think like a "critical reader." This means understanding the passage on two levels: (1) being able to grasp the author's overall argument quickly, and (2) being able to interpret the purpose of the details as you read, and relate them to the big picture.

ACT Reading Comprehension (as its name suggests) is a little more straightforward than SAT Critical Reading. As on the SAT, you're given four reading passages from four different areas—but the passages are longer, more detailed, and more academic than SAT passages. Topics that have previously appeared on the ACT, for example, have included voting patterns in the United States, the appreciation of music, and an analysis of what happens when stars collapse. ACT Reading Comprehension isn't necessarily harder, however. To compensate for the length of the passages, ACT Reading questions often revolve around simply locating details and facts. Here's an example of such a question:

6. The shift in the direction of stratospheric winds that occurs every two years is known as

   F. a facula
   G. the solar flux
   H. North Atlantic storms
   J. the quasi-biennial oscillation

Comprehend This
On ACT Reading Comprehension, you're given 35 minutes to complete a section that includes four passages and 40 questions.

If SAT Critical Reading is like analyzing a debate, ACT Reading is a more like researching a term paper: it's about checking the facts and details, and making sure that you've got accurate information. If you're good at interpretation, you'll do well on the SAT. But if you're more of a quantitative thinker, you might be more comfortable on ACT Reading.

The Math Sections

The SAT and ACT both test you on the arithmetic, algebra, and geometry you've learned in high school, and both permit you to use a calculator as you attempt to answer the questions. But there are some big differences. Being aware of these distinctions, and understanding their implications for you as a test taker, is key to deciding which test is better for you.

Differences in Focus

The majority of the math material on the two exams is comparable, but there are some differences. The following content areas are not tested on the SAT, but are fair game on the ACT: trigonometry; graphs and equations of circles, ellipses, and parabolas; and the quadratic formula.

Beyond these distinctions in content, there is a difference in the focus of the questions. SAT questions often combine several concepts, and part of the challenge is figuring out just what you're asked to do. ACT math questions tend to be more straightforward, requiring you to call on a particular concept or formula. In fact, there's an "information" section included with the directions that head each SAT math section; this information section contains some key mathematic facts and formulas. This indicates that the people who make the SAT are interested in your ability to manipulate this information, not just memorize it.

On the ACT, however, if you don't remember the Pythagorean theorem, you're on your own. If you feel at ease with (and perhaps even enjoy) questions that call upon logical reasoning and visualization, you might prefer the SAT. But if you're more comfortable with straightforward, academically rigorous questions, you might prefer the ACT.

Differences in Format

Another big difference between the exams is in their formats. While all of the 60 ACT Math questions are tested in the five-choice multiple-choice format, there are three different question formats on the SAT.

There are three math sections on the SAT with a total of 60 questions. They're tested in three different question types: Regular Math, which is in the five-choice multiple choice format; Quantitative Comparisons (QCs), which ask you to compare two elements; and Grid-ins, which require you to fill in the answer (no multiple choice). The same content is tested across the board, but each type emphasizes slightly different skills. If the idea of switching gears like this appeals to you, SAT Math may be for you.

Regular Math on the SAT

The emphasis here is on problem solving, and selecting the correct answer from the five given. Having answer choices means that the correct answer is always right there in front of you, and that sometimes you can plug the choices into the question to see which is correct. But having answer choices can also

Question Breakdown

The SAT contains approximately equal numbers of arithmetic, algebra, and geometry questions, as well as some problems classified as "other," which include logical reasoning, probability, etcetera. The ACT provides much more specific information about its content. Each ACT Math subject test includes:

- 24 pre-algebra and elementary algebra questions
- 10 intermediate algebra questions
- 8 coordinate geometry questions
- 14 plane geometry questions
- 4 trigonometry questions

Regular Math
This question type represents all of the 60 ACT Math questions, and the majority of SAT Math questions, accounting for 35 of the 60 questions. These questions appear on two math sections: 25 on a 30-minute section and ten on a 15-minute math section.

mean that you'll be tempted by an appealing but wrong answer choice before giving the problem enough thought. Look at the following example:

7. Liza drives 60 miles to her friend's house at 20 miles per hour, and then later that day she returns home along the same route at 30 miles per hour. What was her average speed for the round trip, in miles per hour?

    (A) 23
    (B) 24
    (C) 25
    (D) 26
    (E) 27

Your first impulse might be to gravitate to choice (C): 20 + 30 = 50, so the average speed must be 25, right? Wrong. You can't just average the two speeds. You need to divide the total distance by the total time. In this case the total distance is 2(60) = 120. Driving 60 miles at 20 mph takes three hours and driving 60 miles at 30 mph takes two hours, for a total of five hours driving time. This means the average speed is $\frac{120}{5} = 24$, choice (B). To succeed on Regular Math questions it's important not to be hasty, and to avoid these kinds of traps by considering the problem instead of picking the first answer that appeals to you.

Quantitative Comparisons
There are 15 QCs in the 30-minute SAT math section. You should take about 10 minutes to do all the QCs, which works out to about 45 seconds each. Of course, you'll spend less time on the early QCs, and a little more on the tougher ones.

Quantitative Comparisons on the SAT

This is a question type that you won't have seen in high school, so it's important to get familiar with it and know what its directions mean before the day of the test. You're given quantities in two columns and are asked to compare them, choosing (A) if the quantity in Column A is greater, (B) if the quantity in Column B is greater, (C) if the quantities are equal, and (D) if you aren't given enough information to decide. Kaplan's QC mantra is, "Compare, don't calculate." These questions are meant to be done quickly, and it is often possible to determine the relationship between the columns without calculating their exact values. You're rewarded for finding quick, inventive ways to compare them, not for plodding through and computing their precise values. Check out the following example:

	Column A	Column B
8.	$1 - \frac{1}{1{,}000{,}000}$	$1 - \frac{1}{1{,}000{,}001}$

You could calculate the value of each column, but it's not necessary to determine the answer. In each column, you're subtracting some fraction from 1. Both fractions have the same numerator, so the larger fraction is the one with the smaller denominator. That means that the fraction in Column B is larger than the one in Column A. Since you're subtracting less in Column A, the result will be greater. So you could solve this QC without putting pencil to paper—or finger to calculator, as the case may be. You won't get any more points for figuring out the exact values in the columns, but you will waste precious time. As you can see, QCs are not about number crunching, but about quickly and intuitively spotting the relationship between expressions. If these are skills you possess, you'll breeze through this section with confidence.

Grid-Ins on the SAT

This is the only question type on the SAT that doesn't include answer choices. The questions vary like those on the Regular Math section, but you have to solve the problem without any prompting from choices and then fill in your answer on the special grid that's provided. Because you don't have choices to pick from, it's especially important to check your work, and watch out for careless mistakes. For this reason, a calculator can be very useful on this question type. Since the test makers don't give you a safety net by providing answer choices, they also don't penalize you for wrong answers. Consequently it really pays to guess on this question type. The nature of the grid makes some kinds of answers, such as negative numbers, impossible. This can alert you to computational errors and also help narrow down your guesses.

Grid-ins
Since Grid-ins don't give you choices, they take a little longer than Regular Math questions. If you move through the QCs at the recommended pace, you'll have about 15 minutes left for the Grid-in section. This will give you about a minute for each question, plus a few minutes to check your work and avoid careless mistakes.

Science Reasoning on the ACT

One of the first things we tell ACT students at Kaplan is that they don't need to be budding Einsteins to ace the ACT Science Reasoning section. You won't have to have the periodic table memorized or dredge up experimental procedures from your chemistry class. All the information you need to answer the questions is provided in the test booklet. What ACT Science Reasoning really tests (as the name implies) is your ability to think like a scientist—to draw conclusions from a set of data, to grasp the purpose of an experiment, or to identify the assumptions underlying a scientific theory. If you've dealt with these issues in science class, you just have to adjust to using them on the ACT. Here's an example:

The Appliance of Science
ACT Science Reasoning requires you to answer 40 questions in 35 minutes.

9. The results of the experiments suggest that an indigo bunting's ability to choose a migration direction depends on:

A. the visibility of familiar stars
B. seasonal temperature variations
C. whether it is raised indoors or outdoors
D. the presence of adult indigo buntings

Answering the Test Question

Whichever test you decide to take (and many students decide to take both!), it's important to make sure you're prepared for Test Day. Now that you've got an overall grasp of what each test is about, it's time to take a closer look at some of the skills and strategies that can earn you extra points. In this next chapter, we'll show you how to translate your understanding of the format of each test into a strategic advantage.

2 SAT or ACT? Strategies for Mastering Each Test

To perform well on standardized tests such as the SAT and ACT, you need to draw on a set of skills that the College Board and ACT do not mention in any of their registration materials: you need to be a good test taker. First and foremost, that means recognizing that the SAT and ACT are different from the tests you have grown accustomed to in high school—where you may often spend more time on difficult questions than you do on easy ones.

In the world of standardized tests, you are rewarded only for answering as many questions as you can correctly, regardless of their difficulty. You may actually lose points by spending more time on hard questions than on easy ones, or for going methodically through the test one question at a time!

In this chapter, we'll explain how understanding the formats of the SAT and ACT can help you develop a strategic approach on the day of the test. Knowing what to expect can save you a lot of anxiety when you sit down to confront the real thing. In addition, understanding how these tests function can also help you decide which test to take when you're applying to college.

The SAT and ACT Are Highly Predictable

The first thing to realize when you're prepping for the SAT and ACT is that you're not alone; millions of students take these tests every year as part of the college admissions process. Every time you take an SAT or ACT, your performance is compared with the performance of every other student who takes your test. In fact, the performance of your peer group is also equated with the scores of students who took the SAT or ACT five, ten or 15 years ago.

Should you be intimidated by the astronomical number of students involved in the testing process? No way. Believe it or not, you can use this fact to your advantage. To make students' scores comparable from one year to the next, the test makers go to great lengths to make sure that every SAT and ACT tests the *same range* of math, verbal, and (on the ACT) science skills. That's why they're called "standardized tests"—because each test is standardized in content and difficulty level.

A Different Kind of Test
The SAT and ACT are not like the tests you take in high school. Often, in school, you might need to get 85 or 90 percent of the questions right in order to get a decent score. On the SAT, you sometimes need to get about 75 percent of the questions correct to get a 1300—a very solid combined score. On the ACT, the average student gets about 50 percent of the questions right.

Because the SAT and ACT follow a standardized format, you can learn the setup of each of these exams in advance. This means that if you invest a little preparation time, there will be no surprises on the day of the test. And it also means that you can develop a strategic approach to each section to maximize your score.

Learn the Directions

One of the easiest things you can do to help your performance on the SAT or the ACT is understand the directions before taking the test. Since the instructions are always the same, there's no reason to waste time on the day of the test reading them. By learning them beforehand as you go through this book, you'll save valuable time. You need every second during the test to answer questions and get points.

For example, your directions for SAT Analogies will look pretty much like this:

> DIRECTIONS: Choose the lettered pair of words that is related in the same way as the pair in capital letters.
>
> FLAKE : SNOW ::
>
> (A) storm : hail
> (B) drop : rain
> (C) field : wheat
> (D) stack : hay
> (E) cloud : fog

Not exactly rocket science, is it? The test makers ask you to figure out which answer choice is related in the same way as FLAKE : SNOW (the answer is (B) drop : rain, because a drop is a unit of rain). Once you've read and understood these directions, there's no reason to read them again on the day of the test. Use the practice sets in this book to get familiar with all SAT and ACT directions.

The Power of Predicting
Don't just wade through the answer choices on the day of the test. Use the format to your advantage by first *predicting* your answer and then looking for an answer choice that matches.

Predict the Answer

The SAT and ACT are both largely multiple choice tests. But can you use this format knowledge to your advantage? You bet. Just consider how the test is constructed. To separate high-scoring students from the rest of the pack, the SAT and ACT test makers purposely include *tempting wrong answer choices* as traps.

The surest way to avoid falling for these traps is to *predict* the answer before you look at the answer choices. For example, if you're answering an SAT Sentence Completion, don't just jump into the answer choices to see which one fits. Instead, read the sentence, *predict* the missing word, and then scan the answer choices to see which one fits. Check out the following example.

Filmed on ---- budget and edited at breakneck speed, Melotti's documentary nevertheless ---- the film critics with its perceptiveness and verve.

(A) a low . . disappointed
(B) an inflated . . distracted
(C) an uneven . . amused
(D) a disproportionate . . appalled
(E) an inadequate . . impressed

If you just launched into the answer choices, you would find that many of the choices *sound* like they fit the overall sense of the sentence: for example, "a *low* budget," "*amused* the film critics." You would also find that plugging in and comparing each of the answer choices for every question is an extremely time-consuming process. Fortunately, there's a better way. If you try to *predict* the answer first, you'll notice that the first blank must be negative (to be consistent with *breakneck speed*), while the second blank must be positive (to be consistent with *perceptiveness and verve*). If you had predicted *wowed* or something similar for the second blank, you would have noticed that only *impressed* in choice (E) matches. And you wouldn't have fallen for any tempting wrong answers.

You Don't Have to Answer Questions in Order

Most students answer SAT and ACT questions in the order in which they're given. This is a perfectly natural tendency; human beings (most of them) like to perform a series of tasks in an orderly fashion. On the SAT and ACT, though, this isn't always the smartest strategy. Depending on your particular strengths, the difficulty level of the questions, and the time remaining, it sometimes pays to skip around.

Within any given section of the SAT and ACT (the ACT English section, for example), you are allowed to skip around and answer the questions in any order that appeals to you. High scorers know this, and use that knowledge to move through the test more efficiently. They don't dwell on any one question, especially a hard one, until they have tried every question at least once. This is important because time is so limited on the SAT and ACT that you need to make sure you have answered all the questions *within your ability level* before you attempt to crack the real tough nuts.

Take control of the test by answering questions that you are comfortable with first. You'll end up earning more points, and it will also boost your confidence. If you spend too much time on one hard question, it tends to undermine your rhythm, and makes you lose your cool on the next few questions.

So what should you do when you see a question that looks impossible (or extremely laborious) on the SAT or ACT? When you run into questions that look tough, circle them in your test booklet and skip them for the time being. Go back and try them again (if you have time) after you have answered all of the more basic ones. On second glance, some of those tough questions might turn out to be surprisingly simple. If you have started working on a tough question and begin to get confused or stuck, quit working on the problem and move on. Dogged persistence pays off in most areas of life—but not on the SAT or ACT.

Time-Tested Strategies

Most high school students develop specific strategies for answering test questions in school. On essay tests, students usually deal first with the topics that they understand the best (or at least have a clue about). Then, they move on to those questions that pose a bigger challenge. Another essay strategy is to answer the question worth the most points first. Either way, the analogy holds up on the SAT and ACT: answer the basic questions first; it's all about getting more points.

Use the Order of Difficulty on the SAT

All questions on the SAT (except Critical Reading questions) are arranged in order of difficulty. In other words, the questions get progressively harder as you work through each question set.

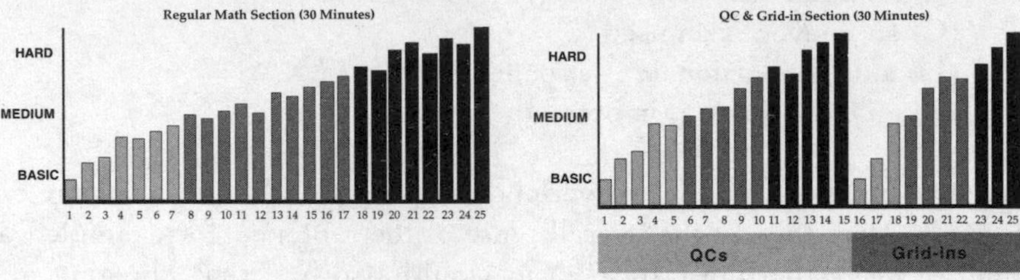

Questions get harder as you move through a section.

Here's how to use this pattern to your advantage. As you work, you should always be aware of where you are in the set. If you're generally uncomfortable with questions at the end of each question set, consider spending *more* time on questions at the beginning of each set—to make sure that you secure these "easy" points.

As you get to the end of the set, you need to become more suspicious. Now, the answers won't come easily—you'll probably have to work around tough vocabulary, or figure out three or four stages in a math problem. If the answer *does* come easily, look at the problem again, because the obvious answer is likely to be wrong. Watch out for the answer that "looks right." It may be a distractor—a wrong answer choice meant to entice you.

Do Question Triage on the ACT

In a hospital emergency room, the triage nurse is the person who evaluates each patient and decides which one gets attention first. Unless you practice the same method on ACT questions, you may run out of time at the end of each test section and require a little medical attention yourself!

Food for Thought

Let's say you took two-and-a-half minutes to get a tough question right. That might make you feel good, but you'd actually be better off if you had skipped the tough question and, in the same amount of time, answered two or three more basic questions correctly.

On the ACT, you don't necessarily have to answer every question correctly to get a good score. At the same time, though, the ACT does throw you a lot of questions in a short period of time. We find that students mostly have trouble finishing Math and Reading sections—on the Math section, because they get hung up figuring out tough problems, and on the Reading section, because of those long and wordy Reading passages.

Practicing question triage on the ACT means making a quick judgment about each question type you encounter: how difficult or time consuming is it? If you're thinking like a smart test taker, you've got three options:

- If it seems to be comprehensible and reasonably doable, do it right away.
- If it seems to be tough and time consuming, but ultimately doable, skip it, circle the number of the question in your booklet, and come back to it later.
- If it looks impossible, skip it, and mark it as "HARD" in your booklet. If you've answered all other questions, you

can come back to it later. Or you can skip it altogether and it will never trouble you again.

Even though we have made a big deal about skipping around, we often hear from students that they don't like to do this. They are typically worried that they will mess up their grids. Which leads us to . . .

Be Careful with the Answer Grid

SAT and ACT scores are based on the answers selected on the answer grid. Even if you were to work out every question correctly on these tests, your score undoubtedly would be lower if you were to "misgrid." So be careful. While filling in the bubbles with your answers might seem to be a mindless exercise, you have to do it in a strategic fashion. This is especially true if you follow our sage advice and answer questions out of order.

It is important to develop a disciplined strategy for filling in the answer grid on either the SAT or ACT. We find that it is smart to grid the answers in groups rather than one question at a time. This is how it works: circle your answer to each question in the booklet as you figure it out. Then transfer those answers to the answer grid in groups of five or more (until you get close to the end of a section, when you should grid in answers one by one—it will help you avoid running out of time).

There are a number of advantages to gridding in this fashion. Gridding in groups cuts down on errors because you can focus on this one task and do it right. Gridding in groups also saves you time you would otherwise spend moving papers around, finding your place, and redirecting your mind. Gridding in groups will also make it easier to skip over the bubbles for questions that you have skipped. We find that students who grid individually on any standardized test are much more likely to forget to do this.

On the SAT, all answer choices are labeled A, B, C, D, and E. But on the ACT, answers for even-numbered questions are labeled F, G, H, J (and, in Math, K). Only odd-numbered questions use A, B, C, D (and, again, E in Math). This might be a bit confusing at first, but you can make it work *for* you. As we've noted, "misgridding" (accidentally entering an answer one row up or down) is a common problem. On the ACT, that won't happen if you pay attention to the letters in the answer. If you're looking for an A and you see only F, G, H, J, and K, you'll know you're in the wrong row on the answer grid.

Grid in Groups
You should, of course, circle the correct answers in your test booklet *as you figure them out.* But don't transfer them onto your grid one by one. On the Math portion of the SAT and ACT, and the short-answer section of the SAT Verbal, grid the questions in blocks of five or one-page increments. On the Critical Reading section of the SAT, and in English, Reading, and Science Reasoning on the ACT, you will probably want to grid in at the end of each passage.

Don't Be Afraid to Guess

Guessing on the SAT

You may have heard other students talking about a "guessing penalty" on the SAT. This is a misnomer. It's really a wrong-answer penalty. If you guess wrong, you get penalized. If you guess right, you're in great shape. The fact is, if you can eliminate one or more answers as definitely wrong, you'll turn the odds in your favor and *actually come out ahead* by guessing.

Kaplan Rules
DON'T GUESS, unless you can eliminate at least one answer choice.
DON'T SKIP IT, unless you have absolutely no idea.

Leave No Bubble Unfilled
On the ACT, never leave blanks on your grid. Even if you can't answer a question or are running out of time, just guess. Since there's no guessing penalty on the ACT, a lucky guess will give you a higher score, and a bad guess will leave you no worse off.

Here's how the penalty works:

- If you get an answer wrong on a Quantitative Comparison question, which has four answer choices, you lose one-third of a point.
- If you get an answer wrong on other multiple-choice questions, which have five answer choices, you lose one-quarter of a point.
- If you get an answer wrong on a Grid-in math question, for which you write in your own answers, you lose nothing.

The fractional points you lose are meant to offset the points you might get "accidentally" by guessing the correct answer. With practice, however, you'll learn that it's often easy to eliminate a few answer choices for some of the difficult problems that you encounter. By learning the techniques for eliminating wrong answer choices, you can actually turn the "guessing penalty" to your advantage.

Guessing on the ACT

On the ACT, there's absolutely *no* guessing penalty. This means that questions left blank and questions answered incorrectly simply don't count when the number of correct answers are tallied. Unlike some other standardized tests, the ACT has no wrong-answer penalty. That's why you should always take a guess on every ACT question you can't answer, even if you don't have time to read it. Although the questions vary enormously in difficulty, hard questions are counted the same as basic questions. So it pays to guess on the questions you find to be too difficult and spend your time on the ones that are doable.

3 SAT VERBAL

THE FORMAT

There are three scored Verbal sections on the SAT. The approximate breakdown of each section is as follows:

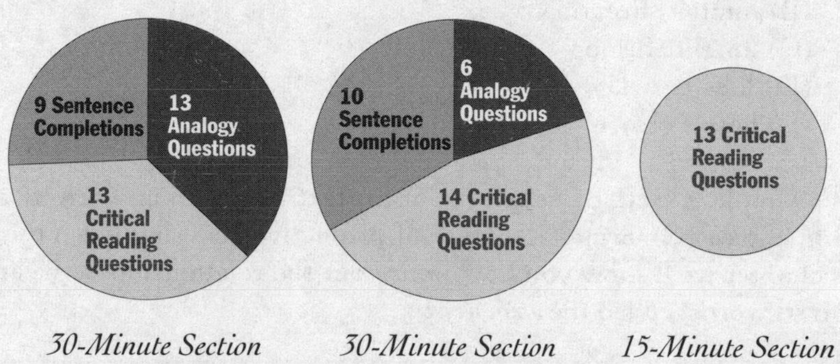

30-Minute Section *30-Minute Section* *15-Minute Section*

- one 30-minute section with nine Sentence Completions, 13 Analogies, and 13 Critical Reading questions
- one 30-minute section with ten Sentence Completions, six Analogies, and 14 Critical Reading questions
- one 15-minute section with 13 Critical Reading questions

Rule of Thumb
Work through the Sentence Completions and Analogies quickly and efficiently. Make sure you get all the points you can there, and then move on to Critical Reading.

The Sentence Completions and Analogy sets are arranged by order of difficulty. The first few questions in a set are meant to be fairly straightforward and manageable. The middle few questions will be a little harder, and the last few are the most difficult. Keep this in mind as you work, and move through the early questions a little more quickly to leave yourself more time for the difficult ones.

Critical Reading is *not* arranged by difficulty. Any time you find yourself beginning to spend too much time on a reading question, you should skip it and return to it later.

How to Approach SAT Verbal

To do well on SAT Verbal, you need to be systematic in your approach to each question type and each of the three Verbal sections. Sentence Completions and Analogies are designed to be done relatively quickly. That means you can earn points fast, so you should do these first. Critical Reading takes a lot longer, so you can't leave yourself just five minutes to do a passage. Remember, you earn just as many points for an easy question as you do for a hard one.

Analogies
There are 19 Analogies on the SAT. Each 30-minute Verbal section contains a set of Analogies. You'll probably see one set of 13 questions and one set of six.

Analogies

The key to testing your best on SAT Analogies is to get familiar with the format first. An odd-looking question type, Analogies test your vocabulary and your ability to figure out the relationships between pairs of words. You're given a pair of capitalized words (for example, POTATO : VEGETABLE), and you're asked to determine their relationship, then identify the answer choice that has the same relationship.

Here's an example:

CRAB : SHELL ::
(A) eagle : beak
(B) hunter : firearm
(C) knight : armor
(D) lobster : claw
(E) head : crown

In this example, a SHELL is a layer of protective covering worn by a CRAB, just as in choice (C), armor is a layer of protective covering worn by a knight. In this chapter we'll show you how figure out the relationship between the two capitalized words, called the *stem words*.

Building Bridges

In every SAT Analogy question, there exists a strong, definite connection between the two stem words—what we at Kaplan call a *strong bridge*. Your task is to identify this relationship, and then to look for a similar relationship between the answer choices.

Strong Bridges

The words *teacher* and *classroom* have a strong, definite connection—a classroom is by definition a place where a teacher conducts lessons. TEACHER : CLASSROOM is typical of the sort of bridges that appear on the SAT.

Burn Weak Bridges
Correct answers on the SAT Analogy section are always strong bridges. Rule out wrong answers that contain weak bridges.

Weak Bridges

The words *teacher* and *pencil* do not have a strong, definite connection—a teacher may or may not possess or use a pencil. Since the two words are not "by definition" related, TEACHER : PENCIL would *not* appear as a stem pair on the SAT, but it might appear on the SAT as a wrong answer choice. At Kaplan, we call such answer choices *weak bridges*. Rule them out on the day of the test, because weak bridges are never the correct answer!

Finding the Bridge

The first step in any Analogy question is to *form a sentence* that expresses the relationship between the two stem words. For example, the relationship between the stem pair POTATO : VEGETABLE would be "a POTATO is a type of VEGETABLE." This strategy is called *building a bridge.* Your bridge sentence should sound like a definition of one of the words.

To Solve an Analogy

1. Build a bridge between the stem words.
2. Plug in the answer choices.
3. Adjust your bridge, if you need to.

Kaplan's Three-Step Method for Analogies

The Kaplan Method for solving Analogies has three simple steps:

1. Build a bridge between the stem words.
2. Plug in the answer choices.
3. Adjust your bridge, if you need to.

Here's typical SAT Analogy question. Let's go over the Kaplan Method step-by-step.

LITER : VOLUME ::
(A) bottle : can
(B) knob : radio
(C) scale : height
(D) gram : weight
(E) juice : vitamin

Step One: Build a Bridge
A LITER is by definition a measure of VOLUME. So the correct bridge here would be "is a measure of."

Step Two: Plug in the Answer Choices
Now plug in answer choices (A) through (E) into the bridge *is a measure of. Be sure to consider every answer choice!* (A): Is a bottle a measure of can? Nope. (B): Is a knob a measure of a radio? Uh-uh. (C): Is a scale a measure of height? Close, but not quite—a scale is an instrument used to measure weight. (D): Is a gram a measure of weight? Yes it is. (E): Is a juice a measure of vitamin? Not at all.

Step Three: Adjust Your Bridge, If You Need To
Sometimes the bridge you think of might not fit any of the answer choices. Or it might fit more than one answer choice. In this case, you might have to rethink the connection between the two words. Here's an example:

FIREPLACE : FLUE ::
(A) labyrinth : entrance
(B) camera : lens
(C) radio : antenna
(D) engine : exhaust
(E) fortress : drawbridge

If your bridge was something vague like, "a FLUE is attached to a FIREPLACE," then you might have picked (C)—"an antenna is attached to a radio." But that's not the precise relationship between FLUE and FIREPLACE. Make a more precise bridge, and try again.

The function of a FLUE, by definition, is to carry smoke out of a FIREPLACE. So your bridge here might be, "a FLUE conducts smoke out of a

Is Your Bridge a Classic?
Five classic bridge types are:

1. Description
2. Type
3. Function
4. Place
5. Part/Whole

FIREPLACE." This makes answer choice (D) pop out, since an exhaust carries smoke out of an engine.

Classic Bridges

SAT Analogies follow a standardized format, like every other question type on the test. So although you can't find out in advance what particular words will show up on your SAT, you *can* get familiar with the types of relationships that will be tested. At Kaplan, we call these frequently occurring relationships *classic bridges.*

Classic bridges take different forms, depending on what parts of speech are used. But the underlying concepts appear from test to test. Don't attempt to memorize the following bridges. Instead use them to learn what types of bridges you can expect to see on the day of the test.

Bridge Type #1: DESCRIPTION
In many Analogies, one stem word is a person, place, or thing, and the other word is a characteristic of that person, place, or thing. Look at these examples:

PAUPER : POOR—A PAUPER is always POOR.
GENIUS : INTELLIGENT—A GENIUS is always INTELLIGENT.
TRAGEDY : SAD—A TRAGEDY is always SAD.

This classic bridge can also describe a person, place, or thing by what it is *not*.

PAUPER : WEALTHY—A PAUPER is never WEALTHY.
GENIUS : STUPID—A GENIUS is never STUPID.
TRAGEDY : HAPPY—A TRAGEDY is never HAPPY.

Here are more types of classic bridges. Fill in each blank with a stem word that will complete the bridge. There is more than one way to fill in each blank. The important thing is to get the right idea (suggested answers follow).

Bridge Type #2: TYPE
The MACARENA is a type of ----.
A PENGUIN is a type of ----.
A TRUCK is a type of ----.

Bridge Type #3: FUNCTION
SCISSORS are used to ----.
A TELEPHONE is used to ----.
A KEY is used to ---- a door.

Bridge Type #4: PLACE
An AUDITORIUM is a place where a ---- is performed.
A PARK is a place people visit for ----.
A ---- is a place where SURGEONS work.

Bridge Type #5: PART/WHOLE
An ENGINE is part of a ----.
A PICTURE is mounted in a ----.
An ELBOW is part of an ----.

Here are some answers to complete the examples of the classic bridge types we just listed. Your answers may vary from our suggested answers. But as long as you've grasped the overall principle, that's OK.

Bridge Type #2: TYPE

The MACARENA is a type of DANCE.
A PENGUIN is a type of BIRD.
A TRUCK is a type of VEHICLE.

Bridge Type #3: FUNCTION

SCISSORS are used to CUT.
A TELEPHONE is used to COMMUNICATE.
A KEY is used to LOCK a door.

Bridge Type #4: PLACE

An AUDITORIUM is a place where a CONCERT is performed.
A PARK is a place people visit for RECREATION.
A HOSPITAL is a place where SURGEONS work.

Bridge Type #5: PART/WHOLE

An ENGINE is part of an AIRPLANE.
A PICTURE is mounted in a FRAME.
An ELBOW is part of an ARM.

Analogy Practice Quiz

Now answer the following Analogy questions to assess your strengths and weaknesses. At the end of the chapter, you'll find an answer key and strategic explanations. Then enter your score on the "SAT or ACT? Score Comparison Chart" at the end of this book.

1. CHANDELIER : CEILING ::

(A) ring : finger
(B) carpet : floor
(C) earring : ear
(D) knob : door
(E) spotlight : stage

Ⓐ Ⓑ Ⓒ Ⓓ Ⓔ

2. DEFINE : NEBULOUS ::

(A) balance : weighty
(B) soothe : lax
(C) discipline : restrained
(D) dignify : circumspect
(E) order : chaotic

Ⓐ Ⓑ Ⓒ Ⓓ Ⓔ

3. EAVESDROP : LISTEN ::

(A) whisper : shout
(B) tell : confide
(C) gossip : speak
(D) spy : watch
(E) pretend : reveal

Ⓐ Ⓑ Ⓒ Ⓓ Ⓔ

4. DILATORY : PROCRASTINATOR ::

(A) benevolent : dictator
(B) hardy : explorer
(C) itinerant : nomad
(D) bellicose : leader
(E) wandering : musician

Ⓐ Ⓑ Ⓒ Ⓓ Ⓔ

Sentence Completions

Of all the SAT Verbal question types, Sentence Completions are probably the most student friendly. Unlike Analogies, Sentence Completions provide you with a context to help you figure out tough vocabulary. And unlike Critical Reading, they only require you to read one sentence at a time. As the name suggests, Sentence Completion questions test your ability to *complete* sentences that are missing one or two key words by selecting the appropriate answer choice.

Here's an example:

> Though the morbid legends attached to the tower give it a ---- aspect at first, the impression is soon ---- by the sight of children playing inside.
>
> (A) forbidding . . dispelled
> (B) romantic . . eschewed
> (C) distinct . . evaporated
> (D) gruesome . . bolstered
> (E) surreal . . enlivened

In this example, the clue word *though* indicates a contrast between the first and second blank; in spite of the ---- aspect given to the tower by morbid legends, this impression is soon ---- by the sight of children playing inside. Choices (A) *forbidding* and (D) *gruesome* both fit the first blank, but only choice (A)'s *dispelled* fits the suggestion that the onlooker's initial impression is proven inaccurate.

Sentence Completions
There are 19 Sentence Completions on the SAT. You'll probably see one set of nine and one set of ten. They appear in both 30-minute Verbal sections.

Picking up on Clues

The key to success on Sentence Completions is to look for "structural clues" that can help you predict the meaning of the blanks. For example, words such as *but*, *although*, and *despite* often show that the sentence contains a contrast. Conversely, words such as *and* and *also* or the use of a colon may show that the missing words are consistent with the sentence. On SAT Sentence Completions, the meaning of the sentence can sometimes depend on a single word!

Get a Clue
Always read the sentence carefully—remember that "structural clue" words can have a significant influence on the meaning of the sentence.

Try using the clue words to predict the missing words in the sentences below.

1. *Although* the professor had a reputation as a harsh disciplinarian, students ---- attending his lectures.
2. *Because* the professor had a reputation as a harsh disciplinarian, students ---- attending his lectures.

Can you see how the meaning of the blank is completely altered just by changing the structural clue word? In the first example, the word *although* indicates a surprising contrast—*although* the professor had a fierce reputation, students *loved* or *enjoyed* attending his lectures. Changing *although* to *because* reverses the situation; you might predict *dreaded* or *avoided* for the second example.

Kaplan's Four-Step Method for Sentence Completions

This is Kaplan's method for solving Sentence Completions:

1. **Read the sentence carefully, looking for clues.**
2. **Predict the answer.**
3. **Select the answer choice that matches your prediction.**
4. **Read it back into the sentence.**

Here's an example:

1. Bach was one of Western music's most ---- composers, producing in his career as a concertmaster a remarkable diversity of church and secular music.

(A) notorious
(B) amiable
(C) prolific
(D) devious
(E) sporadic

Step One: Read the Sentence Carefully, Looking for Clues

What kind of composer was Bach? The key phrase in this example is *remarkable diversity*—it tells you that Bach produced a great deal of church and secular music in his career. So you're looking for a word that means "abundantly productive."

Step Two: Predict the Answer

Don't look at the answer choices yet. You've got to know what you want before you go shopping, and if you don't have a clear idea of the answer in your head, you'll get distracted by tempting wrong answer choices. Try to *predict* an answer that might fit the blank—find a word of your own that makes sense. Here, you might choose *productive, hard working,* or *creative.*

Step Three: Select the Answer Choice That Matches Your Prediction

Now look at the answer choices, and pick the one that matches your prediction. (A): Does *notorious* mean "productive"? No—it means "infamous." (B): Does *amiable* mean "productive"? Uh-uh; *amiable* means "friendly." (C): Does *prolific* mean "productive"? Sounds right. (D): Does *devious* mean "productive"? No—it means "cunning." (E): Does *sporadic* mean "productive"? No, it means "occurring occasionally."

Don't Get Trapped

When working on a Sentence Completion, don't begin by plugging each answer choice into the sentence. That method takes too long and makes you vulnerable to traps. Try to predict the missing word before you look at the answer choices.

Step Four: Read It Back into the Sentence
Now plug your choice into the sentence, and read it through to make sure it really makes sense.

> Bach was one of Western music's most *prolific* composers, producing in his career as a concertmaster a remarkable diversity of church and secular music.

Sounds like a *New York Times* feature on the old boy, doesn't it? You've confirmed that (C) is the correct answer, and are ready to move on to the next question.

Dealing with Two-Blankers

Many Sentence Completions have two blanks, but this doesn't make them twice as hard. Don't be intimidated by two-blankers. Just figure out the easiest blank first, narrow your options, and move on to the second blank. Let's work through the Four-Step Method again, using a second example:

2. Although the television program exposed the UFO sightings as ----, many people will ---- their beliefs about the existence of extraterrestrial life forms.

   (A) legitimate . . abandon
   (B) spurious . . maintain
   (C) inaccurate . . discard
   (D) careless . . promote
   (E) deceitful . . conceal

Two-Blank Strategy
When dealing with two-blankers, don't try to solve both blanks at the same time; divide and conquer is the most strategic approach. Pick the easiest blank, solve it, narrow down your options, and move on to the other blank.

Step One: Read the Sentence Carefully, Looking for Clues
Although is a key structural clue here. It tells you that the second phrase contrasts with the first. So you're told that *although* UFO sightings were exposed, "people will ---- their beliefs."

Step Two: Predict the Answer / Step Three: Select the Answer Choice That Matches Your Prediction
The word *exposed* suggests a negative word for the first blank—something like *fake, false,* or *untrue.* Choices (B) *spurious,* (C) *inaccurate,* and (E) *deceitful* all fit here—but you can rule out choices (A) and (D).

Moving on to the second blank, you would predict a positive word here—something that means "keeping" or "preserving" a belief in extraterrestrials. Of the remaining answer choices, only (B), *maintain,* fits the second blank.

Step Four: Read It Back into the Sentence
Always check that your selected answer sounds right.

> Although the television program exposed the UFO sightings as *spurious,* many people will *maintain* their beliefs about the existence of extraterrestrial life forms.

Using Word Charge

Even if you can't exactly predict the meaning of the missing word, you can often determine whether the word is positive, negative, or neutral in charge (or tone). Use this knowledge to narrow down your choices! Try to identify the charge of the missing words in the following examples:

1. Attila the Hun was a ---- military leader, subjugating all the tribes who stood in his way.
2. A noted ----, the industrialist Andrew Carnegie was celebrated for his charitable donations and patronage of the arts.
3. The journalist adopted a ---- stance towards the peace process, attempting to be fair to both sides involved.

1. *Negative charge!* Unless you're actually a Hun, you wouldn't predict a positive attitude towards the subjugation of thousands of people. So *powerful* or *tyrannical* would be good predictions here.

2. *Positive charge!* If Carnegie gave a lot to charity and to the arts, you would expect a warm and fuzzy word here—something like *benefactor* or *philanthropist.*

3. *Neutral charge.* Here the journalist is striving to be fair, so you would predict a neutral word—something like *objective, neutral,* or *impartial.*

What's the Charge?
If you're stuck on a hard Sentence Completion, try to predict the charge of the missing word(s). Often you can tell whether a missing word has a positive, negative, or neutral charge and use that information to narrow down your choices. You can also use word charge to crack tough vocabulary—just ask yourself whether those ten-cent words sound good or bad.

Sentence Completions Practice Quiz

Now answer the following Sentence Completion questions to assess your strengths and weaknesses. At the end of the chapter, you'll find an answer key and strategic explanations. Then enter your score on the "SAT or ACT? Score Comparison Chart" at the end of this book.

1. Except for certain life stages when they may function as "loners," wolves act as ---- animals, generally living in packs with strong bonds and clear hierarchies.

   (A) carnivorous
   (B) fearsome
   (C) social
   (D) singular
   (E) wild

   A B C D E

2. During China's Han Dynasty, manual work was considered ----; even noblemen felt that they could engage in it without ----.

   (A) distasteful . . difficulty
   (B) erudite . . training
   (C) inexpensive . . remuneration
   (D) intense . . discomfort
   (E) respectable . . dishonor

3. Despite its stated goals of fostering hard work and productivity, the company promotes many ---- and unproductive employees.

   (A) creative
   (B) discontented
   (C) accomplished
   (D) lackadaisical
   (E) meritorious

4. The original American colonies were ---- entities, each having its own government, maintaining its own army, and functioning ----.

   (A) related . . competitively
   (B) independent . . affirmatively
   (C) distinct . . autonomously
   (D) prosperous . . austerely
   (E) united . . expressively

Critical Reading

Improving your SAT Critical Reading score means building skills you already have and applying them to the test. You don't need outside knowledge to answer the Critical Reading questions. And you don't need an amazing vocabulary, since unfamiliar words will be defined for you.

Critical Reading passages and questions are very predictable, since the test makers use a formula to write them. You'll be given four reading passages, 400 to 850 words each, drawn from the arts, humanities, social sciences, sciences, and fiction. One of these is a "paired passage" consisting of two related excerpts. You'll be asked about the overall tone and content of a passage, the logic underlying the author's argument, and the meaning of specific words or phrases. You'll also be asked to compare and contrast the related passages.

Critical Reading
There are only three basic types of Reading questions: Big Picture, Little Picture, and Vocabulary-in-Context. Get to know the strategies for dealing with each type of question.

The Format

Critical Reading instructions tell you to answer questions based on what is stated or implied in the accompanying passage or passages. As with other question types, you should get familiar enough with the Critical Reading format that you don't waste time reading the directions again on the day of the test.

Each reading passage begins with a brief introduction. *Don't skip these introductions*; they'll help you focus your reading. Related questions follow the passage.

Critical Reading questions have a specific order: The first few questions ask about the beginning of the passage, the last few about the end. Questions following "paired passages" are generally ordered as follows. The first few questions relate to the first passage, the next few to the second passage, and the final questions ask about the passages as a pair. You'll learn more about this later in this chapter.

Critical Reading questions are not ordered by difficulty. Unlike the other kinds of questions on the SAT, the location of a Critical Reading question tells you nothing about its potential difficulty. So don't get bogged down on a hard Critical Reading question. The next one might be a lot easier.

Out of Order
Unlike the other Verbal question types, Critical Reading questions are not ordered by difficulty. If you're having trouble answering a question, the next one might be easier.

How to Read the Passages

Some students find Critical Reading passages dull or intimidating. Remember that each passage is written for a purpose—the author wants to make a point, describe a situation, or convince you of his or her ideas. As you're reading, ask yourself, "What's the point of this? What's this all about?" This is active reading, and it's the key to staying focused on the page.

Active reading doesn't mean reading the passage word-for-word. It means reading lightly, but with a focus. Getting hung up on details is a major Critical Reading pitfall. You need to grasp the outline, but you don't need to grasp all the fine details. The questions will help you fill in the details by directing you to important information in the passage.

Seven Critical Reading Strategies

Here are seven strategies to help you get through SAT reading passages quickly and efficiently, extracting just the information you need to answer the questions:

1. Focus on the First One-Third of the Passage
The author usually spells out most of the important issues at the beginning of the passage. Try to establish the topic of the passage and the author's point of view at the outset.

2. Look for the Big Idea
Don't read as if you're memorizing everything. Aim to pick up just the gist of the passage—the author's main idea and the paragraph topics.

3. Be a Critical Reader
As you read, ask yourself critical questions: "What's the author's point? What message is the author trying to get across?"

4. Make It Simple
Despite the fancy language, reading passages are usually about pretty straightforward topics. Don't get bogged down by technical jargon; translate the author's ideas into *your own words*.

5. Use the Paragraph Topics
The first two sentences of each paragraph generally tell you what it's about.

6. Keep Moving
Aim to spend no more than two to three minutes reading each passage. Remember, just reading the passage doesn't score you points.

7. Don't Sweat the Details
Don't waste time reading and rereading parts you don't understand. Make sure you leave time for answering the questions, which is what really counts.

Test your reading skills on the following passage, keeping these strategies in mind.

In Your Own Words
Don't get bogged down in any technical jargon you find in Critical Reading passages. You aren't expected to memorize this jargon. Rephrase it in your own words.

The following passage is from a discussion of the origin of the Cold War between the United States and the Soviet Union.

Could the Cold War have been avoided? Revisionist historians maintain that it was within the power of the United States, in the years during and immediately after the Second World War, to prevent the developing standoff between the United States and the Soviet Union. These historians suggest, for example, that the United States could have officially recognized the new Soviet sphere of influence in eastern Europe instead of continuing to call for self-determination in those countries. A much-needed reconstruction loan could have helped the Soviets recover from the war. In addition, the United States could have sought to assuage Soviet fears by giving up the monopoly of the atomic bomb and turning the weapons over to an international agency (with the stipulation that future nuclear powers do the same).

The implementation of any one of these proposed policies might have changed the course of history in the postwar era. However, the historians' criticism of the United States's course of action fails to take into account the political realities in the United States at the time, and unfairly condemns the American policy makers who did consider each of these alternatives and found them to be unworkable. Recognition of a Soviet eastern Europe was out of the question. Roosevelt had promised self-determination to the eastern European countries, and the American people, having come to expect this, were furious when Stalin began to shape his spheres of influence in the region. The president was in particular acutely conscious of the millions of Polish Americans who would be voting in the upcoming election.

Negotiations had indeed been conducted by the administration with the Soviets about a reconstruction loan, but the Congress refused to approve it unless the Soviets made enormous concessions tantamount to restructuring their system and withdrawing from eastern Europe. This, of course, made Soviet rejection of the loan a foregone conclusion. As for giving up the bomb, the elected officials in Washington would have been in deep trouble with their constituents had that plan been carried out. Polls showed that 82 percent of the American people understood that other nations would develop bombs eventually, but that 85 percent thought that the United States should retain exclusive possession of the weapon. Policy makers have to abide by certain constraints in deciding what is acceptable and what is not. They, and not historians, are in the best position to perceive those constraints and make the decisions.

It's important to learn how to read the passage quickly and efficiently. Remember, though, that reading the passage won't earn you points—it's the questions that count.

Kaplan's Five-Step Method for Critical Reading Questions

Here's Kaplan's proven approach to Critical Reading questions:

1. **Read the question stem.**
2. **Locate the material you need.**
3. **Come up with an idea of the right answer.**
4. **Scan the answer choices.**
5. **Select your answer.**

To Approach Critical Reading

- Read the question stem.
- Locate the material you need.
- Come up with an idea of the right answer.
- Scan the answer choices.
- Select your answer.

Step One: Read the Question Stem

This is the place to really read carefully. Take a second to make sure you understand what the question is asking.

Step Two: Locate the Material You Need

If you are given a line reference, read the material surrounding the line mentioned. It will clarify exactly what the question is asking. If you're not given a line reference, scan the text to find the place to which the question applies, and quickly reread those few sentences. Keep the main point of the passage in mind.

Step Three: Come up with an Idea of the Right Answer

Don't spend time making up a precise answer. You need only a general sense of what you're after, so you can recognize the correct answer quickly when you read the choices.

Step Four: Scan the Answer Choices

Scan the choices, looking for one that fits your idea of the right answer. If you don't find an ideal answer, quickly eliminate wrong choices by checking back to the passage. Rule out choices that are too extreme or go against common sense. And get rid of answers that sound reasonable but don't make sense in the context of the passage.

Step Five: Select Your Answer

You've eliminated the obvious wrong answers. One of the few remaining should fit your ideal. If you're left with more than one contender, consider the passage's main idea, and make an educated guess.

Now try these questions about the Cold War passage.

1. The primary purpose of the passage is to

   (A) explode a popular myth
   (B) criticize historical figures
   (C) refute an argument
   (D) analyze an era
   (E) reconcile opposing views

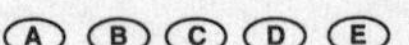

2. In line 6, the word *recognized* most nearly means

(A) identified
(B) noticed
(C) acknowledged
(D) distinguished
(E) remembered

3. The author refers to the Polish Americans (lines 22–24) chiefly to illustrate that

(A) the president had an excellent rapport with ethnic minorities
(B) immigrants had fled from eastern European countries to escape communism
(C) giving up the idea of east European self-determination would have been costly in political terms
(D) the Polish people could enjoy self-determination only in America
(E) the political landscape of the United States had changed considerably since the president was elected

4. A fundamental assumption underlying the author's argument in the second and third paragraphs is that

(A) the Soviets were largely to blame for the failure of conciliatory U.S. initiatives
(B) the American public was well informed about the incipient Cold War situation
(C) none of the proposed alternatives would have had its intended effect
(D) the American public was overwhelmingly opposed to seeking peace with the Soviets
(E) the government could not have been expected to ignore public opinion

5. The phrase *certain constraints* in lines 35–36 most likely refers to

(A) the etiquette of international diplomacy
(B) the danger of leaked information about atomic bombs
(C) the views of the electorate
(D) the potential reaction of the enemy
(E) the difficulty of carrying out a policy initiative

[See the following section for an explanation of each question and its answer.]

Three Critical Reading Question Types

One helpful strategy for handling Critical Reading questions is to get familiar with the three basic question types that appear on the test. While there are 40 reading questions on each SAT Verbal section, there are only three basic types of reading questions: Big Picture, Little Picture, and Vocabulary-in-Context. Let's look at these question types in reviewing the sample reading passage and questions above.

Big Picture Questions

Big Picture questions test your overall understanding of the passage's main points. Big Picture questions ask you about:

- the main point or purpose of a passage
- the author's overall attitude or tone
- the logic underlying the author's argument
- how different parts of a passage relate to each other

While Big Picture questions ask you to step back and take a look at the whole passage, you'll often find it necessary to focus on the first 15 lines of the passage—that's where the author generally defines the topic and maps out his or her plan of attack. To identify Big Picture questions, look for question stems such as:

- The primary focus of the passage is . . .
- This passage serves mainly to . . .
- Which of the following titles best describes the passage . . .

Let's look at the first question from the sample passage and questions above:

1. The primary purpose of the passage is to

   (A) explode a popular myth
   (B) criticize historical figures
   (C) refute an argument
   (D) analyze an era
   (E) reconcile opposing views

This Big Picture question is about the main purpose of the passage. The author of this passage has one overarching strategy: set up the arguments of the revisionist historians and then knock 'em down—choice (C). Let's look at how the argument develops paragraph-by-paragraph.

In the first paragraph, the author explains the things that, according to the revisionists, could have been done to avoid the Cold War. The United States could have just accepted Soviet domination in eastern Europe, given the Soviets money for reconstruction, and given up its monopoly of the bomb. The second and third paragraphs outline the author's counterarguments; he concentrates on the American political atmosphere as the main reason that the revisionists' proposals would not have worked at the time.

Choice (E) is wrong because the author is definitely not interested in reconciling his view with that of the revisionists. Choice (A) is wrong because the ideas of the revisionists are not, as far as we know, a popular myth. Choice (B) is out because the author is defending historical figures—the policy makers—for what they did, not criticizing them. Choice (D) is too neutral a choice for this passage. The author does engage in analysis of the era of the beginning of the Cold War, but his purpose is to do far more than just analyze events. He wants to refute revisionist theories.

Vocabulary-in-Context Questions

Vocabulary-in-Context questions test your ability to figure out the meaning of specific words from the surrounding lines. These questions do not test your ability to define hard words such as *archipelago* or *garrulous*. They do test your ability to infer the meaning of a word from context.

Check That Line Reference

Vocabulary-in-Context questions always have a line reference, and you should always use it.

In fact, the words tested in these questions will probably be familiar to you—they are usually fairly common words with more than one definition. Many of the answer choices will be definitions of the tested word, but only one will work in context. Vocabulary-in-Context questions always have a line reference, and you should always use it. It's crucial that you refer to the line in which the vocabulary word appears in order to figure out its meaning!

Let's look at the second question from the sample passage and questions above:

2. In line 6, the word *recognized* most nearly means

(A) identified
(B) noticed
(C) acknowledged
(D) distinguished
(E) remembered

This Vocabulary-in-Context question (like many of its kind) tests a secondary definition of a familiar word. *Recognized* generally means (A) "identified" or (B) "noticed." But that's not what it means here. One great strategy for Vocabulary-in-Context questions is to think of them as Sentence Completions:

> These historians suggest, for example, that the United States could have officially ---- the new Soviet sphere of influence in eastern Europe . . .

When historians say that the United States could have recognized the Soviet influence in eastern Europe, they mean that the United States could have formally acknowledged this Soviet presence, making (C) correct. Notice that none of the other choices makes sense if you plug it into the context.

Little Picture Questions

More than two-thirds of Critical Reading questions on the SAT are Little Picture questions. Little Picture questions ask you about small chunks of the passage—most often, they're about the point of a particular phrase or example. Little Picture questions usually give you a line reference to refer you to a specific paragraph—a strong clue to where the answer is located in the passage. Little Picture questions commonly ask about:

- the meaning of a particular phrase or example
- the author's logic at a specific point in the passage
- the topic of a particular paragraph

To answer Little Picture questions, always put the phrase or example in context by reading the lines that surround it. Don't just read the lines quoted—try to relate the details to the topic of the paragraph in which they appear. Success in Critical Reading is all about connecting those little details to the author's overall argument. To identify Little Picture questions, look for question stems like these:

- The author refers to Wordsworth's use of metaphor (lines xx–xx) chiefly to illustrate the . . .
- In lines xx–xx, the phrase "van Gogh knew only too well" emphasizes the point that . . .
- The author mentions her experience in "leaving China for the last time" (line xx) in order to suggest that . . .

Let's look at the third, fourth, and fifth questions from the sample passage and questions above:

3. The author refers to the Polish Americans (lines 22–24) chiefly to illustrate that

(A) the president had an excellent rapport with ethnic minorities
(B) immigrants had fled from eastern European countries to escape communism
(C) giving up the idea of east European self-determination would have been costly in political terms
(D) the Polish people could enjoy self-determination only in America
(E) the political landscape of the United States had changed considerably since the president was elected

This Little Picture question is about the purpose of an example: why does the author mention Polish Americans? As on many Little Picture questions, the answer is strongly implied. To research the answer, check back to the last two sentences of the second paragraph. The author says there that Roosevelt could never have recognized a Soviet eastern Europe because the American people did not like the idea of the Soviets holding sway in that region. In particular, the president would have lost the votes of the Polish Americans who, you can infer, did not want the Soviets controlling their country of origin. Choice (C) spells out this point. None of the other choices is really supported by the end of the paragraph.

4. A fundamental assumption underlying the author's argument in the second and third paragraphs is that

(A) the Soviets were largely to blame for the failure of conciliatory U.S. initiatives
(B) the American public was well informed about the incipient Cold War situation
(C) none of the proposed alternatives would have had its intended effect
(D) the American public was overwhelmingly opposed to seeking peace with the Soviets
(E) the government could not have been expected to ignore public opinion

In the second and third paragraphs, the author refutes the suggestions of the revisionists primarily by saying that the policy makers couldn't do what was necessary to avoid the Cold War because the American people were against it. The assumption the author makes is that the policy makers "could not have been expected to ignore public opinion," choice (E).

5. The phrase *certain constraints* in lines 35–36 most likely refers to

(A) the etiquette of international diplomacy
(B) the danger of leaked information about atomic bombs
(C) the views of the electorate
(D) the potential reaction of the enemy
(E) the difficulty of carrying out a policy initiative

This question is closely linked to the previous one. The author refers to certain constraints at the end of the third paragraph, in the midst of the discussion of the impact of public opinion on the policy makers. From context, then, you know that the constraints the author is talking about are the opinions of the people—in other words, "the views of the electorate," choice (C). If you didn't put the sentence about constraints in context, any of the other choices might have looked appealing.

Paired Passages—A (Not-So) Special Case

Don't let the paired passages worry you—they're not twice as hard as the single reading selections. In fact, students often find the paired passages the most interesting on the test. With paired passages, focus as you read on the relationship between the two passages. Just as with single passages, the questions following paired passages can help fill in the big picture.

Questions following paired passages tend to be ordered, with the first few questions relating to the first passage, the next few to the second passage, and the final questions asking about the passages as a pair. This is the best way to tackle the questions in any case, even if the test makers mix in a question about both passages amidst questions on the first passage (it's been known to happen).

How to Do Paired Passages

- Skim the first passage, looking for the drift (as you would with a single passage).
- Do the questions that relate to the first passage.
- Skim the second passage, looking for the drift and thinking about how the second passage relates to the first.
- Do the questions that relate to the second passage.
- Now you're ready to do the questions that ask about the relationship between the two passages.

Critical Reading Practice Quiz

Now read the following Critical Reading passage and answer the following questions to assess your strengths and weaknesses. At the end of the chapter, you'll find an answer key and strategic explanations. Then enter your score on the "SAT or ACT? Score Comparison Chart" at the end of this book.

The following passage discusses the impact that Native Americans had on the New World landscape.

In the mid-1600s, the English colonists came up with two justifications for taking the Native Americans' lands. First, they argued that colonists would "civilize" the Native Americans. The other part of the rationale was that Europeans could put the land to a "higher use," making it more productive by intensive cultivation and by bringing in livestock.

The idea that Europeans might put the land to higher use required downplaying how native people were using it. This was somewhat problematic, because the land the settlers desired most was the best land, which the Native Americans had already cleared for their own crops of beans, corn, pumpkins, squash, and tobacco. The English were able, however, to construct an image of the Indians as nomadic hunters who did not change the landscape.

But New World people had changed the landscape. Along the east coast of North America, the lands that the English sought for tobacco cultivation had been planted for thousands of years. As fertility declined in some fields, the Native Americans opened up others, leaving the older ones to lie fallow. Later they might return to previously used fields, whose overgrowth of brush and small trees was easier to clear than climax forest. By the time the colonists arrived, the eastern woodlands had become a mosaic of Native American fields, some in use, some overgrown with brush, some nearly forests again.

Fire was a useful tool for renovating farming plots: it not only cleared the undergrowth but it also returned nutrients from the vegetation to the soil. Native Americans used fire widely in eastern North America to change the forests. English settlers recorded a marked shift in the forest vegetation after the Native Americans retreated farther west. At first the forest was described as "parklands," with little vegetation at ground level. After the Native Americans died or moved away, the Europeans began describing the forest as dense and scrubby, with impenetrable thickets of vegetation beneath the woodland canopy.

Farther west, Native Americans used fires to turn forests into grasslands and, in drier areas, to keep prairies from becoming chaparral or scrub deserts. Archaelogist Henry Lewis has described how, for thousands of years, the Native Americans modified landscapes in western Canada, and how present-day environmental agencies are rediscovering the advantages of controlled burning. The catastrophic fires in Yellowstone National Park in the summer of 1988 showed that fire is an inherent part of the forest ecosystem, without which some species cannot survive or reproduce. They also showed the dangers of suppressing natural fires for decades.

In what is now the southwestern United States and northern Mexico, people rerouted the flow of rivers to create environments capable of supporting large populations. For example, in about A.D. 1000, Hohokam Indians built an elaborate system of canals and irrigated fields in the floodplains of the Gila and Salt rivers (south of modern Phoenix). On a larger scale, Central and South American peoples, such as the Aztecs, the Incas, and their predecessors, transformed landscapes with thousands of miles of canals and extensive drained or irrigated farm fields.

The possibility that early Native Americans were responsible for the extinction of the large animals of the Western Hemisphere has been hotly debated. Many animals that were around at the end of the last glaciation 12,000 years ago — mastodons, giant sloths, camels, giant beavers, and others — disappeared soon after the climate warmed. The weapons and tools found with the bones of these animals make it hard to argue that humans played no role in these extinctions. In the Caribbean the extermination of such species as giant flightless owls can be more closely tied to the arrival of the first humans.

While some scholars have documented the effect New World peoples had on their environment, others have sought to cast them as conservationists, people who knew the inner workings of ecosystems and lived without changing them. This view, which emerged in the nineteenth century, has gained widespread favor in this century. People who call Native Americans conservationists probably intend this as a compliment to their sophistication. The ability to wreak havoc on the environment is no longer regarded as a measure of civilization. But this compliment retains a note of condescension, assuming the Europeans had the ability to subdue the land, even if unwisely, while native peoples merely adapted to it, finding ways of surviving without changing things.

Native Americans have been conceived of in many ways, as both savage and noble. The latest stereotype, as "ecological Indians," oversimplifies their interaction with their environment. The important lesson they offer is that they changed the New World continents in ways that made the land more productive, and yet they carefully avoided the destruction of the ecosystems of the Americas.

1. The information in lines 1–12 suggests that the idea that the Europeans could put the Native Americans' land to "higher use" was

(A) based on the Europeans' ignorance of the extent of Native American farming
(B) conceived by colonists who had only altruistic intentions
(C) put forward although it had little or no basis in fact
(D) dispelled quickly once settlers saw the farmland of the Native Americans
(E) downplayed by the Native Americans who wished to keep their land

Ⓐ Ⓑ Ⓒ Ⓓ Ⓔ

2. According to the author, the image of the Native Americans as "nomadic hunters who did not change the landscape" (lines 11–12) was primarily a result of the

(A) fact that English colonists took the best farming land from the Native Americans
(B) observation of Europeans that the Native Americans had limited farming
(C) attempt by the Europeans to justify taking the Native Americans' land
(D) naive comparison of Native American culture with European culture
(E) English colonists' misunderstanding of Native American ways of farming

Ⓐ Ⓑ Ⓒ Ⓓ Ⓔ

3. Which of the following best explains why the Native Americans used a farming pattern that turned the eastern woodlands into a "mosaic"?

(A) They wished to establish the fact that they were not merely nomadic hunters.
(B) The fertility of the soil declined rapidly.
(C) This pattern of farming distinguished their land from that of the English colonists.
(D) They had no choice but to clear away some of the forest to get to the best land.
(E) This pattern of farming allowed them to use their land productively without ruining it.

Ⓐ Ⓑ Ⓒ Ⓓ Ⓔ

4. In line 25, the word *marked* most nearly means

(A) delineated
(B) drawn
(C) striking
(D) circular
(E) intended

Ⓐ Ⓑ Ⓒ Ⓓ Ⓔ

5. In the fifth paragraph, the author mentions the fires in Yellowstone in 1988 in order to emphasize which point?

(A) The devastation that resulted merely strengthened the resolve of the environmental agencies to prevent natural fires.
(B) The Native Americans were correct in viewing fire as having a beneficial effect on forests.
(C) Present-day environmental agencies have begun to mine the vast store of knowledge of the Native Americans.
(D) Forest fires have proved to be a dangerous element of nature that cannot be entirely tamed.
(E) Allowing forest fires to occur frequently is essential to the livelihood of our forest ecosystems.

6. In the seventh paragraph, the author includes information about the extinctions of North American animals mainly in order to

(A) prove that Native Americans lived in the New World over 12,000 years ago
(B) broaden the picture of the environmental impact of Native Americans
(C) challenge the image of Native Americans as nomadic hunters
(D) substantiate the modern view of Native Americans as conservationists
(E) discredit the view that Native Americans caused wildlife extinctions

7. The author uses the final paragraph to do all of the following EXCEPT

(A) identify misconceptions
(B) suggest further study
(C) counter a prevalent view
(D) reemphasize an earlier point
(E) give an assessment

8. The author objects to the characterization of Native Americans as conservationists for which reason?

(A) The Native Americans did change their environment and its ecosystems.
(B) There is no historical account of much of the life of the Native Americans.
(C) Conservationism is a relatively modern phenomenon.
(D) The Native Americans had not attained the requisite level of civilization to be conservationists.
(E) The characterization is presumptuous and disdainful.

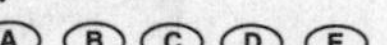

SAT Verbal Practice Quizzes: Explanations

Analogies

Answers
1. C 2. E 3. D 4. C

1. **C** You need to define your bridge carefully in this one, because if you don't, more than one choice will fit into it. A **CHANDELIER** is a decorative piece that hangs from a **CEILING**. The only choice that fits into this bridge is (C): an **earring** is a decorative piece that hangs from an **ear.** If you started out with a more broadly defined bridge, say "a chandelier is attached to a ceiling," then both (C) and (D) would work; "a knob is attached to a door." When this happens, you know you have to redefine your bridge. Choice (E) is wrong because though a chandelier does light up a ceiling, a spotlight doesn't have to be used to light up a stage.

2. **E** *Nebulous* means "vague" or "lacking in definition," so the bridge could be expressed as follows: "Something **NEBULOUS** is hard to **DEFINE.**" In a similar way, something that's **chaotic** is difficult to **order**. Choice (A) is the closest wrong answer. Something that's weighty may be difficult to balance, but weighty things are not by definition difficult to balance. Choice (C) has a bridge that is the opposite of the stem bridge. Something that's restrained is easy to discipline. The word *circumspect* in (D) means "prudent" or "cautious."

3. **D** To **EAVESDROP** is to **LISTEN** secretly, while to **spy** is to **watch** secretly. None of the other choices works in the bridge. Choice (C) comes close: someone who is gossiping may be speaking secretly, but the word *gossip* does not mean "to speak secretly." Choice (B) has a bridge that is nearly the reverse of the stem bridge: to confide in someone is to tell that person something confidentially.

4. **C** This is an especially difficult question because it has more than a few tough vocabulary words. A **PROCRASTINATOR** is someone who is continually putting things off that should be done, and **DILATORY** means "characterized by procrastination." A procrastinator, then, is by definiton, dilatory. The choice that fits this bridge is (C). A **nomad** is a person who wanders from place to place, without a fixed home; **itinerant** means "traveling from place to place." Thus a nomad is by definition itinerant. Choices (A), (B), and (E) may tempt you because they are familiar-sounding phrases, but dictators are never benevolent, explorers are not always hardy, and musicians are not always wandering. In (D), *bellicose* means "inclined to start quarrels," which is not true of all leaders.

Sentence Completions

Answers

1. C 2. E 3. D 4. C

1. **C** You can predict what the word in the blank should be from two clues. First, the phrase *Except for* alerts you that the blank is the opposite of *loners*, and second, the phrase *generally living in packs with strong bonds* virtually defines the missing word in blank. **Social** (C) is the word that fits the bill. Some of the other words may be strongly associated with wolves, but they don't work in the sentence.

2. **E** The two halves of the sentence are connected by a semicolon, which signals consistency of meaning between the two. The view of the noblemen in the second half has to jibe with the general opinion about manual work expressed in the first half of the sentence. Thus, (A) and (D) don't work because the general opinion that manual work is distasteful or intense won't lead noblemen to think that they can do it without difficulty or discomfort. Choices (B) and (C) don't make sense when you know that *erudite* means "learned" and *remuneration* means "compensation or pay." Choice (E) works because if manual work was considered **respectable**, noblemen could engage in it without **dishonor**.

3. **D** The word *despite* signals that there is a contrast between the stated goals of the company and the type of employee it promotes. Since the company says it wants industrious and productive workers, you can predict that the workers they promote are lazy or **lackadaisical**, choice (D). These workers certainly won't be meritorious, (E), and there's no reason to think they are creative, (A), discontented, (B), or accomplished, (C).

4. **C** The repetition of the word *own* emphasizes that the colonies functioned separately or individually, either of which would have been a good prediction for the second blank. An entity is something with a distinct existence, so *separate* or *independent* would be a good bet for the first blank, too. So both of the words in the correct answer should have to do with separateness or independence. The best choice is **distinct . . autonomously**. *Autonomously* means "separately and independently." In (A), *related* is wrong for the first blank. *Independent* is fine in (B), but *affirmatively* doesn't fit the prediction. Neither of the words in (D) matches the prediction; *austerely* means "very simply or sternly, without frills or extras." Finally, in (E), *united* is just the opposite of what's needed.

Critical Reading

Answers

1. C 2. C 3. E 4. C 5. B 6. B 7. B 8. A

1. **C** According to the first paragraph, English colonists justified taking the Native Americans' lands by arguing that they could put the land to "higher use" by cultivating it. Downplaying how the native people were using the land was problematic, though, because the Native Americans were already successfully planting crops on it. The author clearly suggests that the idea that Europeans could put the land to "higher use"

had little or no basis in fact, choice (C). Choice (A) is wrong because the author's implying that the Europeans were aware of the extent of Native American farming. Choices (B) and (D) also contradict the passage; the colonists were not altruistic, and did not stop spreading propaganda once they became aware of the facts. No mention is made of what the Native Americans thought about the "higher use" idea, so (E) is out.

2. **C** This question is very similar to the last and is drawn from the same part of the passage, so you might have been able to answer it without going back to the passage. The image of the Native Americans as nomadic hunters was, just like the idea of putting their land to "higher use," the result of the colonists' attempt to justify taking their land, choice (C)—not a misunderstanding, (E). The author never says what happened when the colonists took the Native Americans' land, so (A) is wrong. Choice (B) contradicts the assertion that the Indians had farmed extensively. Choice (D) can be eliminated because the English were not naively comparing Native American culture with European culture; they deliberately constructed the "nomadic hunter" image of the Native Americans in order to justify taking their land.

3. **E** The third paragraph discusses the Native Americans' "mosaic" farming pattern. The Native Americans plant fields until the fertility declines, then let them lie fallow and open up others. When they return to the previously used fields, these are easy to clear and cultivate again. In this way, they are using their land productively without ruining it, choice (E). Notice that the correct choice here fits not only the third paragraph but the theme of the entire passage. Choices (A) and (C) are wrong because the author never says the Native Americans were using their farming pattern to show that they were not merely nomadic hunters or to distinguish their land from that of the colonists. Although the Native Americans did use the pattern to allow fields with declining fertility to recover, this does not mean that the fertility of the soil declined rapidly, (B). Choice (D) is no doubt a true statement, but it does not explain why the Native Americans used the particular farming pattern they did.

4. **C** The "marked shift" in question is the change in forest vegetation after the Native Americans left—we're told that parklands became impenetrable thickets. So the change was a striking one—choice (C). Some of the other choices may be possible alternate meanings of *marked*, but they don't work in context.

5. **B** The fires in Yellowstone "showed that fire is an inherent part of the forest ecosystem. . . ." (lines 37–38). Observing the effects of these fires is how environmental agencies are rediscovering the advantages of controlled burning. Since the Native Americans used controlled burning first, the author is emphasizing that they were correct in viewing fire as having a beneficial effect on forests, (B). Choice (A) contradicts the information in the paragraph. Choice (C) is too broad; the environmentalists aren't investigating everything the Native Americans knew. Choice (D) exaggerates the dangerous aspect of forest fires; the passage

only discusses the danger of preventing them for too long. Finally, (E) is wrong because it is too extreme. Occasional forest fires, not frequent forest fires, are essential to the livelihood of forest ecosystems.

6. **B** In the seventh paragraph, the author discusses the possibility that early Native Americans caused the extinction of the large animals of the western hemisphere. Once again, this particular point fits in with the overall discussion; the author's purpose is not to take a strong stand on this issue but to show another way that Native Americans had an impact on their environment, (B). The author doesn't talk about the extinctions to prove that Native Americans were living in North America over 12,000 years ago, (A). Furthermore, the information in the paragraph certainly doesn't challenge the image of the Native Americans as nomadic hunters, (C), substantiate the modern view of Native Americans as conservationists, (D), or discredit the view that Native Americans caused wildlife extinctions (E).

7. **B** To answer this question, you have to go back and reread the last paragraph, which fortunately is not very long. The author says that the stereotype of Native Americans as "ecological Indians" is an oversimplification. So two things the author does are identify misconceptions, ruling out (A), and counter a prevalent view, ruling out (C). When the author goes on to point out that Native Americans changed their environment without destroying it, he is reemphasizing an earlier point, (D), and giving an assessment (E). What the author does *not* do is suggest further study (B).

8. **A** The eighth and ninth paragraphs deal with the idea that the Native Americans were conservationists—a misconception, according to the overall message of the passage, because the Native Americans had an extensive impact on their environment. The author rejects this characterization because it oversimplifies the Native Americans' interaction with the environment. They didn't just adapt to the land; they changed the landscape, without destroying its ecosystems. Choice (A) is correct. Choice (B) is out because no lack of historical evidence is mentioned. Choice (C) misses the point of why the author objects to the conservationist label. Choice (D) distorts lines 64–65, where the author ironically suggests that the ability to destroy the environment is the mark of civilization. Finally, (E) overexaggerates the author's tone here. He says there's a note of condescension in this characterization—not that it's presumptuous and disdainful.

4 ACT VERBAL

THE FORMAT

The two ACT Verbal sections contain English and Reading questions that together constitute 50 percent of your composite score. Here's the breakdown you'll see on the test:

- one 45-minute section with 75 English questions
- one 35-minute section with 40 Reading questions

Unlike "short Verbal" questions on the SAT, Verbal questions on the ACT are *not* arranged by order of difficulty, which means that you should use a "question triage" approach to each English and Reading question: whenever you find yourself spending too much time on any one question, skip it and return to it later.

ENGLISH

The English test is 45 minutes long and includes 75 questions. That works out to about 30 seconds per question, but in practice you should spend less time on more basic questions and more on harder questions. The test is divided into five passages, each with about 15 questions.

Students nearly always get more questions correct in English than in any other section. That tends to make students think that English is a lot easier than the rest of the ACT. But alas—it's not that simple. Because most students do well, the test makers have much higher expectations for English than for other parts of the test. They *know* that it's generally easier to get English questions right than, say, Science Reasoning questions. They've got a whole department of little statistician elves who keep track of things like this. That's why, to earn an average English subscore (a 20, say), you have to get almost two-thirds of the questions right, while on the rest of the test you need to get only about half right.

The good news about ACT English is that it's not just a test of grammar. Questions on ACT English test your ability to spot redundancy, use your logic and common sense, and apply just a few hard-and-fast grammar rules.

The Question Types
The three main question types in ACT English are:

- economy questions
- sense questions
- technicality questions

There are three main question types you'll encounter in ACT English:

- economy questions—these test your understanding of whether material is strictly essential to the passage, or whether it could be said more simply or economically.
- sense questions—these ask you to identify and correct logical flaws in the passage—statements that just don't make sense.
- technicality questions—these check your knowledge of key punctuation, grammar, and usage issues.

Almost all ACT English questions follow a standard format. First, a word, phrase, or sentence in a passage is underlined. You're given four options: to leave the underlined portion alone ("NO CHANGE," which is always the first choice), or to replace it with one of three alternatives (the ones proposed in the other three choices). For example:

. . . Pike's Peak in Southwest Colorado is named <u>before Zebulon Pike, an early explorer.</u> (1) He traveled through the area, exploring. . . .

1. A. NO CHANGE
   B. before Zebulon Pike became an explorer,
   C. after Zebulon Pike, when,
   D. after Zebulon Pike.

The best answer for this question is choice D. The other choices all have various problems—grammatical, stylistic, logical. They make the passage look and sound like it was written by your baby brother. Only choice D makes the sentence sensible and correct. That's why it's the answer.

Nonstandard Format Questions

Some ACT English questions—usually about ten per exam—don't follow this standard format. These items pose a question and offer four possible responses. In many cases, the responses are either "yes" or "no," with an explanation. Pay attention to the reasoning.

. . . Later, Pike fell while valiantly defending America in the War of 1812. [2] He actually died near York (now called Toronto). . . .

2. Suppose the author considered adding the following sentence at this point: "It goes without saying that this occurred after he discovered Pike's Peak." Given the overall purpose of the passage, would this sentence be appropriate?

F. No, because the sentence adds nothing to the meaning of the passage.
G. No, because the passage is not concerned with Pike's achieve-ments.
H. Yes, because otherwise the sequence of events would be unclear.
J. Yes; though the sentence is not needed, the author recognizes this fact by using the phrase "it goes without saying."

The correct answer for this question is choice F. Though choice G correctly indicates that the sentence doesn't belong in the passage, it offers a pretty inappropriate reason. The passage *is* concerned with Pike's achievements. Choices H and J are wrong because they recommend including a sentence that's clearly redundant.

When in Doubt . . .

On the ACT, more than 20 questions—almost a third of all the English items—test your awareness of redundancy, verbosity, relevance, and similar issues. For these questions—which we call *economy questions*—the shortest answer is very frequently correct. What that means is:

The "Short" Cut
For "economy" questions in ACT English, very often the shortest answer is the right one.

- If you're not sure whether an idea is redundant, it probably is, so take it out.
- If you're not sure whether a sentence or phrase is verbose, it probably is, so take it out.
- If you're not sure whether an idea is relevant, it probably isn't, so take it out.

In other words, when in doubt, take it out.

Keep It Short—on *All* English Questions

Questions in which the lengths of the answers vary greatly, or that contain the answer choice "OMIT," are usually economy questions. For these questions, you should be especially inclined to pick the shortest choice. For the other questions, the shortest answer is not nearly as often the correct choice. But even for these other questions, the shortest answer is frequently your best bet.

Because these issues of writing economy are so important to English questions of all kinds, we've made them the linchpin for our recommended approach to ACT English. When approaching English questions, the very first question you should ask yourself is: "Does this stuff belong here? Can the passage or sentence work *without* it?"

Reading English Passages

Before launching in and starting to correct the prose on an ACT English passage, it usually pays to skim each paragraph to get a sense of how it's shaped and what it's about. For most students, that makes correcting the underlined portions a little easier, since you'll have a better sense of the context. The skimming technique is simple: you skim a paragraph, then do the questions it contains, then skim the next paragraph, do the questions *that* one contains, etcetera. Some students even find it helpful to skim the entire passage before starting on the questions.

Try the following passage, and then we'll go over Kaplan's Four-Step Method for English questions.

The character of Frankenstein did not originate in Hollywood. Rather, the legendary mad scientist who sought to reanimate lifeless bodies were [1] the creation of Mary Wollstonecraft Shelley. Her *Frankenstein: or the Modern Prometheus*, published in 1818—is [2] considered one of the greatest horror tales of all time.

1. A. NO CHANGE
   B. bodies was
   C. bodies, was
   D. bodies' is

(A) (B) (C) (D)

2. F. NO CHANGE
   G. 1818 was
   H. 1818, is
   J. 1818. It's

(F) (G) (H) (J)

Mary Shelley conceived of her nightmarish subject in response to a wager. She, and her husband, [3] along with Lord Byron and Byron's physician, had a contest to see who could write the best "ghost story" because it was begun [4] in such a whimsical fashion, her tale became a serious examination of the fate of an individual who decides to overstep moral and social bounds.

3. A. NO CHANGE
   B. She and, her husband,
   C. She, her husband too
   D. She and her husband,

(A) (B) (C) (D)

4. F. NO CHANGE
   G. story." If it begun
   H. story" although it was begun
   J. story." Although it was begun

(F) (G) (H) (J)

She tells the story of a German scientist, Frankenstein, who discovers the secret of bringing dead corpses [5] back to life and so creates

5. A. NO CHANGE
   B. how to turn dead corpses
   C. bringing the dead
   D. restoring the dead

(A) (B) (C) (D)

a monster. Despite the monster's gruesome 6 appearance, he is basically good. The monster becomes evil only when his creator refuses acceptance and care 7 him. When the rejected monster kills members of Frankenstein's family, the scientist pursues his creation to the North Pole, where the two of them both lose their lives? 8

Numerous popularizations have been made of Shelley's intellectual "ghost story." Horror stories are exciting movies. 9 Perhaps the most familiar is the classic 1931 version starring that master of cinematic horror, Boris Karloff, 10 as the monster.

6. F. NO CHANGE
   G. monsters' gruesome
   H. monsters gruesome
   J. monster's gruesomely horrible

   (F) (G) (H) (J)

7. A. NO CHANGE
   B. to accept, and care for
   C. to accept and care for
   D. to accept and care over

   (A) (B) (C) (D)

8. F. NO CHANGE
   G. Pole, where both lose their lives.
   H. Pole; where the two of them lose their lives.
   J. Pole, and where their live's are lost.

   (F) (G) (H) (J)

9. A. NO CHANGE
   B. Horror stories make exciting movies.
   C. Horror stories, so exciting, are popular with audiences.
   D. OMIT the underlined portion.

   (A) (B) (C) (D)

10. F. NO CHANGE
    G. horror Boris Karloff,
    H. horror, Boris Karloff
    J. horror Boris Karloff

    (F) (G) (H) (J)

[See the following section for answers and explanations.]

Kaplan's Four-Step Method for English Questions

1. When in doubt, take it out.

2. Make it make sense.

3. Use your ears.

4. Look for pitfalls.

Step One: When in Doubt, Take It Out

Almost a third of ACT English questions are economy questions—they test your ability to to identify whether the underlined sections are actually relevant to the passage. You can solve these questions by simply checking to see if the underlined material doesn't belong in the passage, or is too wordy. Often the correct answer is the shortest, simplest way of expressing an idea. Here's an example:

> She tells the story of a German scientist, Frankenstein, who discovers the secret of bringing dead corpses [5] back to life and so creates a monster.

Question 5 tests redundancy. Since a corpse by definition is a dead body, there's no need to say "dead corpses." Only choice C eliminates the error. Choice D introduces another redundancy: *restoring . . . back* means the same thing as *restoring.*

> Numerous popularizations have been made of Shelley's intellectual "ghost story." Horror stories are exciting movies. [9] Perhaps the most familiar is the classic 1931 version . . .

Question 9 is also about irrelevant information. While the underlined statement may be true, it's not relevant to the development of this paragraph. When in doubt, leave it out. A good clue that choice D is the answer is that choices A, B, and C are all grammatically correct; the problem must be something else. And that problem is redundancy.

Step Two: Make It Make Sense

Remember that good grammar makes good sense. Since grammatical problems often show up as nonsensical statements, asking yourself if a particular sentence is *logical* can help you uncover errors. For example:

> The monster becomes evil only when his creator refuses acceptance and care [7] him.

You probably could tell that the sentence containing segment 7 didn't make sense. Look for a simpler, clearer choice. Choice B is better, but there's no reason to include a comma in the phrase *accept and care*. Read the sentence out loud, and you'll hear the problem. Choice C leaves out the offending comma. Choice D isn't idiomatic. You don't care over someone, you care for them, or about them.

Use Your Ears
Use your ears when working on English passages. Does the sentence sound like it doesn't fit into the passage? Does it sound like it runs on?

> When the rejected monster kills members of Frankenstein's family, the scientist pursues his creation to the North Pole, where the two of them both lose their lives? (8)

Even though the word *where* appears in the underlined fragment of this sentence, the sentence is not a question. So the question mark is wrong. Also, there's a redundancy problem. If you say *two of them* you don't need to say *both* as well. Choice H is not redundant, but it incorrectly uses a semicolon to separate the incomplete thought at the end of the sentence. Choice J uses the possessive *live's* when the plural *lives* is needed. Correct choice G is not redundant, and separates the two parts of the sentence correctly.

Step Three: Use Your Ears
Often you can *hear* problems in an ACT English passage. The test makers might throw a formal sentence in an informal passage, or omit a comma where you would normally pause for breath. You can train your ear to listen for these errors. But don't forget to use your eyes, too. For example:

> Her *Frankenstein: or the Modern Prometheus*, published in 1818—is (2) considered one of the greatest horror tales of all time.

Do you see something funny in this sentence? Something unbalanced? The phrase *published in 1818* is set off by a comma on the left and a dash on the right. The comma isn't underlined, so we can change only the dash. Only H has a second comma to match the one before *published*.

> She, and her husband, (3) along with Lord Byron and Byron's physician, had a contest . . .

Here's another one that tests your knowledge of punctuation. Four people have a contest, but they are presented in the sentence as a compound subject ("she and her husband") and a prepositional phrase ("*with* Lord Byron and Byron's physician"). This phrase should be set off by commas, as it is in choice D. Choices A and C separate a pair of subjects. We say: "John and Mary are here," not "John, and Mary are here." In Choice B, there's no reason to put a comma after *and*.

Here's another example of an error that your ears could have easily picked up:

> . . . along with Lord Byron and Byron's physician, had a contest to see who could write the best "ghost <u>story" because it was begun</u> [4] in such a whimsical fashion, her tale became a serious examination of the fate of an individual who decides to overstep moral and social bounds.

This is a run-on sentence that includes a nonsensical connecting word. *Because* signals a cause-and-effect relationship, but what the author wants to signal is really a contradiction: although it began as a joke, the book became a very serious project. Choice G is wrong for the same reason. Choice H uses the right connecting word, but creates a run-on sentence. Choice J separates the run-on into two sentences, and gives you the right connecting word—*although.*

Step Four: Look for Pitfalls
A certain number of questions test classic grammar pitfalls. It's a good idea to prepare for the test by creating a "flag list" of errors that teachers often find in your own papers—using *who* instead of *whom,* for instance, or confusing *there, they're,* and *their.* For example:

> Rather, the legendary mad scientist who sought to reanimate lifeless <u>bodies were</u> [1] the creation of Mary Wollstonecraft Shelley.

Here, *were* is the plural form of the verb—which is wrong, since the subject is *scientist.* Choice B provides the correct, singular form *was.*

Don't Be Afraid of No Change

A certain number of questions will also contain no error. So don't be afraid to select choice A or F. Here are two examples:

> Despite the <u>monster's gruesome</u> [6] appearance, he is basically good.

> Perhaps the most familiar is the classic 1931 version starring that master of cinematic <u>horror, Boris Karloff,</u> [10] as the monster.

Sometimes, They're Right
Don't feel that you must find the mistake when working on an ACT English question. The NO CHANGE choice is there for a reason.

English Practice Quiz

Now answer the following English questions to assess your strengths and weaknesses. At the end of the chapter, you'll find an answer key and strategic explanations. Then enter your score on the "SAT or ACT? Score Comparison Chart" at the end of this book.

The late twentieth century may well be remembered as the Age of the "Yuppie" (young urban professional). Our society seems obsessed with the notion of social mobility. There are two different types of social mobility: horizontal and vertical. (1) If there is a change in occupation, but no change in social class, it is called *horizontal mobility.* One example of this would be a lawyer who changes law firms that are comparable in pay and salary and prestige. (2) A change in role involving a change in social standing is called "vertical mobility" (3) and can be either upward or downward.

1. A. NO CHANGE
   B. mobility horizontal, and vertical.
   C. mobility; horizontal and vertical.
   D. mobility: being horizontal and vertical.

   (A) (B) (C) (D)

2. F. NO CHANGE
   G. in pay and prestige.
   H. with pay, salary and prestige.
   J. pay in terms of salary and prestige.

   (F) (G) (H) (J)

3. A. NO CHANGE
   B. it's called "vertical mobility"
   C. they're called "vertical mobility"
   D. it is called "vertical mobility"

   (A) (B) (C) (D)

The extent of change can vary greatly. At one pole, social mobility may affect only one member of a society. At the other extreme, it may change the entire social system. The Russian Revolution of 1917, therefore, (4) altered an entire class structure.

4. F. NO CHANGE
   G. nonetheless
   H. for instance
   J. consequently

   (F) (G) (H) (J)

[1] In addition to involving degrees of change, (5) social mobility occurs at a variety of rates. [2] The "American dream" is based in part on the notion of rapid social mobility, in which an unknown individual becomes an "overnight success." [3] One example of rapid social mobility would be the young guitar player who becomes an instant rock star. [4] The athlete who wins an Olympic gold medal too. (6) [5] For instance, each generation in a family may be a little better off than the generation before it. [6] Social mobility may also be accomplished by more gradual changes. [7]

5. A. NO CHANGE
   B. In addition, it involved differing degrees of change,
   C. In addition to the fact that it involved change's differing degrees,
   D. It involves degrees of change,

Ⓐ Ⓑ Ⓒ Ⓓ

6. F. NO CHANGE
   G. is another example.
   H. is too.
   J. OMIT the underlined portion and end with a period.

Ⓕ Ⓖ Ⓗ Ⓙ

7. For the sake of unity and coherence, Sentence 6 should be placed:

   A. where it is now.
   B. after Sentence 2.
   C. after Sentence 4.
   D. at the beginning of the next paragraph.

Ⓐ Ⓑ Ⓒ Ⓓ

The results of mobility are difficult to measure in that. (8) Some view large-scale mobility in a negative light, claiming that it disintegrates class structure and puts an end to meaningful traditions. Accordingly (9)

8. F. NO CHANGE
   G. in.
   H. on.
   J. OMIT the underlined portion and end the sentence with a period.

Ⓕ Ⓖ Ⓗ Ⓙ

9. A. NO CHANGE
   B. (Begin new paragraph) Similarly,
   C. (Begin new paragraph) Likewise,
   D. (Do NOT begin new paragraph) On the other hand,

Ⓐ Ⓑ Ⓒ Ⓓ

others claim that they're attempting to rise validate and therefore reinforce the class system. They see mobility as a positive thing, enabling individuals to improve their own lives and the lives of their families. [11]

Still others see social mobility as destroying, rather than reinforced—the class system yet they feel this is a positive change. According to them, society will benefit from the breakdown like a flat tire of a social system in which material wealth is given so much importance.

10. F. NO CHANGE
G. they
H. those who are
J. their

11. Suppose that at this point in the passage the writer wanted to add more information. Which of the following additions would be most relevant to the paragraph?
A. A discussion of the problems of the educational system in America
B. A listing of average salaries for different occupations
C. Some examples of the benefits of social mobility
D. A discussion of a rock star's new video

12. F. NO CHANGE
G. reinforcing, the class system; yet
H. reinforced. The class system; and
J. that it reinforces the class system

13. A. NO CHANGE
B. (such as a flat tire)
C. (like the kind a flat tire gets)
D. OMIT the underlined portion.

Whether we view it positively or negatively, social mobility is a basic fact of modern industrial society. The crowd of yuppies hitting the shopping malls, credit cards in hand, show [14] that vertical mobility is very much with us and so will a lot of other things be. [15]

14. **F.** NO CHANGE
G. shows
H. showing
J. to show

(F) (G) (H) (J)

15. **A.** NO CHANGE
B. and there they will be for some time to come.
C. and will be for some time to come.
D. OMIT the underlined portion and end the sentence with a period.

(A) (B) (C) (D)

Reading

The ACT Reading test is 35 minutes long and includes 40 questions. The test contains four passages, each of which is followed by ten questions. When you factor in the amount of time you'll initially spend on the passages, this works out to about 30 seconds per question—again, more for the tough ones, less for the basic ones.

There are four categories of reading passages: social studies, natural sciences, humanities, and prose fiction. You'll get one passage in each category. The passages are about 1,000 words long and are written at about the same difficulty level as college textbooks and readings. The social studies, natural sciences, and humanities passages are usually well-organized essays. Each has a very specific theme. Questions expect you to recognize this theme, to comprehend specific facts contained in the passage, and to understand the structure of the essay. Prose fiction passages require you to understand the thoughts, feelings, and motivations of fictional characters.

You don't need a Ph.D. in Romance literature to do well on the ACT Reading section. To turn in a good score, you need to be able to read and digest the ACT's lengthy Reading passages quickly and efficiently. Then you need to patiently research each Reading question by going back to the passage. Fortunately, the questions are fairly straightforward once you get used to the format. There are three main question types you'll encounter on the ACT Reading section:

- Specific Detail questions
- Inference questions
- Big Picture questions

Three Types of Reading Questions
The three main types of ACT Reading questions are:

- Specific Detail questions
- Inference questions
- Big Picture questions

Specific Detail Questions

Specific Detail questions ask about things stated explicitly in the passage. The challenge with these questions is, first, finding the proper place in the passage in which the answer can be found (sometimes you'll be given a line reference, sometimes not), and second, being able to match up what you see in the passage with the correct answer, which will probably be worded differently.

Inference Questions

Most Reading sections also include a large number of Inference questions, which require you to make an inference from the the passage—to "read between the lines." Inference questions are a little harder than Specific Detail questions because the answers are not directly stated in the passage—you have to draw conclusions about the author's underlying point.

Big Picture Questions

Although the majority of Reading questions are Specific Detail and Inference questions, the Reading subtest also includes another type of question that we call *Big Picture questions.* Some Big Picture questions ask about the passage as a whole, requiring you to find the theme, tone, or structure of the passage.

The Key to ACT Reading

The real key to ACT reading is to read quickly but actively, getting a sense of the gist or "main idea" of the passage and seeing how everything fits together to support that main idea. You should constantly try to think ahead. Look for the general outline of the passage—determine how it's structured. Don't worry about the details. You'll come back for those later.

Kaplan's Three-Step Method

1. **Preread the passage.**
2. **Consider the question stem.**
3. **Research the passage (before looking at the choices).**

Step One: Preread the Passage

Prereading means quickly working through the passage before trying to answer the questions. Remember to "know where you're going," anticipating how the parts of the passage fit together. In this preread, the main goals are to:

- Understand the "gist" of the passage (the "main idea").
- Get an overall idea of how the passage is organized—a kind of road map—so that it will be easier to refer to later.

You may want to underline key points, jot down notes, circle structural clues—whatever it takes to accomplish the two goals above. You may even want to label each paragraph, to fix in your mind how the paragraphs relate to one another and what aspect of the main idea is discussed in each.

Step Two: Consider the Question Stem

Most test takers have an almost irresistible urge to jump immediately to the answer choices to see what "looks okay." That's not a good idea. Don't let the answer choices direct your thinking. The test makers intentionally design the answers to confuse you if they can. In Reading, you should think about the question stem (the part above the answer choices) without looking at the choices. In most questions, you won't be able to remember exactly what the passage said about the matter in question. That's okay. In fact, even if you *do* think you remember, don't trust your memory. Instead . . .

Step Three: Research the Passage (Before Looking at the Choices)

You won't be rereading the whole passage, of course. But refer to a specific paragraph to research your answer (the question stem will sometimes contain a line reference to help you out; otherwise, rely on your map of the passage). Your chosen answer should match the passage—not in exact vocabulary, perhaps, but in *meaning*.

Now practice the Three-Step Method on the sample Reading passage that follows, and then we'll review the questions, highlighting strategies for each question type.

Think

As you work on the questions, remember to refer to the passage. Don't trust your memory. But don't confine yourself to the exact words the passage uses. This is a common trap. Think about what they mean.

The first truly American art movement was formed by a group of landscape painters that emerged in the early nineteenth century called the Hudson River School. The first works in this style were created by Thomas Cole, Thomas Doughty, and Asher Durand, a trio of painters who worked during the 1820s in the Hudson River Valley and surrounding locations. Heavily influenced by European Romanticism, these painters set out to convey the remoteness and splendor of the American wilderness. The strongly nationalistic tone of their paintings caught the spirit of the times, and within a generation the movement had mushroomed to include landscape painters from all over the United States. Canvases celebrating such typically American scenes as Niagara Falls, Boston Harbor, and the expansion of the railroad into rural Pennsylvania were greeted with enormous popular acclaim.

One factor contributing to the success of the Hudson River School was the rapid growth of American nationalism in the early nineteenth century. The War of 1812 had given the United States a new sense of pride in its identity, and as the nation continued to grow, there was a desire to compete with Europe on both economic and cultural grounds. The vast panoramas of the Hudson River School fitted the bill perfectly by providing a new movement in art that was unmistakably American in origin. The Hudson River School also arrived at a time when writers in the United States were turning their attention to the wilderness as a unique aspect of their nationality. The view that the American character was formed by the frontier experience was widely held, and many writers were concerned about the future of a country that was becoming increasingly urbanized. The Hudson River School painters profited from this nostalgia because they effectively represented the continent the way it used to be.

In keeping with this nationalistic spirit, even the painting style of the Hudson River School exhibited a strong sense of American identity. Although many of the artists studied in Europe, their paintings show a desire to be free of European artistic rules. Regarding the natural landscape as a direct manifestation of God, the Hudson River School painters attempted to record what they saw as accurately as possible. Unlike European painters who brought to their canvases the styles and techniques of centuries, they sought neither to embellish nor to idealize their scenes, portraying nature with the care and attention to detail of naturalists.

1. The first works in the Hudson River School style were produced in:

A. the late 1700s.
B. 1800.
C. 1812.
D. the 1820s.

Ⓐ Ⓑ Ⓒ Ⓓ

2. The passage implies that Hudson River School paintings "fitted the bill perfectly" (lines 19–20) because they :

F. depicted famous battle scenes.
G. were very successful commercially.
H. reflected a new pride in the United States.
J. were favorably received in Europe.

Ⓕ Ⓖ Ⓗ Ⓙ

3. Which of the following is NOT described as a feature of Hudson River School painting?

A. portraying the splendor of the wilderness.
B. celebrating the expansion of the railroad.
C. idealizing the everyday life of rural people.
D. recording natural scenery as accurately as possible.

Ⓐ Ⓑ Ⓒ Ⓓ

4. The main point of the second paragraph is that:

F. the Hudson River School paintings appealed to widespread nationalistic sentiments.
G. many early nineteenth-century painters took their inspiration from writers.
H. Hudson River School painters were forced to compete with European painters.
J. nineteenth-century painters influenced by Romanticism exploited a nostalgia for the past.

Ⓕ Ⓖ Ⓗ Ⓙ

5. Which of the following best describes the attitude of the Hudson River School painters towards European artistic traditions?

A. A successful businessman who changes careers and who becomes a teacher.
B. A sculptor who imitates the technique of a more famous sculptor.
C. A trained surgeon who rejects existing methods of operating and develops a new method.
D. A newly recruited soldier who always obeys her officers' orders.

Ⓐ Ⓑ Ⓒ Ⓓ

Step One: Prereading the Passage

How did you do? This passage is a humanities passage about the Hudson River School of painters, the first "truly American art movement." Your "mental map" of the passage should have read something like this: Paragraph 1 describes the origins of the movement and the contents of its paintings. Paragraph 2 picks up on an idea introduced in Paragraph 1—the way in which a growing nationalism in the United States contributed to the popularity of the Hudson River School paintings. Paragraph 3 states that the painters of the Hudson River School developed a uniquely American style of painting, even though many of them studied in Europe.

Steps Two and Three: Considering the Question Stem and Researching the Passage

Question 1 is a Specific Detail question. The passage lists only two dates (which can quickly be located by scanning the text): the 1820s and 1812. Lines 4–6 say that the first works of the Hudson River School were painted in the 1820s (choice D). The year 1812 (choice C) marks the beginning of the War of 1812. Neither of the other dates—the late 1700s (A) or 1800 (B)— is mentioned in the passage.

Question 2 is an Inference question. The phrase *fitted the bill perfectly* comes a few lines after the passage states that the "War of 1812 had given the United States a new sense of pride in its identity" (choice H). In other words, the nationalistic paintings of the Hudson River School reflected America's mood in the wake of the war. Choice F is flatly contradicted by the passage, which indicates that the artists of the Hudson River School painted landscape, not battle, scenes. The passage doesn't comment on either the Hudson River School's *commercial* success (G) or its reception in Europe (J).

Question 3 is also an Inference question. This question asks you to pick the choice that's *not* characteristic of the Hudson River School. The best way to get the answer to a question like this one is to use the process of elimination—find the *true* choices and strike them off. The last sentence of the first paragraph says that wilderness (A) and railroad (B) scenes were characteristic of this school. Likewise, the last sentence of the third paragraph states that Hudson River School painters had a habit of "portraying nature with the care and attention to detail of naturalists" (D). Thus, the answer must be choice C. Indeed, the text never mentions that humans were part of the landscapes painted by Hudson River School artists.

Question 4 is a Big Picture question about the second paragraph. The first sentence of the second paragraph says, "One factor contributing to the success of the Hudson River School was the rapid growth of American nationalism in the early nineteenth century." The rest of the paragraph goes on to explain this statement. So choice F is correct. Choice J is too broad in scope; the second paragraph discusses Hudson River School painters, not *all* nineteenth-century painters. Choices G and H draw conclusions that aren't supported in the passage.

Question 5 is an Inference question. The third paragraph outlines the relationship of Hudson River School painters to European painters. This paragraph says that, although Hudson River School painters were trained in Europe, they developed their own style of painting. This is most similar to a "trained surgeon who rejects existing methods of operating and develops a new method" (choice C).

Reading Practice Quiz

Now answer the following Reading questions to assess your strengths and weaknesses. At the end of the chapter, you'll find an answer key and strategic explanations. Then enter your score on the "SAT or ACT? Score Comparison Chart" at the end of this book.

In the 500 years since Leonardo, two ideas about man have been especially important. The first is the emphasis on the full development of the human personality. The individual is prized for himself. His creative powers are seen as the core of his being. The unfettered development of individual personality is praised as the ideal, from the Renaissance artists through the Elizabethans, and through Locke and Voltaire and Rousseau. This vision of the freely developing man, happy in the unfolding of his own gifts, is shared by men as different in their conceptions as Thomas Jefferson and Edmund Burke. . . .

Thus the fulfillment of man has been one of the two most formative grand ideas. . . . Men have seen themselves entering the world with a potential of many gifts, and they have hoped to fulfill these gifts in the development of their own lives. This has come to be the unexpressed purpose of the life of individuals: fulfilling the special gifts with which a man is endowed.

The self-fulfillment of the individual has itself become part of a larger, more embracing idea, the self-fulfillment of man. We think of man as a species with special gifts, which are the human gifts. Some of these gifts, the physical and mental gifts, are elucidated for us explicitly by science; some of them, the aesthetic and ethical gifts, we feel and struggle to express in our own minds; and some of them, the cultural gifts, are unfolded for us by the study of history. The total of these gifts is man as a type or species, and the aspiration of man as a species has become the fulfillment of what is most human in these gifts.

This idea of human self-fulfillment has also inspired scientific and technical progress. We sometimes think that progress is illusory, and that the devices and gadgets which have become indispensable to civilized men in the last 500 years are only a self-propagating accumulation of idle luxuries. But this has not been the purpose in the minds of scientists and technicians, nor has it been the true effect of these inventions on human society. The purpose and the effect has been to liberate men from the exhausting drudgeries of earning their living, in order to give them the opportunity to live. From Leonardo to Franklin, the inventor has wanted to give, and has succeeded in giving, more and more people the ease and leisure to find the best in themselves which was once the monopoly of princes.

Only rarely has a thinker in the last 500 years gone back from the ideal of human potential and fulfillment. Calvin was perhaps such a thinker who went back, and believed as the Middle Ages did, that man comes into this world as a complete entity, incapable of any worthwhile development. And it is characteristic that the state which Calvin organized was, as a result, a totalitarian state. For if men cannot develop, and have nothing in them which is personal and creative, there is no point in giving them freedom.

The second of the two grand formative ideas is the idea of freedom. We see in fact that human fulfillment is unattainable without freedom, so that these two main ideas are linked together. There could be no development of the personality of individuals, no fulfillment of those gifts in which one man differs from another, without the freedom for each man to grow in his own direction.

What is true of individuals is true of human groups. A state or a society cannot change unless its members are given freedom to judge, to criticize, and to search for a new status for themselves. Therefore the pressure of ideas has been toward freedom as an expression of individuality. Sometimes men have tried to find freedom along quiet paths of change, as the humanists did on the eve of the Reformation, and as the dissenting manufacturers of the eighteenth century did. At other times, the drive for freedom has been explosive: intellectually explosive in the Elizabethan age and the Scientific Revolution, economically explosive in the Industrial Revolution, and politically explosive in the other great revolutions of our period, from Puritan times to the age of Napoleon.

. . .Freedom is a supple and elusive idea, whose advocates can at times delude themselves that obedience to tyranny is a form of freedom. Such a delusion ensnared men as diverse as Luther and Rousseau, and Hegel and Marx. Philosophically, there is indeed no unlimited freedom. But we have seen that there is one freedom which can be defined without contradiction, and which can therefore be an end in itself. This is freedom of thought and speech: the right to dissent.

1. The authors mention Calvin in the fifth paragraph (lines 38–44) in order to:

A. introduce the topic of the Middle Ages.
B. praise an unusual thinker.
C. present a counterexample.
D. illustrate a point made in the previous paragraph.

(A) (B) (C) (D)

2. As it is used in line 19, the word *elucidated* means:

F. decided
G. revealed
H. invented
J. judged

(F) (G) (H) (J)

3. The passage implies that, in the past 500 years, history has revealed two intellectual traditions that are:

A. equally important, even though mutually exclusive.
B. similarly important and closely tied together.
C. only now being seen as particularly important.
D. less important than freedom of thought and speech.

(A) (B) (C) (D)

4. In the fourth paragraph (lines 26–29) the authors' point about "devices and gadgets" is that:

F. all technological progress is an illusion.
G. all inventors attain self-fulfillment.
H. these inventions have allowed people to work less.
J. these inventions are a necessary evil.

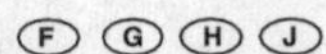

5. What do the authors suggest was "once the monopoly of princes" (line 36)?

A. political power to create totalitarian states
B. vast amounts of wealth for personal use
C. leisure time for self-fulfillment
D. brilliant inventions to spur human progress

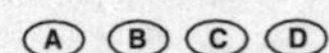

6. In the final paragraph, the authors indicate that the idea of freedom:

F. always involves some element of political dissent.
G. is actually a delusion.
H. has, at times, been defined as obedience to tyranny.
J. is sometimes seriously flawed.

7. Which of the following opinions concerning "the self-fulfillment of the individual" (line 16) would the authors most likely reject?

A. Self-fulfillment requires a degree of leisure.
B. Self-fulfillment is a praiseworthy but unreachable goal.
C. Self-fulfillment is an ideal shared by diverse thinkers.
D. Self-fulfillment means pursuing one's creative potential.

8. The authors clearly indicate that they believe freedom is:

F. essential if societies are to progress.
G. the product of stable societies only.
H. a prerequisite for world peace.
J. only attainable through revolution.

9. According to the passage, Luther, Rousseau, Hegel, and Marx have in common that they were:

A. misled by a false idea of freedom.
B. believers in unlimited freedom.
C. supporters of the right to dissent.
D. opponents of tyranny.

10. The authors' attitude toward intellectual, econonomic, and political revolutions is best characterized as:

F. detached.
G. concerned.
H. suspicious.
J. approving.

Ⓕ Ⓖ Ⓗ Ⓙ

ACT Verbal Practice Quizzes: Explanations

English

Answers
1. A 2. G 3. A 4. H 5. A 6. G 7. C 8. J 9. D 10. H
11. C 12. G 13. D 14. G 15. D

1. **A** The sentence is correct as it stands. There is clearly a pause between *mobility* and *horizontal,* so we need some form of punctuation between the two words. Choice C uses a semicolon, but semicolons connect two phrases that could be sentences by themselves. The phrase *horizontal and vertical* could not be a sentence. Choices A and D correctly use a colon, which introduces a list or definition. However, choice D unnecessarily inserts the word *being.* Don't add what you don't need.

2. **G** The words *pay* and *salary* have approximately the same meaning. It is redundant to use both (choices F and H). Choice J produces the phrase *firms that are comparable pay in terms of salary and prestige,* which makes no sense.

3. **A** Think about what the sentence is saying. Choice B, C, and D add unnecessary pronouns to the sentence. The subject, *change,* is right there, so it's wrong to throw in the pronoun *they* or *it.*

4. **H** The mention of the Russian Revolution illustrates the point made in the preceding sentence, that social mobility "may change the entire social system." *For instance* (choice H) correctly indicates this. Choices F, G, and J are wrong because this sentence does not offer a conclusion based on the preceding sentence.

5. **A** I hope your ear told you that choices B and D sound funny. Since choices B and D are complete sentences in themselves, you can't connect them to another complete sentence, "social mobility occurs at a variety of rates," with a comma. I also hope you steered clear of choice C, with its incorrect and confusing phrase "change's differing degrees."

6. **G** The underlined word occurs in an incomplete sentence that lacks a verb. Choices F, H, and J are incorrect because they do not create complete sentences. Choice H adds the verb *is,* but doesn't tell us what the athlete is. Choice G, however, adds a verb and completes the meaning.

7. **C** Sentence 6 says that gradual changes can accomplish social mobility, so it makes the most sense before sentence 5, which gives an example of a gradual change. Choice C is correct.

8. **J** The phrase *in that* (choice F) sounds funny and makes the sentence incomplete. Changing the phrase to *in* (choice G) or *on* (choice H) still doesn't complete the sentence. Omitting the phrase, however, leaves a complete sentence.

9. **D** The preceding sentence stated that some people view large-scale mobility negatively. This sentence offers a contrasting opinion. The words "accordingly" (A), "similarly" (B), and "likewise" (C) are incorrect because they imply agreement. The phrase "on the other hand" (D) correctly introduces a differing thought.

10. **H** Your ear can help on this one. You might say, "They attempt," but not "They attempting" (choice G). In choice F, the phrase *they are attempting* sounds OK until you keep reading. Ask yourself what the phrase *they are attempting to rise validate* means.

11. **C** The main theme of the passage is social mobility. The American educational system (choice A), salary ranges (choice B), and a rock video (choice D) have nothing to do with this. The correct choice is C, since it talks about some benefits of social mobility.

12. **G** The sentence compares two verbs: *destroy* and *reinforce.* Things that are compared need to be in the same form. *Destroying* ends in *-ing,* so we need the *-ing* form of *reinforce.* Only choice G uses this form.

13. **D** OMIT the underlined portion (choice D). It's not clear how a flat tire benefits anyone. Choices B and C don't help.

14. **G** The subject of the sentence is *crowd,* not *yuppies.* A crowd is singular, no matter how many yuppies are in it, so we need the singular *shows,* instead of *show.*

15. **D** The point of the sentence is that vertical mobility is not a passing phenomenon. The underlined portion is not necessary and only distracts from this point.

Reading

Answers

1. C 2. G 3. B 4. H 5. C 6. H 7. B 8. F 9. A 10. J

This humanities passage deals with the connection between two "grand ideas": human self-fulfillment and freedom. Here's a mental map to the passage: the first and second paragraphs provide some historical perspective about the ideal of human self-fulfillment. The third paragraph explains what the authors have in mind when they speak of human self-fulfillment. The fourth paragraph mentions that self-fulfillment has led to scientific and technical progress, which, in turn, has made individual self-fulfillment easier. The fifth paragraph discusses one thinker, Calvin, who did not believe in human self-fulfillment, and the consequences of this attitude. The sixth and seventh paragraphs tie together the ideals of human self-fulfillment and freedom, saying that the former is not possible without the latter, and introduces some historical examples to support this thesis. Finally, the eighth paragraph mentions some thinkers who distorted the idea of freedom, and the importance of freedom of thought and speech.

1. **C** The passage talks about self-fulfillment and freedom and what these great ideas have inspired. Paragraph five (lines 37–44) begins with the sentence: "Only rarely has a thinker . . . gone back from the ideal of human potential and fulfillment." The next sentence, which introduces Calvin, says "Calvin was perhaps such a thinker who went back, and believed . . . that man [is] . . . incapable of any worthwhile development" (lines 38–41). Calvin, therefore, is a counterexample offered to show that not everyone over the past 500 years has believed in the ideals of self-fulfillment and human potential.

2. **G** Reread the lines surrounding the word *elucidated* in line 19 to get its meaning. Lines 20–21 say "aesthetic and ethical gifts, we feel and struggle to express in our own minds. . . ." Lines 21–22 say "cultural gifts, are unfolded for us by the study of history." Considering this, "revealed," choice G, best captures this idea of unfolding and struggling to express gifts.

3. **B** Lines 46–47 explain that "human fulfillment is unattainable without freedom, so that these two main ideas are linked together." The sixth paragraph begins talking about freedom by describing it as "the second of the two grand formative ideas." This follows the first five paragraphs, which discuss fulfillment. This information supports choice B as the correct answer.

4. **H** Lines 31–33 explain that, "The purpose and the effect [of devices and gadgets] has been to liberate men from the exhausting drudgeries of earning their living. . . ." Choice H best paraphrases these ideas.

5. **C** Lines 33–36 indicate that, before the development of all sorts of work-saving devices and gadgets, princes alone had the "leisure to find the best in themselves."

6. **H** In lines 62–63 Bronowski and Mazlish explain that "freedom . . . advocates can at times delude themselves that obedience to tyranny is a form of freedom." Therefore, the author's ideas are best expressed by choice H.

7. **B** You can find the answer to this question using the process of elimination (remember, you're looking for the choice that the authors would *reject*). Choice A is supported by the discussion in paragraph four (lines 25–36): people are able to find the best in themselves when they have more leisure time. Choice C is supported by paragraph one (lines 1–9). The authors mention various people in diverse professions in various eras who have all praised the development of the individual. Choice D is supported in lines 42–43, where the author contends that men develop by having something in them "which is personal and creative." This leaves choice B. Nowhere in the text do the authors say or imply that

"self-fulfillment is a praiseworthy but unreachable goal." Indeed the authors seem to believe that self-fulfillment is possible.

8. F Lines 46–47 say that freedom is necessary for human fulfillment. Lines 25–26 talk about self-fulfillment inspiring progress. The final paragraph talks about the importance of freedom of thought and speech. Thus, the authors would undoubtedly contend that freedom is necessary for a society to make progress.

9. A Lines 63–65 talk about the delusion that "ensnared" Luther, Rousseau, Hegel, and Marx. According to the authors, all of them confused freedom with obedience to tyranny. Choice A, therefore, is the answer.

10. J The authors make it clear throughout the passage that they feel freedom is a valuable ideal. In the seventh paragraph, they suggest that revolutions have often made societies more free. Considering this, choice J is the best answer.

5 SAT Math

How SAT Math Is Set Up

There are three scored Math sections on the SAT:

- one 30-minute section with 25 Regular Math questions
- one 30-minute section with a set of 15 QCs and a set of ten Grid-ins
- one 15-minute section with ten Regular Math questions

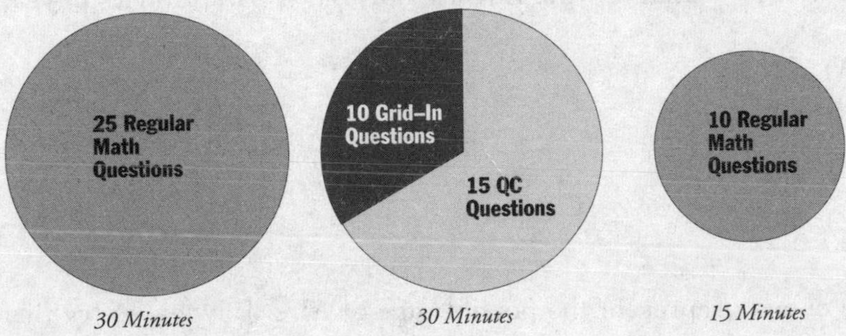

Difficulty Level

All sets of SAT Math questions are designed to start off basic and gradually increase in difficulty.

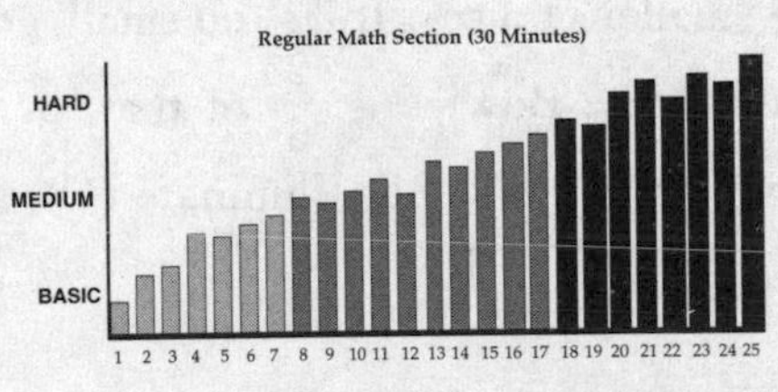

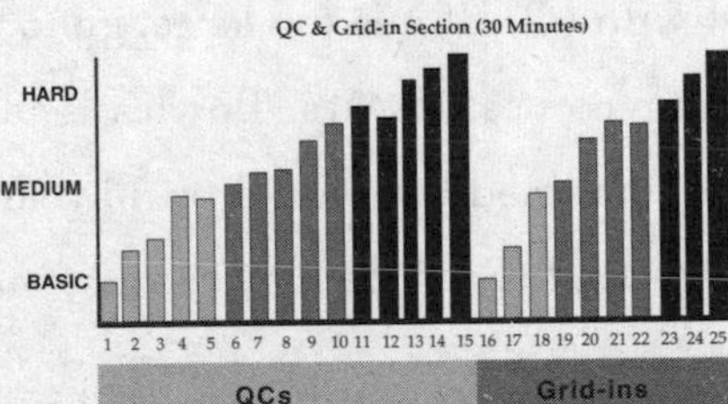

The ten Regular Math questions also get more difficult.

Always be aware of the difficulty level as you go through a question set. Easy problems call for different strategies. The harder the questions, the more traps you will encounter. If you know you're dealing with a hard question (even though it may look easy), you'll be prepared.

The three basic content areas tested on the SAT are arithmetic, algebra, and geometry. These topics are tested in each of the three question types. But you need more than content knowledge to do well on SAT Math. We'll give you strategic advice for each of the three question types to help you succeed.

Regular Math

This question type accounts for over half of the math questions on the SAT. Each question gives you five answers from which to choose, and you lose one-quarter point for a wrong answer. What's important to remember about this question type is that the right answer is always on the page in front of you. Here are a couple of Kaplan strategies that help you take advantage of this fact: backsolving and picking numbers.

Backsolving

When you're stuck on a Math question that contains numerical answer choices, you can plug the choices into the question to see which works. Start with the middle-range number when you backsolve. Since answer choices are listed in increasing or decreasing order, that means starting with choice (C). If (C) is too large, move on to the smaller choices. If it's too small, move to the bigger choices.

Try this sample question:

1. The combined age of Mr. and Mrs. Bowles is 60 years. If the age of Mr. Bowles is $\frac{2}{3}$ that of Mrs. Bowles, how old is Mrs. Bowles in years?

 (A) 12
 (B) 24
 (C) 30
 (D) 36
 (E) 40

The five choices represent the possible age of Mrs. Bowles, so try them in the question stem. The choice that gives a combined age of 60 years, with Mr. Bowles $\frac{2}{3}$ the age of Mrs. Bowles, is the correct answer.

Start with (C). If it is too large, go to the smaller choices. If it's too small, go to the larger ones. If Mrs. Bowles is 30, then Mr. Bowles is $\frac{2}{3}$ of that, or 20. Their combined age would be 50 years, which is too small. Eliminate (C), and also (A) and (B) since they're even smaller.

Either (D) or (E) will be the answer. If you try (D) and it works, you know it's correct. If (D) doesn't work, you know that (E) must be correct. Either way, you have to check only one more choice to find the answer. Try (D). If Mrs. Bowles is 36 years old, then Mr. Bowles would be $\frac{2}{3}$ of that, or 24. Adding 24 to 36 gives us 60, so choice (D) is correct.

Picking Numbers

Picking numbers is an easy way to make an abstract problem more concrete. Rather than trying to figure out remainders using variables and algebra, or trying to find a percent of some value of x, picking numbers lets you work with numbers to find the answer. You can use this strategy for many different types of questions. Some of the best questions to pick numbers on are remainder, percent, even/odd, and rate questions.

Think Small and Easy
Use numbers that are small and easy to work with. It's less important to use numbers that are realistic for a given situation (such as the price of an item) than it is to keep your calculations simple.

Try this sample question:

2. For x dollars it is possible to buy $p - 1$ picture frames. At this rate, how many dollars would it take to buy p picture frames?

(A) $x + 1$

(B) $x - 1$

(C) $\dfrac{xp}{p-1}$

(D) $\dfrac{x+1}{p}$

(E) $\dfrac{x(p-1)}{p}$

The only thing that's hard about this question is that it uses variables instead of numbers. So make it real. Pick numbers for the variables that are easy to work with. Say $p = 3$ and $x = 4$. With 4 dollars you can buy $3 - 1 = 2$ frames. That is, each frame costs 2 dollars. Three frames will therefore cost $3 \times 2 = 6$ dollars. When $p = 3$ and $x = 4$, the correct answer should equal 6. Plug those values into the answer choices and see which yield 6:

(A) $x + 1 = 4 + 1 = 5$

(B) $x - 1 = 4 - 1 = 3$

(C) $\dfrac{xp}{p-1} = \dfrac{(4)(3)}{3-1} = \dfrac{12}{2} = 6$

(D) $\dfrac{x+1}{p} = \dfrac{4+1}{3} = \dfrac{5}{3} = 1\dfrac{2}{3}$

(E) $\dfrac{x(p-1)}{p} = \dfrac{4(3-1)}{3} = \dfrac{4(2)}{3} = \dfrac{8}{3} = 2\dfrac{2}{3}$

Choice (C) is the only one that yields 6, so it must be correct.

When picking numbers for an abstract word problem like this one, it's important to try all five answer choices. Sometimes more than one choice will yield the correct result, in which case one or more choices work coincidentally with the numbers you picked. When this happens, pick another set of numbers to weed out the coincidences. Avoid picking 0 and 1 for these types of problems, since they tend to give several "possibly correct" answers.

Quantitative Comparisons

In Quantitative Comparisons, instead of solving for a particular value, you need to compare two quantities. At first, QCs may seem really difficult because of their unfamiliar format; however, once you become used to them, they can be quicker and easier than the other question types.

Answer Choices

In each question, you'll see two mathematical expressions, one in Column A, the other in Column B. You have to compare them. Some questions include additional information about one or both quantities. This information is centered above the two columns, and is essential to making the comparison.

For each QC, answer:

(A) if Column A is greater
(B) if Column B is greater
(C) if the columns are equal
(D) if more information is needed to determine the relationship

There is no choice (E) for QCs. A response of (E) will be treated as an omission. Since QCs have only four choices, you lose one-third of a point for a wrong answer.

Choices (A), (B), and (C) represent definite relationships between the quantities in Column A and Column B. But choice (D) represents a relationship that cannot be determined. Here are two things to remember about choice (D) to help you decide when to pick it.

1. Choice (D) is never correct if both columns contain only numbers. The relationship between numbers is unchanging, but choice (D) means more than one relationship is possible.
2. Choice (D) is correct if you can demonstrate two different relationships between the columns. Suppose you ran across the following QC:

The QC Facts
- 15 questions
- 40 seconds per question
- Rule of thumb: compare—don't calculate!

	Column A	Column B
3.	x	x^2

If $x = 1$, both columns contain 1 and are therefore equal. But if $x = 2$, 4 in Column B is greater than 2 in Column A. Since more than one relationship is possible, the answer is (D). In fact, as soon as you find a second possibility, stop work and pick choice (D).

QCs are all about comparing, as their name suggests. It is often possible to determine the relationship between the columns without calculating their exact values. Now that you have a good grasp of the meanings of the four answer choices, we'll introduce four strategies to help you move quickly and efficiently through the QC section.

The Basic Approach

- Don't read the directions.
  - Know what (A), (B), (C), and (D) mean.
  - Don't get bogged down in unnecessary calculations.
- Be quick.

Compare Piece by Piece

	Column A	Column B
4.	$\frac{2}{3}+\frac{3}{5}+\frac{4}{7}$	$\frac{5}{11}+\frac{6}{13}+\frac{7}{15}$

You could find the sum in each column, but that would mean a lot of calculations. You would either have to find common denominators to add the fractions, or convert the fractions to decimals and add them. Even with your calculator, this would take some time. There's a faster way: comparing piece by piece. Compare the values of "pieces" in each column. If every "piece" in one column is greater than a corresponding "piece" in the other column, the column with the greater individual values will have the greater total value.

Look at the first fraction in each column. In Column A you have $\frac{2}{3}$ and in Column B you have $\frac{5}{11}$. Since $\frac{2}{3}$ is greater than $\frac{1}{2}$ and $\frac{5}{11}$ is less than $\frac{1}{2}$, $\frac{2}{3}$ is greater than $\frac{5}{11}$. As it turns out, all of the fractions in Column A are greater than $\frac{1}{2}$, while all the fractions in Column B are less than $\frac{1}{2}$. Therefore, all the fractions in Column A are greater than all the fractions in Column B, and Column A is greater.

Picking Numbers

	Column A	Column B
5.	x^2	x^3

If a QC involves variables, try picking numbers to make the relationship clearer. At first glance you might think that Column B is greater, because raising the same number to a higher power must result in a larger number. This is true if $x = 2$, for example. In this case Column A would equal 4 while Column B would equal 8.

But that doesn't mean that Column B is always greater and that the answer is (B). It does mean that the answer is not (A) or (C). The answer could still be (D)—not enough information to decide. If time is short, guess and pick (B) or (D). But if there's time, pick another number and plug it in again.

Negative Numbers and Fractions
Some surprising things can happen when you play around with negative numbers and fractions. Keep things like this in mind:

- When you square a positive fraction less than 1, the result is smaller than the original fraction.
- When you square a negative number, the result is a positive number.
- When you square 0 and 1 they stay the same.

As best as you can, try to find a different number that will alter the relationship. Can you think of a number that will make the columns equal? It's important not to assume that all variables represent positive integers. Unless you're told otherwise, variables can represent zero, negative numbers, or fractions. Since different kinds of numbers behave differently, always pick a different kind of number the second time around.

If $x = 1$, then both columns amount to 1 and are equal. Can you think of a number that will make Column A greater? What if x is a positive fraction less than 1? Try $x = \frac{1}{2}$: then Column A is $\frac{1}{4}$ and Column B is $\frac{1}{8}$, so Column A is greater. And if x is any negative number, then Column A is greater because a negative raised to an even power is positive, while a negative raised to an odd power is negative. Since more than one relationship is possible, the answer is (D).

As soon as you find a second possibility, stop work and pick choice (D). We tried a few more numbers here just to give you examples of the kinds of numbers to pick.

Avoiding the Obvious

	Column A	Column B
	Two sides of a right triangle have lengths 3 and 4.	
6.	The length of the third side	5

Many people would look at this question, choose (C) as the answer, and confidently move on. However, these people would be wrong. They would have fallen for the obvious assumption that the triangle described is a 3-4-5 right triangle. As such, it would have legs of 3 and 4, and the third side, the hypotenuse, would be 5—equal to 5 in Column B. But this isn't necessarily true. There's nothing in the question to indicate 3 and 4 are the lengths of the legs, and that the third side is the hypotenuse. The hypotenuse of the right triangle could just as easily be 4. In this case, the third side would be a leg of the triangle and would necessarily be less than the hypotenuse. If the third side were less than 4 it would certainly be less than 5, in which case Column B would be greater. Since there's more than one possibility, the correct answer is (D).

As this example illustrates, it's important to stay alert and consider possibilities other than the obvious.

GRID-INS

The Grid-in section on the SAT is a lot like the math tests you're already used to taking. Unlike other questions on the SAT, Grid-ins have no multiple-choice answers, and there's no penalty for wrong answers. You have to figure out your own answer and fill it in on a special grid. Some Grid-ins have only one correct answer, while others have several, or even a range of correct choices.

For each question, you'll see a grid with four boxes and a column of ovals beneath each. First write your numerical answer in the boxes, one digit, decimal point, or fraction bar per box. Then fill in the corresponding ovals below.

Only the Ovals Count

The computer registers only the ovals that are filled in, not what you've written at the top of the grid.

However, writing in your answer helps ensure that you'll accurately fill in the correct ovals.

Filling in the Grid

The grid cannot accommodate:

- negative answers
- answers with variables
- answers greater than 9,999

If you come up with an answer that fits into any of the above categories, you'll know that you did something wrong. Check your work and try again. Since you don't have answer choices, it's especially important to be careful about your calculations. Using your calculator can help you avoid careless mistakes.

What follows are descriptions of a few more idiosyncrasies of filling in answers on the grid.

Don't Grid Mixed Numbers

If your answer to a Grid-in question is $5\frac{1}{5}$, you need to convert it to an improper fraction or a decimal before you can grid it in. If you grid $5\frac{1}{5}$ as 51/5, the scoring computer will read it as $10\frac{1}{5}$. Instead, grid in 26/5 or 5.2.

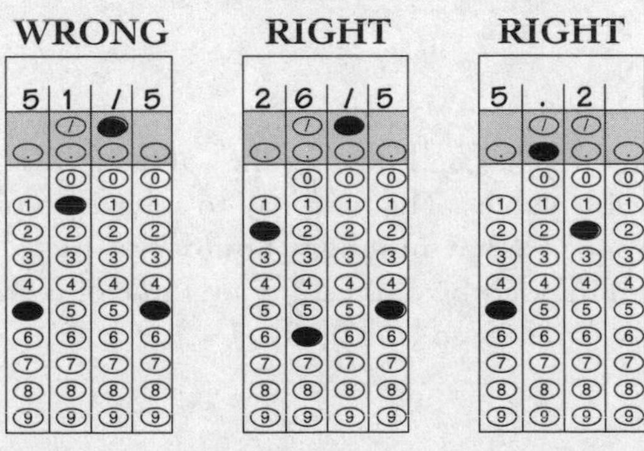

It's Worth a Guess

Remember, there's no penalty for wrong answers on Grid-ins. So even if you're unsure of the answer, it's really worth your while to guess.

Top Grid-In Mistakes

- gridding in mixed numbers
- making rounding errors
- writing an answer but forgetting to fill in the ovals
- double-bubble: gridding two numbers in the same column (the computer reads this as an omission)
- filling in the wrong oval under the right number—it's still considered a wrong answer

Grid Decimals Accurately

If your answer to a Grid-in is .2468 and you grid it in as 0.2 or .24 or .25, your answer will be marked as wrong. You have to grid as many digits as possible, so you should start as far left on the grid as you can, and grid .246. Technically, .247 is closer, but you will get credit whether you grid .246 or .247, so don't worry about rounding up. It's never necessary. It's also unnecessary to reduce fractions to simplest terms, unless the fraction won't fit on the grid.

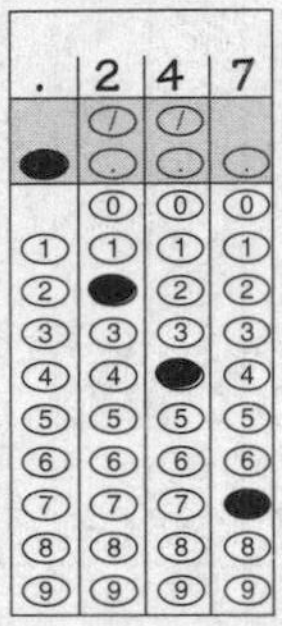

. 2 4 7

More Than One Answer Is Possible

Some Grid-ins have more than one possible answer. Suppose the question asks for an integer greater than 200 and less than 300 that's a multiple of both 5 and 6. You could answer 210, 240, or 270, and any of the three would be correct. If you come up with an answer of $x > 5$, you can grid in any number greater than 5. Gridding in 5, however, would be wrong.

Classic Questions

Here are five questions typical of those that turn up with frequency on the SAT math sections, along with the Kaplan strategies to solve them. These classic question types could turn up as any of the three question types. For instance, the combined-percent-increase/decrease example on the next page is a Regular Math question, but this concept could just as easily be tested in the QC format.

Remainders

The following is a typical remainders question:

7. When n is divided by 5 the remainder is 4. What is the remainder when $3n$ is divided by 5?

   (A) 0
   (B) 2
   (C) 3
   (D) 4
   (E) 12

This question doesn't depend on knowing the value of n. In fact, n has an infinite number of possible values. The best way to solve is to pick a number for n and see what happens. What number should you pick? Since n leaves a remainder of 4 when divided by 5, pick any multiple of 5 and add 4. The easiest multiple to work with is 5, so let n be $5 + 4 = 9$.

To see what the remainder is when $3n$ is divided by 5, plug in $n = 9$:

$$3(9) \div 5 =$$
$$27 \div 5 =$$
$$\frac{27}{5} = 5 \text{ remainder } 2$$

So the remainder is 2 when $n = 9$, and the correct answer is (B). The remainder will also be 2 when $n = 14, 19, 24$, etcetera.

Speed Tip
When picking a number for a remainders problem, add the remainder to the number you're dividing by.

Combined Percent Increase/Decrease

The following is a typical combined-percent-increase/decrease question:

8. From 1980 through 1985, the population of Country X increased by 100%. From 1985 through 1990, the population increased by 50%. What was the combined percent increase from 1980 through 1990?

    (A) 50%
    (B) 150%
    (C) 200%
    (D) 250%
    (E) 300%

This kind of problem usually appears at the end of a question set, and often tricks many test takers. Many students will figure that an increase of 100% followed by an increase of 50% results in an overall increase of 150%, and pick (B) as the answer. They would be wrong.

When a quantity undergoes more than one percent increase (or decrease), you cannot simply add (or subtract) the percents to get the answer. In this question, the first increase is a percent of the starting population, and the second increase is a percent of the new, larger population. Percents can be added and subtracted only when they are percents of the same amount.

The way to avoid falling into this trap is to pick a number for the starting amount, apply the percent changes to it, and see what happens. And since it's easy to calculate percents of 100, that's the best number to pick for the starting amount. If the original population were 100, an increase of 100% would mean an increase of 100 people. This would bring the population to 100 + 100 = 200. This population is then increased by 50%. Since 50% of 200 is 100, the population becomes 200 + 100 = 300. The original population was 100, so the overall increase is 300 – 100 = 200. And since the original amount was 100, an increase of 200 is the same as an increase of 200%, choice (C).

Work with 100
Pick 100 for percent problems. Don't worry about whether or not it's a realistic number for the situation. What matters is that it's the easiest number to work with.

Patterns

The following is a typical patterns question:

9. What is the units' digit of 3^{598}?

Think you can just plug this one in on your calculator to find the answer? Think again. Most calculators can't handle a number this big. If you don't get an "ERROR" message, the result will probably be given in scientific notation, which won't help you out here. So what should you do? Look for a pattern.

Find the first few powers of 3—your calculator will be a big help on this:

$3^1 = 3$ $3^5 = 243$
$3^2 = 9$ $3^6 = 729$
$3^3 = 27$ $3^7 = 2{,}187$
$3^4 = 81$ $3^8 = 6{,}561$

Notice how the units' digits repeat a pattern of 3, 9, 7, 1. If you figure out which term in this pattern corresponds to 3^{598}, you can find its units' digit. There are four repeating terms in the pattern, so divide the exponent by 4 to see how many times this pattern repeats itself:

$$598 \div 4 = 149, \text{ remainder } 2$$

So there are 149 complete groups of this pattern, and since the remainder is 2, the pattern continues through to the second term of the pattern. So the units' digit of 3^{598} corresponds to the second term of the pattern, which is 9.

There are some variations on this type of question; for example, you might be asked to find a particular term in a repeating decimal. That kind of question is even easier, since the pattern is already identified for you.

By the way, the question above would be a good Grid-in to guess on. You're asked to find the units' digit of a number, so there are only ten possible answers: 0, 1, 2, 3, 4, 5, 6, 7, 8, and 9. So even if you had no clue about how to solve, you should fill in one of these numbers. Remember, you're not penalized for wrong answers on this question type. If you recognized the pattern but then were uncertain about how to proceed, you would have narrowed down your choices to 3, 9, 7, or 1, and would stand an even better chance of guessing correctly.

System of Equations

The following is a typical system-of-equations question:

$$x + 3y = 11$$
$$3x - y = 3$$

10. In the system of equations above, what is the value of $2x + y$?

(A) –3
(B) 2
(C) 3
(D) 7
(E) 20

In order to get a numerical value for each variable, you need as many different equations as there are variables to solve for. In this case, you have two different equations with two variables, so you can solve. The question is, what's the best way to solve?

You could solve for x in terms of y, plug in that expression to solve for the value of y, then plug in the value of y to solve for the value of x, and then finally plug these values into the expression $2x + y$. But that's a lot of work, which will take a lot of time, and provide a lot of chances for computational mistakes.

The fact that the question asks you to solve not simply for x or y, but for an expression containing both variables, is a hint that there's a better way to solve. In such cases there's usually a way to combine the equations, by adding or subtracting them, to come up with the desired expression or some multiple of it.

In this case, if you simply add the equations, you find that $4x + 2y = 14$. Dividing both sides by 2, you see that $2x + y = 7$, choice (D).

Length/Area Ratio

The following is a typical length/area ratio question:

	Column A	Column B
	Circle A has a radius of x. Circle B has a radius of $2x$.	
11.	Twice the area of circle A	The area of circle B

You might think that because the radius of circle B is twice the radius of circle A, its area must be twice the area of circle A, which would make the columns equal. You would, however, be wrong.

In proportional figures, the ratio of the areas is not the same as the ratio of the lengths. The ratio of the areas is the square of the ratio of corresponding linear measurements. In other words, since the ratio of the radius of circle A to the radius of circle B is 1:2, the ratio of their respective areas is therefore $1^2:2^2$, or 1:4. Therefore the area of circle B is four times as great as that of circle A, so Column B is greater.

If you understand and remember this concept, you'll avoid this common mistake. If not, you can always pick numbers to see what happens. Let $x = 1$. The radius of circle A would be 1, making its area $\pi(1)^2 = \pi$. The radius of circle B would be 2, making its area $\pi(2)^2 = 4\pi$. That leaves you comparing $2(\pi)$ or 2π in Column A with 4π in Column B, so Column B is clearly greater.

SAT Math Practice Quiz

Now answer the following SAT Math questions to assess your strengths and weaknesses. At the end of the quiz, you'll find an answer key and strategic explanations. Then enter your score on the "SAT or ACT? Score Comparison Chart" at the end of this book.

Regular Math

1. The total cost of four books is \$70, and a fifth book costs \$20. What is the average (arithmetic mean) cost of all five books?

   (A) \$17.50
   (B) \$18.00
   (C) \$22.50
   (D) \$45.00
   (E) \$90.00

2. Which of the following is an expression for "12 greater than the square root of the product of 10 and *a*"?

   (A) $12 + \sqrt{10a}$
   (B) $12 + \sqrt{10 + a}$
   (C) $12\sqrt{10a}$
   (D) $12 + 10\sqrt{a}$
   (E) $\sqrt{10a + 12}$

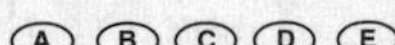

3. 75% of 12 is equal to $\frac{1}{3}$ of what number?

   (A) 3
   (B) 9
   (C) 24
   (D) 27
   (E) 36

Ⓐ Ⓑ Ⓒ Ⓓ Ⓔ

4. If $c = 6$ and $\frac{c}{\partial} = 2$, which of the following is the value of $\frac{c + \partial}{\partial}$?

   (A) 7

   (B) 5

   (C) 3

   (D) $\frac{8}{3}$

   (E) $\frac{4}{3}$

Ⓐ Ⓑ Ⓒ Ⓓ Ⓔ

5. What is the units' digit of 3^{155}?

(A) 1
(B) 3
(C) 5
(D) 7
(E) 9

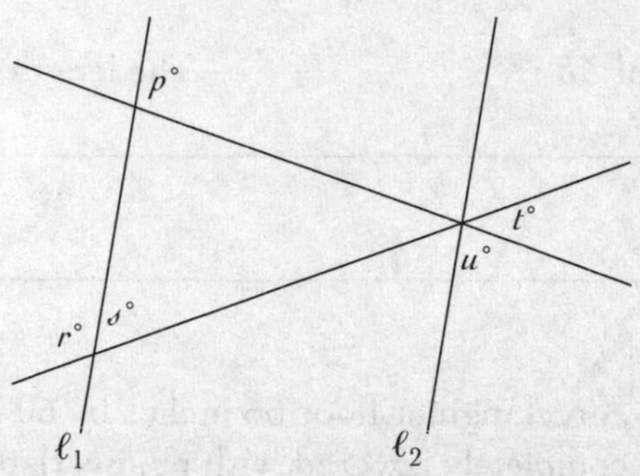

6. In the figure above, if $\ell_1 \parallel \ell_2$, which of the following must be equal to p ?

(A) $180 - s$
(B) $r + s$
(C) $r + t$
(D) $s + t$
(E) $t + u$

7. Increasing n by 70 percent and decreasing the result by 50 percent is equivalent to which of the following?

(A) Increasing n by 20 percent
(B) Increasing n by 15 percent
(C) Increasing n by 5 percent
(D) Decreasing n by 15 percent
(E) Decreasing n by 20 percent

Quantitative Comparisons

	Column A	Column B
	There are 25 students in Class A. There are 35 students in Class B.	
8.	The number of boys in Class A	The number of boys in Class B
9.	$\frac{1}{2} \cdot \frac{2}{3} \cdot \frac{3}{4} \cdot \frac{4}{5} \cdot \frac{5}{6} \cdot \frac{6}{7}$	$\frac{1}{7}$

	Column A	Column B

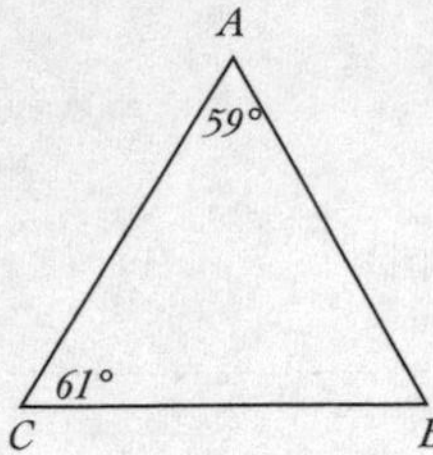

	Column A	Column B
10.	The length of AB	The length of AC
		Ⓐ Ⓑ Ⓒ Ⓓ Ⓔ
11.	x	$6x^2$
		Ⓐ Ⓑ Ⓒ Ⓓ Ⓔ

Grid-Ins

12. A rectangular floor 56 inches by 60 inches is to be completely covered with nonoverlapping rectangular tiles, each 6 inches by 8 inches. How many tiles are needed to cover the floor?

13. If $4^{n+1} = 64$, then $n^3 =$

14. If $4n < 3$ and $8n > 5$, what is one possible value for n?

15. The average of 12 numbers is 15. If one number is deleted, the average of the remaining 11 numbers is 14. What number was deleted?

SAT Math Practice Quiz: Explanations

Answers

1. B 2. A 3. D 4. C 5. D 6. D 7. D 8. D 9. C 10. A 11. D
12. 70 13. 8 14. $\frac{5}{8} < n < \frac{3}{4}$ (or $.625 < n < .75$) 15. 26

1. **B** Average = $\frac{\text{Sum of Terms}}{\text{Number of Terms}}$. Four books add up to \$70, and the fifth costs \$20, so the total cost of the five books is \$90. Divide that sum by 5 and you get \$18 for the average cost.

2. **A** This is an exercise in translation. "12 greater than" refers to adding 12 to something, but what? To translate "the square root of the product of 10 and *a*" we must first notice that "10 and *a*" cannot be written as 10 + *a*, because "the product of 10 + *a*" makes no sense. To get a product, 10 must be multiplied by something else. So "the product of 10 and *a*" must be translated as 10 times *a*, or 10*a*. So the square root of the product of 10 and *a* is 10*a* with a radical sign over it. That means the whole phrase must translate as $12 + \sqrt{10a}$.

3. **D** 75% of 12 is 9, which is $\frac{1}{3}$ of 27.

4. **C** If $c = 6$ and $\frac{c}{\partial} = 2$, then $\partial = 3$. Plug $c = 6$ and $\partial = 3$ into the expression

$$\frac{c+\partial}{\partial} \text{ and you get } \frac{6+3}{3} = \frac{9}{3} = 3.$$

5. **D** The SAT is a timed test—even the most difficult and complicated problem can be solved in not much more than a minute. One way to find the units' digit of 3^{155} would be to multiply 3 times 3 times 3 times 3, etcetera, but the result is too big for your calculator, and it would clearly take too much time to multiply it out yourself. There has to be a better (that is, faster) way.

The key is to find the pattern. Start raising 3 to ever higher powers (your calculator can help here) and see what happens to that last digit:

$$\begin{aligned} 3^1 &= \underline{3} \\ 3^2 &= \underline{9} \\ 3^3 &= 2\underline{7} \\ 3^4 &= 8\underline{1} \\ 3^5 &= 24\underline{3} \\ 3^6 &= 72\underline{9} \\ 3^7 &= 218\underline{7} \\ 3^8 &= 656\underline{1} \end{aligned}$$

Do you see the pattern in the units' place? 3, 9, 7, 1, 3, 9, 7, 1 . . . Every fourth power of 3 has a units' digit of 1, so the units' digit of 3^{156} is 1, and therefore the units' digit of 3^{155} would be the number just before the 1 in the pattern. The units' digit of 3^{155} is 7.

6. **D** When a transversal crosses two parallel lines, all the acute angles formed are equal, and all the obtuse angles formed are equal. Since the problem concerns angle p, an obtuse angle, let's just consider the transversal that created angle p. This transversal creates two more obtuse angles when it crosses ℓ_2, although these obtuse angles are each cut into two smaller angles by the other transversal line. Nevertheless, the angle made up of angle t together with the unmarked angle above it is an obtuse angle created by the same transversal that created angle p. So angle t, plus the unmarked angle above it, must be equal to angle p.

The unmarked angle above t is an acute angle created by the other transversal. The angle marked s is also an acute angle created by that transversal. So the unmarked angle above t must have a degree measure of s, and $p = s + t$.

An alternate way to solve the problem is to focus on the triangle formed by the intersecting lines. The angle marked t is vertical to one of the interior angles in the triangle, so we can mark that angle t as well. Angle p is an exterior angle of this triangle, and the exterior angle theorem states that an exterior angle is equal to the sum of the two remote interior angles. The two interior angles now marked s and t are the remote interior angles relative to angle p, so once again, $p = s + t$.

Notice that the angles marked r and u were not part of either solution, and the fact that the lines are parallel wasn't needed to find the answer using the second method. Remember, it's your job to decide which information matters, and stay focused on that.

7. **D** Maybe you thought, "Up 70 percent and down 50 percent—that's a net gain of 20 percent." Wrong! That's the trap the test maker wants you to fall for. A Kaplan grad would know better than to fall for such a "too-good-to-be-true" answer choice.

A good way to do a problem like this is to pick numbers. Suppose $n = 100$. After a 70 percent increase, you're up to 170. Now, what's 50 percent less than 170? Fifty percent less means half; half of 170 is 85. Going from 100 to 85 is a net 15 percent decrease.

Why is a 70 percent increase followed by a 50 percent decrease equivalent to a 15 percent decrease? Because the 70 percent increase and the 50 percent decrease are from different wholes.

8. **D** While there are more students in Class *B* than Class *A*, we are given no information about the number of boys in either. Class *A* might contain 24 boys and one girl, while *B* contains one boy and 34 girls, or both classes could each have 20 boys, etcetera. Since we cannot determine a single relationship between the number of boys in each class, the answer must be choice (D).

9. **C** Compare—don't calculate! You're wasting precious time if you multiply all the numerators and denominators in Column A. Try canceling first. The numbers 2, 3, 4, 5, and 6 all appear on both top and bottom, so they cancel, leaving $\frac{1}{7}$, the same as Column B, so the answer is (C).

10. **A** You can normally trust the looks of a diagram when there's no note saying, "Figure not drawn to scale," but here the differences among the angles and sides are so slight that you can't see the differences with the naked eye.

If you remembered from geometry that longer sides are found opposite bigger angles, you knew right away that *AB* is longer than *AC*, because *AB* is opposite the larger angle. (Angle *B* measures 60 degrees because the three angles of a triangle add up to 180 degrees.) But what if you didn't remember that geometry theorem? Then you could have tried redrawing the diagram, exaggerating the crucial difference. Look what happens if you make the 61-degree angle look a lot bigger than the 59-degree angle:

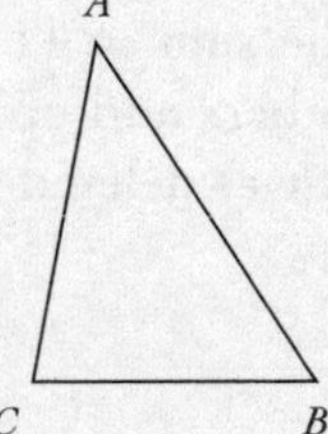

11. **D** It's tempting to pick *B* for this one because most numbers that you might try for x would make Column B bigger. If $x = 1$, $6x^2 = 6$. If $x = -2$, $6x^2 = 24$. But you should be skeptical. Can you find a number to plug in for x such that $6x^2$ is *not* bigger? How about 0? If $x = 0$, $6x^2 = 0$, and the columns are equal. That's enough to demonstrate that the answer is (D).

12. **70**

Since the tiles cover the floor completely without overlap, we can find the number of tiles needed by dividing the area of the floor by the area of one tile. If the rectangular floor is 56 inches by 60 inches, the area of the floor is $56 \times 60 = 3{,}360$. To find the number of 6×8–inch tiles that will fit into an area that's 3,360 square inches, we divide 3,360 by 6×8 and get 3,360/48, which equals 70.

13. **8**

If $4^{n+1} = 64$, it makes sense for us to change 64 to a power of 4. Since $4 \times 4 \times 4 = 64$, rewrite 64 as 4^3. So $4^{n+1} = 4^3$. Since the bases are the same, $n + 1$ must equal 3, and $n = 2$. Now we plug in 2 for n in the expression n^3 to get 2^3, or $2 \times 2 \times 2 = 8$.

14. **$\frac{5}{8} < n < \frac{3}{4}$ or $.625 < n < .75$**

In inequality problems, the solution is a range of values. In this case, we have two conditions for the variable n. The first is that $4n < 3$. To solve for n, we divide both sides by 4, which gives us $n < \frac{3}{4}$ or .75 in decimal form. The second condition for n is that $8n > 5$. To solve for n, we divide both sides by 8 and get $n > \frac{5}{8}$ or .625 in decimal form. If we put both of these conditions together we get $\frac{5}{8} < n < \frac{3}{4}$ or $.625 < n < .75$, so any value that fits within these limits is acceptable. (**Note:** It's better to use decimals when the answer can be anywhere within a range of values, because it's easier to see which values fit the given conditions.)

15. **26**

The key to most averages questions is to use the sum. If you know that the average of 12 numbers is 15, then, even though you don't know what any of the 12 numbers are, you know that they must add up to 12×15, or 180. Likewise, the sum of 11 numbers whose average is 14 is 11×14, or 154. If 12 numbers add up to 180 and 11 of them add up to 154, then the number that was deleted is $180 - 154$, or 26.

6 ACT MATH

The ACT Math section is 60 minutes long and includes 60 questions. That works out to a minute a question, but you'll want to spend less time on basic questions and more on the tough ones. Unlike the SAT, there is no wrong-answer penalty on the ACT. That means that you should answer every single question on the test, guessing on questions that stump you or that you don't have time to do.

THE FORMAT

All of the ACT Math questions have the same basic, multiple-choice format. They ask a question and offer five possible choices, unlike questions on the other three subject tests, which have only four choices each. Since the ACT math questions are in the same format as the Regular Math questions on the SAT, some of the same strategies apply. Both backsolving and picking numbers are very useful for ACT questions, so review those strategies in the SAT Math chapter.

The questions cover a full range of math topics from pre-algebra and elementary algebra through intermediate algebra, coordinate geometry, plane geometry, and even trigonometry.

Although the Math questions, like those in the other sections, aren't ordered in terms of difficulty, questions drawn from elementary school or junior high tend to come earlier in the section, while those from high school math tend to come later. But this doesn't mean that the basic questions come first and the hardest ones come later. We've found that high school subjects tend to be fresher in most students' minds than things they were taught years ago, so you may actually find the later questions easier. (Do you remember the math you learned in seventh grade?)

QUESTION BREAKDOWN

The ACT Math section includes:

- 24 pre-algebra and elementary algebra questions
- 10 intermediate algebra questions
- 8 coordinate geometry questions
- 14 plane geometry questions
- 4 trigonometry questions

Kaplan's Three-Step Method for ACT Math

At Kaplan, we've developed our take-time-to-save-time philosophy into a three-step method for tackling ACT Math problems. The method is designed to help you find the fast, inventive solutions that the ACT rewards. The steps are:

1. **Understand**
2. **Analyze**
3. **Select**

Step One: Understand

Focus first on the question stem (the part before the answer choices), and make sure you understand the problem. Sometimes you'll want to read the stem twice, or rephrase it in a way you can better understand. Think to yourself, "What kind of problem is this? What am I looking for? What am I given?" Don't pay too much attention to the answer choices yet, though you may want to give them a quick glance just to see what form they're in.

Step Two: Analyze

Think for a moment, and decide on a plan of attack. Don't start crunching numbers until you've given the problem a little thought. Ask, "What's a quick and reliable way to find the correct answer?" Look for patterns and shortcuts, using common sense and your knowledge of the test to find the creative solutions that will get you more right answers in less time. Try to solve the problem without focusing on the answer choices.

Step Three: Select

Once you get an answer—or once you get stuck—check the answer choices. If you got an answer and it's listed as one of the choices, chances are it's right. Fill in the appropriate oval and move on. But if you didn't get an answer, narrow down the choices as best you can by process of elimination and then guess.

Each of these steps can happen in a matter of seconds. And it may not always be clear when you've finished with one step and moved onto the next. Sometimes you'll know how to attack a problem the instant you read and understand it.

The Kaplan Three-Step Method
1. Understand
2. Analyze
3. Select

The Kaplan Three-Step Method is not a rigid procedure. It's a set of guidelines that will keep you on track, moving quickly, and evading pitfalls. Just remember to think before you solve. Focus on the question stem first and save the answer choices for later.

Appyling the Three-Step Method

Here's the Three-Step Method applied to a typical ACT question.

1. If the average of five consecutive odd integers is equal to their sum, what is the greatest of the five integers?

    A. 3
    B. 7
    C. 9
    D. 15
    E. 21

Step One: Understand

Before you can begin to solve this problem, you have to figure out what it's asking, and to do that you need to know the meanings of *average, sum, consecutive, odd,* and *integer*. You're looking for five consecutive odd integers whose average and sum are equal. You're dealing with the average of consecutive integers, and that's a special case. The average of consecutive integers is equal to the middle term. So what the question stem is really saying is that when you add up these five odd integers and divide the sum by five, you get the middle integer.

Step Two: Analyze

How are you going to figure out what these five numbers are? You could set up a complicated algebraic equation, but that would take some time. Come up with a better way.

Stop and think logically about the question for a moment. How can five numbers add up to the middle value? What you need to remember is that the term *odd integers* can include nonpositive integers. There is only one set of five consecutive odd integers that will add up to their middle number, and that's –3, –1, 0, 1 and 3. Their average and sum are both 0.

Step Three: Select

The question asks for the greatest of the five integers, which is 3, choice A.

Know When to Skip

At any point in the Three-Step Method you could choose to cut bait and skip the question. Almost everyone should skip at least some questions the first time through.

If you know your own strengths and weaknesses, you can sometimes choose to skip a question while still in Step One (Understand). For example, suppose you never studied trigonometry. Maybe you think that a secant is something that sailors sing while climbing up the yardarms. Well, every form of the ACT includes exactly four trigonometry questions, and it's not hard to spot them. Why waste a second on such a question? Skip it! You don't need those four measly questions to get a great score. And since you know a second visit later won't help any, you might as well go ahead and make some random guesses.

It can be harder to decide to skip a question if you understand it, but then get stuck in Step Two (Analyze). Suppose you just don't see how to solve it. Don't give up too quickly. Sometimes it takes a half-minute or so before you see the light. But don't get bogged down, either. Never spend more than a minute on a question the first time through the section. No single question is worth it. Be prepared to leave a question and come back to it later. Often, on the second try, you'll see something you didn't see before. That old light bulb over your head will light up and you'll be on your way.

Of course, eventually you're going to pick an answer choice for every question, even the ones you don't understand. The first time through the section, however, you should concentrate on the questions you do understand.

No Loitering

Never spend more than a minute on a question during the first pass. If you think you might be able to come up with an answer later, then mark it as a question for your second pass.

Kaplan's Two-Pass Plan for ACT Math

We recommend that you plan two "passes" through the Math section.

- First Pass: Examine each problem in order. Do every problem you understand. Don't skip too hastily—sometimes it takes a few seconds of thought before you figure out how to do it—but don't get bogged down. Never spend more than a minute on any question in the first pass. This first pass should take about 45 minutes.
- Second Pass: Use the last 15 minutes to go back to the questions that stumped you the first time through. Sometimes a second look is all that you need; after going away and then coming back, you'll suddenly see what to do. In most cases, though, you'll still be stumped by the question stem, so it's time to give the answer choices a try. Work by process of elimination, and guess. Be sure to select an answer for every question, even if it's just a blind guess.

Never plan on visiting a question a third time. It's inefficient to go back and forth that much. Every time you leave a question and come back to it, you have to refamiliarize yourself with the problem. Always pick an answer choice on the second pass—even if it's just a wild guess. At the end of the second pass, every question should be answered.

Don't worry if you don't work on every question in the section. The average ACT test taker gets fewer than half the questions right. You could score in the top quarter of all ACT test takers even if you were to do only half of the problems on the test, get every single one of them right, and guess blindly on the other half. If you were to do only one-third of the problems, get every one right, and then guess blindly on the other 40 problems, you would still earn an average score. And if you had time to make smart guesses—eliminating choices that are way off—you would score even better.

Do What You Can
Don't worry about the ones you can't do. Get your points where you can, and don't expect miracles in the hard problems. Guess and move on.

The following five problems are representative of the general ACT Math content, and are accompanied by strategic explanations.

Pre-Algebra and Elementary Algebra

2. If $9^{2x-1} = 3^{3x+3}$, then x = ?

F. -4

G. $-\frac{7}{4}$

H. $-\frac{10}{7}$

J. 2

K. 5

Sometimes you look at a question and it's not immediately clear what you have to do to solve it. Often, the way to get over that stymied feeling is to change your perspective. When you get stuck, try looking at the problem from a different angle. Try rearranging the numbers, or changing fractions to decimals, or factoring, multiplying out, or redrawing the diagram, or anything that might give you the fresh perspective you need to uncover a good solution. In order to solve the problem above, you need to reexpress the left side of the equation so that both sides have the same base.

$$9^{2x-1} = 3^{3x+3}$$
$$\left(3^2\right)^{2x-1} = 3^{3x+3}$$
$$3^{4x-2} = 3^{3x+3}$$

Now that the bases are the same, just make the exponents equal:

$$4x - 2 = 3x + 3$$
$$4x - 3x = 3 + 2$$
$$x = 5$$

So choice K is correct.

Don't Worry. Be Happy!
If you were to skip half of the questions on the test, you would double the amount of time available to work on the rest of the problems—virtually ensuring that you would make no careless mistakes.

INTERMEDIATE ALGEBRA

3. A formula for the area A of a triangle is:

$$A = \sqrt{S(S-a)(S-b)(S-c)}$$

where a, b, and c are the lengths of the sides and $S = \frac{1}{2}(a+b+c)$. What is the area, in square inches, of a triangle with side lengths of 5, 6, and 7 inches?

A. 9
B. $9\sqrt{2}$
C. $6\sqrt{6}$
D. $\sqrt{210}$
E. 18

Sometimes it's hard to see the quick and reliable method immediately because the true nature of the problem is hidden behind a disguise. At first glance, this looks like a horrendously esoteric geometry question. Who ever heard of such a formula?

But when you look at the question a bit, you realize that you don't really have to understand the formula. You certainly don't have to remember it—it's right there in the question. In fact, this is not really a geometry question at all. It's really just an "evaluate the algebraic expression" question in disguise. First, use the given values of a, b, and c to find S:

$$S = \frac{1}{2}(a+b+c)$$

$$= \frac{1}{2}(5+6+7) = \frac{1}{2}(18) = 9$$

Now plug the given values and $S = 9$ into the formula:

$$A = \sqrt{S(S-a)(S-b)(S-c)}$$

$$= \sqrt{9(9-5)(9-6)(9-7)} = \sqrt{9(4)(3)(2)}$$

$$= \sqrt{9} \times \sqrt{4} \times \sqrt{(3)(2)} = 3 \times 2 \times \sqrt{6}$$

$$= 6\sqrt{6}$$

So choice C is correct.

Coordinate Geometry

4. One of the following is an equation for the circle sketched in the standard (x, y) coordinate plane below. Which one?

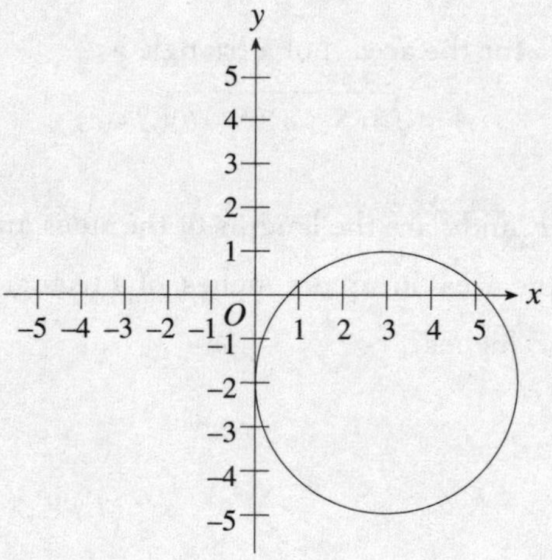

F. $(x+3)^2+(y+2)^2=3$

G. $(x-3)^2+(y-2)^2=3$

H. $(x-3)^2+(y+2)^2=9$

J. $(x+3)^2+(y-2)^2=9$

K. $(x-3)^2+(y-2)^2=9$

If you remember the general form of the equation of a circle, this one's easy. Here the center is (3, –2) and the radius is 3. Plug those numbers in:

$$(x-h)^2+(y-k)^2=r^2$$

$$(x-3)^2+(y+2)^2=3^2$$

$$(x-3)^2+(y+2)^2=9$$

And choice H is the correct answer. If you were careless plugging in you might have incorrectly come up with G as the answer. In this case the y-coordinate of the center is –2, and plugging it into the formula, a negative minus a negative results in a positive.

Alternatively, you could find the correct equation by taking a couple of points from the graph and plugging their coordinates into the answer choices, eliminating the choices that don't work. If you try the point (0, –2), for example, you'll find that choice H is the only choice that works.

PLANE GEOMETRY

5. If the length of one side of a triangle is 5 inches and the length of another side is 8 inches, which of the following could NOT be the length, in inches, of the third side?

   A. 3
   B. 5
   C. 8
   D. 11
   E. 12

When you know the lengths of two sides of a triangle, you know something about the length of the third side: it's less than the sum and greater than the difference of the two known lengths. Given lengths of 5 inches and 8 inches, you know that the third length must be less than 5 + 8 = 13 inches and greater than 8 – 5 = 3 inches. The question asks which could *not* be the length of the third side, so the answer that's impossible is 3, choice A. The third side must be *greater* than 3—it cannot actually equal 3.

TRIGONOMETRY

6. In the figure below, what is the tangent of $\angle C$?

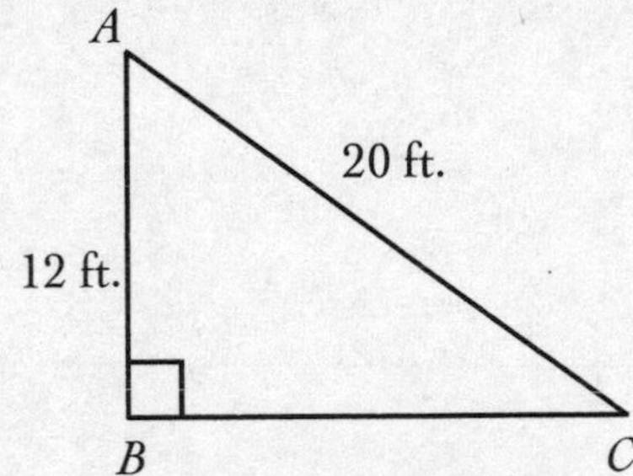

   F. $\frac{3}{5}$

   G. $\frac{3}{4}$

   H. $\frac{12}{13}$

   J. $\frac{13}{12}$

   K. $\frac{4}{3}$

From SOHCAHTOA*, remember that tangent = $\frac{\text{Opposite}}{\text{Adjacent}}$. Here the leg opposite $\angle C$ is labeled as 12, but the leg adjacent isn't given. That means you'll have to find it. You could use the Pythagorean theorem, but you would save time if you noticed that the ratio of the given leg to the hypotenuse is 3:5. This means that *ABC* is a 3-4-5 right triangle—with each side quadrupled—so $BC = 16$. Now that you have the lengths of both the opposite and adjacent sides, just plug them in: $\tan C = \frac{12}{16} = \frac{3}{4}$. So choice G is correct.

*The abbreviation for the definition of sine, cosine, and tangent: sine equals opposite over hypotenuse; cosine equals adjacent over hypotenuse; tangent equals opposite over adjacent

ACT Math Practice Quiz

Now answer the following ACT Math questions to assess your strengths and weaknesses. At the end of the quiz, you'll find an answer key and strategic explanations. Then enter your score on the "SAT or ACT? Score Comparison Chart" at the end of this book.

1. Jimmy's school is 10 miles from his house, on the same street. If he walks down his street directly from the school to his house, he passes a candy store and a grocery store. The candy store is 2.35 miles from the school and the grocery store is 3.4 miles from the candy store. How many miles is it from the grocery store to Jimmy's house?

   A. 3.75
   B. 4.25
   C. 4.75
   D. 5.25
   E. 5.75

   (A) (B) (C) (D) (E)

2. Randy scored 150, 195, and 160 in three bowling games. What should she score on her next bowling game if she wants to have an average score of exactly 175 for the four games?

   F. 205
   G. 195
   H. 185
   J. 175
   K. 165

   (F) (G) (H) (J) (K)

3. What is the sum of the solutions of the equation $2y^2 - 4y - 6 = 0$?

   A. –4
   B. –2
   C. –1
   D. 2
   E. 4

   (A) (B) (C) (D) (E)

4. In ΔDEF below, $\overline{DE} = 1$ and $\overline{DF} = \sqrt{2}$. What is the value of tan x ?

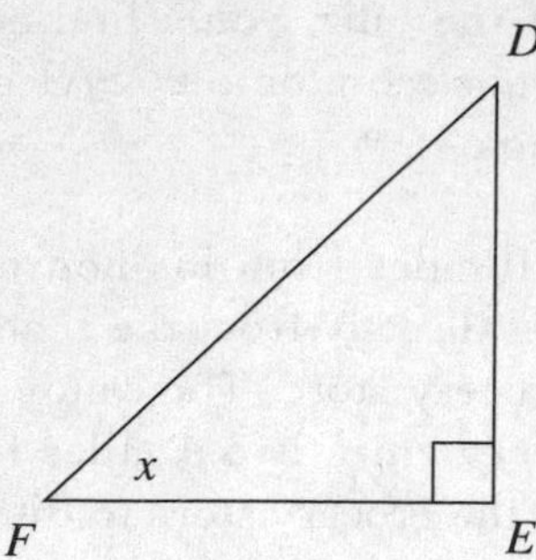

F. $\frac{\sqrt{2}}{2}$

G. 1

H. $\sqrt{2}$

J. $\sqrt{3}$

K. 2

Ⓕ Ⓖ Ⓗ Ⓙ Ⓚ

5. For all r, s, t, and u, $r(t + u) - s(t + u) = ?$

A. $(r + s)(t + u)$

B. $(r - s)(t - u)$

C. $(r + s)(t - u)$

D. $(r - s)(t + u)$

E. 0

Ⓐ Ⓑ Ⓒ Ⓓ Ⓔ

6. In the figure below, $\angle ABC$ is a right angle and $\overline{DF}$ is parallel to $\overline{AC}$. If $\overline{AB}$ is 8 units long, $\overline{BC}$ is 6 units long, and $\overline{DB}$ is 4 units long, what is the area in square units of ΔDBF ?

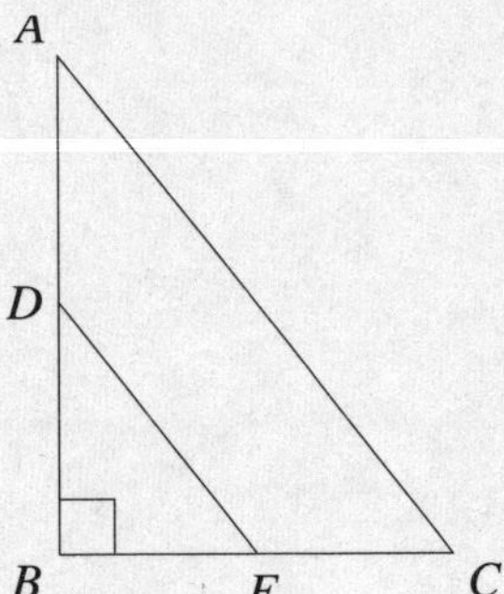

F. 6
G. 12
H. 16
J. 24
K. 48

Ⓕ Ⓖ Ⓗ Ⓙ Ⓚ

7. In the figure below, O is the center of the circle, C and D are points on the circle, and C, O, and D are collinear. If the length of $\overline{CD}$ is 10 units, what is the circumference, in units, of the circle?

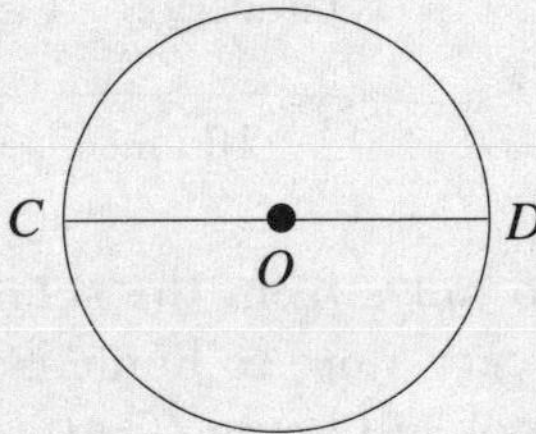

A. 10π
B. 20π
C. 25π
D. 40π
E. 100π

Ⓐ Ⓑ Ⓒ Ⓓ Ⓔ

8. Line T in the standard (x, y) coordinate plane has y-intercept -3 and is parallel to the line determined by the equation $3x - 5y = 4$. Which of the following is an equation for line T?

F. $y = -\frac{3}{5}x + 3$

G. $y = -\frac{5}{3}x - 3$

H. $y = \frac{3}{5}x + 3$

J. $y = \frac{5}{3}x + 3$

K. $y = \frac{3}{5}x - 3$

Ⓕ Ⓖ Ⓗ Ⓙ Ⓚ

Practice Quiz Answers

1. B 2. G 3. D 4. G 5. D 6. F 7. A 8. K

ACT MATH PRACTICE QUIZ: EXPLANATIONS

1. **B** Draw a diagram

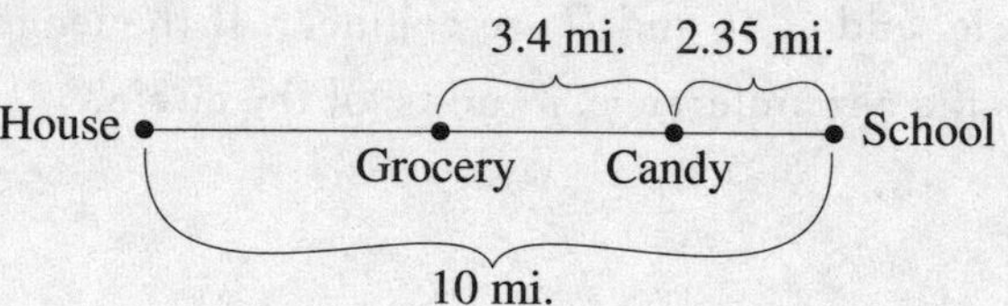

It is $2.35 + 3.4 = 5.75$ miles from the school to the grocery store. The distance from the grocery store to home is the remaining portion of the 10 miles between school and home. That is, 10 miles – 5.75 miles = 4.25 miles.

2. **G** Average $= \dfrac{\text{Sum of Terms}}{\text{Number of Terms}}$. In this case she needs an average of 175.

Let the score on the next game be x. Then $175 = \dfrac{150 + 195 + 160 + x}{4}$.

$$175 \times 4 = 150 + 195 + 160 + x$$
$$700 = 505 + x$$
$$700 - 505 = x$$
$$195 = x$$

So she must score 195 on the next game for an average of 175.

3. **D** $2y^2 - 4y - 6 = 0$ is of the form $ax^2 + bx + c = 0$, and so its roots can be found from:

$$\frac{-b \pm \sqrt{b^2 - 4ac}}{2a}$$

$$= \frac{-(-4) \pm \sqrt{(-4)^2 - 4 \times 2 \times (-6)}}{2 \times 2}$$

$$= \frac{4 \pm \sqrt{16 + 48}}{4}$$ $= 1 \pm 2$, 3 and –1, in this case. The sum of 3 and –1 is 2.

4. **G** Since $\tan = \frac{\text{opposite}}{\text{adjacent}}$, you need to know the length of the side opposite x, $\overline{DE}$, and the side adjacent to x, $\overline{FE}$.

Since $DE = 1$ and $DF = \sqrt{2}$, this must be an isosceles right triangle with sides in the ratio $1 : 1 : \sqrt{2}$. (You could also show this by using the Pythagorean theorem.) So $DE = FE = 1$.

$$\tan x = \frac{\text{opposite}}{\text{adjacent}} = \frac{DE}{FE} = \frac{1}{1}$$

5. **D** Notice that in the expression $r(t + u) - s(t + u)$, both r and s are being multiplied by $t + u$. Factor this out to get $(r - s)(t + u)$.

If you didn't see this, you could have tried picking numbers. Let $r = 2$, $s = 3$, $t = 4$, and $u = 5$. Then $r(t + u) - s(t + u) = 2(4 + 5) - 3(4 + 5) = 18 - 27 = -9$. Any of the answer choices that does not give a value of –9 for these values of r, s, t, and u may be discarded.
A: $(r + s)(t + u) = (2 + 3)(4 + 5) = (5)(9) = 45$—discard.
B: $(r - s)(t - u) = (2 - 3)(4 - 5) = (-1)(-1) = 1$—discard.
C: $(r + s)(t - u) = (2 + 3)(4 - 5) = (5)(-1) = -5$—discard.
D: $(r - s)(t + u) = (2 - 3)(4 + 5) = (-1)(9) = -9$—this may be correct.
E: 0—discard.
So answer choice D is the only one that gives a value of –9 for the chosen values, and it must be correct.

6. **F** $DB = 4$, that is $\overline{DB}$ is half the length of $\overline{AB}$.

ΔABC and ΔDBF are similar, since corresponding angles are of the same measure. Therefore their sides are in the same ratio, that is $\frac{AB}{BC} = \frac{DB}{BF}$, or $\frac{8}{6} = \frac{4}{BF}$ so $BF = 3$. The area of a triangle is $\frac{1}{2}(\text{base} \times \text{height}) = \frac{1}{2}(3 \times 4) = 6$.

Note: You could have discarded answer choices J and K by logic—the area of the smaller triangle must be less than the area of the larger triangle, which is $\frac{1}{2}(6 \times 8) = 24$.

7. **A** The circumference of a circle is $\pi\partial$, where ∂ is the diameter. Here the diameter is 10, so the circumference is 10π.

8. **K** All answers are in the form of the slope-intercept equation, $y = mx + b$, where m is the slope and b is the y-intercept. Line T has a y-intercept of -3, so in this case $b = -3$. (Discard answer choices F, H, and J.) Since T is parallel to $3x - 5y = 4$, they have the same slope. Find the slope of $3x - 5y = 4$:

$$3x - 5y = 4$$
$$-5y = -3x + 4$$
$$y = \frac{3}{5}x - \frac{4}{5}$$

So the slope is $\frac{3}{5}$ and line T has equation $y = \frac{3}{5}x - 3$.

7 ACT Science Reasoning

It's an Open-Book Test

The good news is, you don't have to be a scientist to succeed on the ACT Science Reasoning test. You don't have to know the atomic number of cadmium or the preferred mating habits of the monarch butterfly. All that's required is common sense (though a knowledge of standard scientific processes and procedures sure does help). You'll be given passages containing various kinds of scientific information—drawn from the fields of biology, chemistry, physics, geology, astronomy, and meteorology—that you'll have to understand and use as a basis for drawing conclusions.

The Format

On most Science Reasoning tests, there are six passages that present scientific data, often based on specific experiments. Also, there's usually one passage in which two scientists state opposing views on the same issue. Each passage will generate between five and seven questions. A warning: Some passages will be very difficult to understand, but the test makers usually make up for that fact by having many basic questions attached to them. They do show some mercy once in a while.

There are three main question types on the ACT Science section:

- Data-analysis questions. These require you to read data from tables, graphs, and diagrams and recognize patterns in data. Look for patterns in the data, and try to predict the answer before you look at the choices.
- Experiment questions. These require that you understand the way experiments are designed and what they prove. Try to identify the control group, and the factor that is being varied from one experiment to the next.
- Principle questions. These require you to either logically apply a principle, or identify ways of defending or attacking a principle. This includes making predictions based on a given theory, or showing how a hypothesis might be strengthened or weakened by particular findings.

Thirty Seconds Each

The Science Reasoning test is 35 minutes long and includes 40 questions. The test contains seven passages, each with five to seven questions. Factoring in the amount of time you'll initially spend on the passage, that will give you a little more than 30 seconds for each question.

DATA ANALYSIS QUESTIONS

About a third of the questions in the Science section require you to read data from graphs or tables. In easier questions, you need only report the information. In harder questions, you may need to draw conclusions or note patterns in the data. For example:

A scientist has developed a means of extracting valuable elements from radioactive nuclear power plant effluent using a certain organic reagent. Below are extraction curves for the six different elements: tungsten (W), molybdenum (Mo), ytterbium (Yb), erbium (Er), thulium (Tm), and europium (Eu).

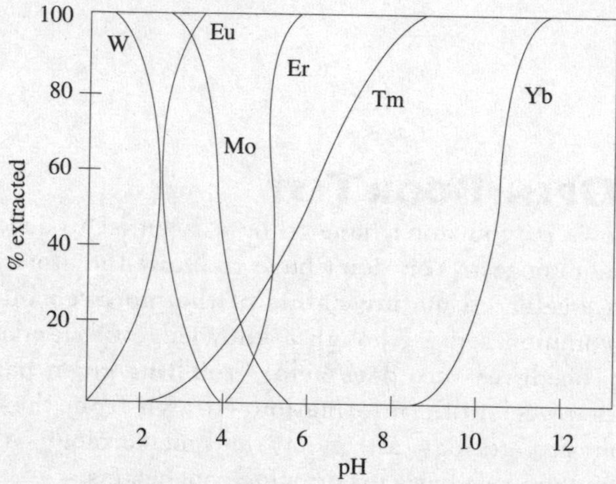

1. Which of the elements in the table can be completely extracted (100%) at a pH of 8.5?

   A. Ytterbium only
   B. Tungsten and molybdenum only
   C. Europium, erbium, and thulium only
   D. Europium, erbium, thulium, and ytterbium only

2. Based on the data given, which of the following conclusions can be drawn about the effect of pH on the percentage extracted?

   F. The percentage of an element extracted increases as pH increases.
   G. The percentage of an element extracted decreases as pH increases.
   H. The percentage of an element extracted is independent of pH.
   J. The effect of pH is different for different elements.

What sort of things did you notice about the graph? First, you should determine what is being represented: the percentage extracted (for six different elements) from the effluent at various pH levels. Notice that each line represents one element. Look at each line on the graph. The slopes of the tungsten and molybdenum lines are negative, that is, the percentage extracted decreases as the pH increases, while the slopes of all the other lines are positive, that is, the percentage extracted increases as the pH increases.

The correct answer to the first question is C. A good way to approach this question would be to draw a vertical line on the graph at pH 8.5. The question could now be interpreted as, "Which elements to the left of this line have reached maximum extraction at pH 8.5?" The only elements that fit into this category are europium, erbium, and thulium, choice C. Choice B is wrong because tungsten and molybdenum have downward slopes, so at pH 8.5, they can't be extracted.

In the second question, the correct answer is J. In the graph, there are two types of slopes: one in which the percentage of an element extracted increases as the pH increases (positive) and one in which the percentage of an element extracted decreases with increasing pH (negative). Since there are two types of slopes, J is the correct response.

Experiment Questions

Other Science Reasoning questions require that you understand the way experiments are designed and what they prove. For example, part of a passage might describe an experiment as follows:

> A process has been developed by which plastic bottles can be recycled into a clear, colorless material. This material, called *nu-PVC,* can be used to form park benches and other similar structures. A series of experiments was performed to determine the weathering abilities of nu-PVC.
>
> Experiment 1
> Fifteen boards of nu-PVC, each 150 × 25 × 8 cm. in size, were sprayed with distilled water for ten hours a day for 32 weeks. All 15 boards remained within 0.1 cm. of their original dimensions. The surfaces of the boards displayed no signs of cracking, bubbling, or other degradation.

3. Based on the results of Experiment 1, which of the following conclusions concerning the effect of rain on nu-PVC is valid?
   - **A.** The material absorbs water over time causing it to permanently swell.
   - **B.** The material will be useful only in areas where there is no acid rain.
   - **C.** The material's surface does not appear to require a protective coating to avoid water damage.
   - **D.** The material loses flexibility after prolonged exposure to precipitation.

This research summary presents the results of an experiment that was done on the material nu-PVC. The purpose of the experiment was to "determine the weathering abilities of nu-PVC," so you can assume that each of the experimental conditions was designed to simulate some aspect of extreme weather. The answer to the question is C. According to the results of Experiment 1, nu-PVC does not suffer any kind of damage when exposed to water for a long period of time. It seems safe to say, then, that nu-PVC would not need a protective coating to avoid water damage, choice C.

Principle Questions

The remaining Science questions require you to either logically apply a principle or identify ways of defending or attacking a principle. Often, the question will involve two scientists stating opposing views on the same subject. But this is not always the case. For example, a passage might describe a theory accounting for the extinction of the dinosaurs during the Cretaceous-Tertiary period. If the scientist argued that the dinosaurs were wiped out by climatic changes caused by massive volcanic eruptions, then the following question might be asked:

4. Which of the following discoveries would most weaken the scientist's theory about the extinction of the dinosaurs?

   F. Certain other species were wiped out in the same period by tidal waves.
   G. The disappearance of dinosaur fossils does not coincide with major volcanic activity.
   H. The impact of an asteroid could also account for the dinosaurs' extinction.
   J. Massive volcanic activity does not always bring about climatic changes.

Principle questions are a lot like ACT Reading questions—you have to summarize the author's argument first, and then identify whether evidence supports or weakens it. The answer here is G. Since the scientist is arguing a link between massive volcanic eruptions and dinosaur extinction, evidence that the two events did not happen at the same time would certainly weaken the author's argument.

You Don't Have to Be a Science Whiz

Knowing science is great, and it certainly can help your work in the Science Reasoning test. But you don't need to know a truckload of scientific facts to answer ACT Science questions. They can be answered by referring to the information *in the passage.*

Dealing with Science Passages

Many ACT takers tend to rely too heavily on what they've learned in school when approaching the Science Reasoning test. But "remembering" is not a mindset that the ACT will reward. You couldn't possibly know the answers to ACT Science Reasoning questions in advance; you have to pull them out of the passages. All the information you need to answer the questions is right on the page. You just have to find it and use it.

Kaplan's Three-Step Method for Science Reasoning

Here's Kaplan's Three-Step Method for ACT Science passages. If it reminds you of the Three-Step Method for ACT Reading, it's because Science passages reward the same systematic approach!

1. **Preread the passage.**
2. **Consider the question stem.**
3. **Refer to the passage (before looking at the choices).**

Step One: Preread the Passage

Almost all Science Reasoning passages have the same general structure. They begin with an introduction. Always read through the introduction first to orient yourself. Some passages relate to material you might have already studied in high school. If you're familiar with the concepts in the passage, you might not need to do more than skim the introduction. Remember, don't focus on details. Try to get a sense of the overall situation.

After reading the introduction, quickly scan the rest of the passage. How is the information presented? Graphs? Diagrams? Are there experiments? What seems to be important? Size? Shape? Temperature? Speed? Chemical composition? Don't worry about details, and don't try to remember it all. Plan to refer to the passage just as you would in Reading.

As you preread the passage, you also want to make sure you know what any tables and graphs in the passage are meant to represent. Feel free to take notes, mark up the test booklet, or circle important information. Get a sense of what kind of data is contained in each graph and table, but don't read the data carefully yet! You may want to take note of general trends in the data, but don't waste time taking in information that may not be relevant to the questions.

Don't Peek

As in ACT Reading, it's tempting to avoid the process of actually answering the question and instead just look at the answer choices and see which one sounds best. Don't do it.

Step Two: Consider the Question Stem

Most of your time in Science Reasoning will be spent considering questions and referring to the passage to find the answers. Here's where you should do most of your really careful reading. It's essential that you understand exactly what the question is asking. Then, go back to the passage and get a sense of what the answer should be *before* looking at the choices.

Step Three: Refer to the Passage (Before Looking at the Choices)

As in Reading, you have to be diligent about referring to the passage. Your prereading of the passage should have given you an idea of where particular kinds of data can be found. Sometimes the questions themselves will direct you to the right place.

Be careful not to mix up units when taking information from graphs, tables, and summaries. Make sure you don't confuse *decreases* and *increases*. Many questions will hinge on whether you can correctly identify the factors that decrease and the ones that increase. Read the questions carefully!

Try the questions on the following passage, keeping in mind the Three-Step Method:

> Optical fibers are strands of highly transparent glass used for communication transmissions. When light is transmitted through optical fibers, power is lost along the way. The power lost depends on the distance traveled, the wavelength of the light transmitted, the glass used, and any impurities present. The following attenuation (power loss in db/km) curve, which was recorded for a fluoride glass optical fiber, includes the attenuation caused by three different impurities commonly present in fluoride glass fibers.

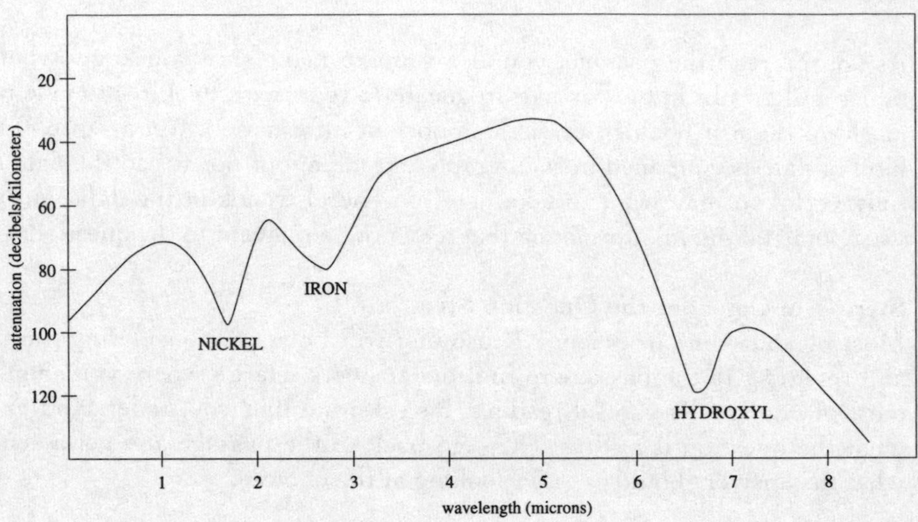

5. In this fiber, copper impurities can lead to an attenuation of roughly 95 decibels per kilometer at wavelengths near 1.6 microns. Such impurities, if graphed as above, would produce an attenuation response similar to that of:

A. nickel.
B. iron.
C. hydroxyl.
D. none of the impurities in the graph.

Ⓐ Ⓑ Ⓒ Ⓓ

6. According to the graph, in a fiber without any impurities, as wavelength increases, power loss will:

F. decrease then increase.
G. increase then decrease.
H. remain the same.
J. fluctuate randomly.

Ⓕ Ⓖ Ⓗ Ⓙ

7. If a researcher using a 6.6 micron laser wished to limit power loss, this fluoride glass fiber would be:

 A. ideal, because attenuation is at a minimum at this wavelength.
 B. impossible, because the fiber does not conduct light at this wavelength.
 C. inefficient, because of interference from hydroxyl groups at this wavelength.
 D. unaffected by the laser's wavelength.

Ⓐ Ⓑ Ⓒ Ⓓ

8. Suppose a scientist were able to develop a fluoride glass fiber without any hydroxyl impurities. Which of the following predictions would most likely be true?

 I. There will be less power lost in the range between 6 and 7 microns.
 II. The attenuation due to iron impurities would increase.
 III. The fiber's overall power loss would decrease.

 F. I only
 G. I and III only
 H. II and III only
 J. I, II, and III

Ⓕ Ⓖ Ⓗ Ⓙ

How did you do? This passage was a data-representation passage about the power loss (attenuation) in optical fibers due to impurities. The graph you're given to interpret shows the attenuation curve for fluoride glass fibers. At certain ranges in wavelength, as you can see, impurities cause a sharp increase in attenuation; for example, nickel causes a power loss of about 95 db/km at 1.5 microns.

The important thing to keep in mind when reading this graph is that attenuation in db/km (the *y*-axis) increases as you move downward. This means, for example, that hydroxyl causes greater power loss than either of the other two impurities.

For Question 5, take a look at the graph and locate the point that corresponds to 1.6 microns and 95 db/km. As it turns out, this is where the line dips—and attenuation sharply increases—due to the presence of nickel impurities. Therefore, copper impurities have an attenuation response similar to that of nickel, choice A.

In order to answer Question 6, you have to envision what the attenuation curve would look like without the sharp dips due to the impurities. It looks as though the curve would rise steadily going from left to right until it reached 5 microns and 30 db/km, at which point it would start to fall. Once you saw this, you might have been tempted to answer that power loss will "increase then decrease," but remember that the power loss increases as you go down the y-axis. This means that power loss is actually decreasing and then increasing, choices F, as you move along the curve from left to right.

To answer Question 7, look at what happens near the 6.6 micron wavelength. At 6.6 microns, according to the graph, hydroxyl impurities in a fluoride glass fiber cause an attenuation of nearly 120 db/km. That's a considerable loss of power. Someone who wished to limit power loss at this wavelength would not choose to use fluoride glass fiber because of "the interference from the hydroxyl groups at this wavelength," choice C. This does not mean, though, that a fluoride glass fiber does not conduct any light at this wavelength at all, as choice B suggests; it's just that a lot of power is lost.

Question 8 is a follow-up to the last one. You already know that hydroxyl impurities in fluoride glass fibers cause power loss in the range between 6 and 7 microns. It stands to reason, then, that if you could get rid of these impurities there would be less power loss both in the range of 6 to 7 microns (Statement I) and in the fiber overall (Statement III). There is no reason to think that the attenuation due to iron impurities would increase, however, so Statement II is false. That makes choice G correct.

SCIENCE REASONING PRACTICE QUIZ

Now answer the following Science Reasoning questions to assess your strengths and weaknesses. At the end of the quiz, you'll find an answer key and strategic explanations. Then enter your score on the "SAT or ACT? Score Comparison Chart" at the end of this book.

Passage 1

Medical researchers and technicians can track the characteristic radiation patterns emitted by certain inherently unstable isotopes as they spontaneously decay into other elements. The half-life of a radioactive isotope is the amount of time necessary for one-half of the initial amount of its nuclei to decay. The decay curves of isotopes ${}_{39}Y^{90}$ and ${}_{39}Y^{91}$ are graphed below as functions of the ratio of N, the number of nuclei remaining after a given period, to N_0, the initial number of nuclei.

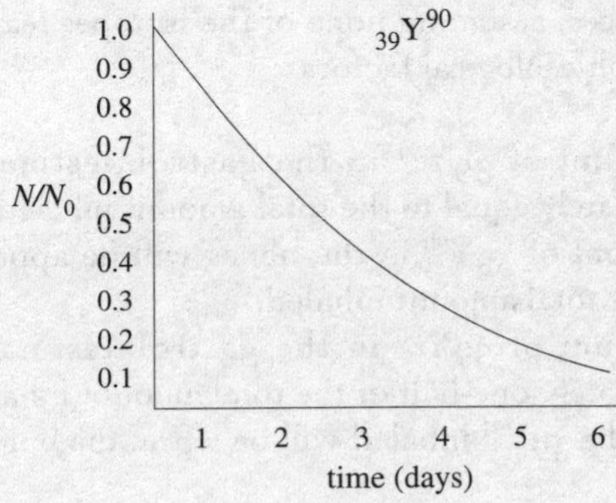

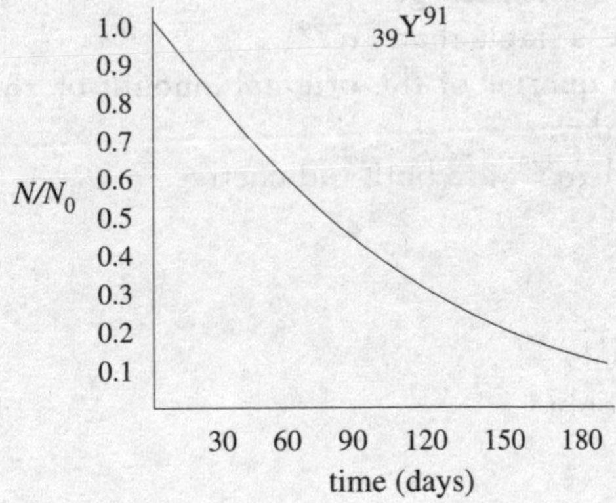

1. The half-life of ${}_{39}Y^{90}$ is approximately:

   A. 2.7 days.
   B. 5.4 days.
   C. 27 days.
   D. 58 days.

Ⓐ Ⓑ Ⓒ Ⓓ

2. What will the approximate ratio of $_{39}Y^{90}$ to $_{39}Y^{91}$ be after 2.7 days if the initial samples of the two isotopes contain equal numbers of nuclei?

   F. 1:1
   G. 1:2
   H. 2:1
   J. 10:1

3. When inhaled by humans, $_{39}Y^{90}$ accumulates in the gastrointestinal tract, whereas $_{39}Y^{91}$ accumulates in the bones. If the total amount of each isotope inhaled goes to the specified area, which of the following situations will exist three days after a patient inhales these substances, assuming none of the isotopes leave the specified areas due to physiological factors?

   A. The amount of $_{39}Y^{91}$ in the gastrointestinal tract will be approximately equal to the total amount inhaled.
   B. The amount of $_{39}Y^{90}$ in the bones will be approximately one-half of the total amount inhaled.
   C. The amount of $_{39}Y^{90}$ in the gastrointestinal tract will be approximately one-half of the total amount inhaled.
   D. None of the $_{39}Y^{91}$ inhaled will be left in the bones.

(A) (B) (C) (D)

4. Which of the following conclusions is(are) supported by the information given in the passage?

   I. $_{39}Y^{90}$ is less stable than $_{39}Y^{91}$
   II. Only one-quarter of the original amount of $_{39}Y^{90}$ will remain after 116 days.
   III. $_{39}Y^{90}$ and $_{39}Y^{91}$ are both radioactive.

   F. I only
   G. III only
   H. I and II only
   J. I and III only

(F) (G) (H) (J)

Passage 2

The reaction of a certain cobalt complex with sodium nitrite ($NaNO_2$) can yield two different products. Product A is a light orange solid with a melting point measured at approximately 90.5° C; Product B is a dark pink solid with a melting point of 68° C. A series of experiments was performed to determine the reaction conditions that favor each product.

Experiment 1

Two separate solutions of the cobalt complex were prepared as follows. Solution 1 was acidified to pH 5.5; Solution 2 was made basic to pH 8.5. All other conditions were identical for the two solutions. When $NaNO_2$ was added to Solution 1, a dark pink solid with a melting point of 68° C was formed. Adding $NaNO_2$ to Solution 2 produced a white solid with a melting point of 81° C.

Experiment 2
Two separate solutions of the cobalt complex were prepared as above. After addition of $NaNO_2$, the solutions were heated to 110° C for 20 minutes. Solution 1 produced a dark pink solid with a melting point of 68° C. Solution 2 produced a light orange solid that melted at 91° C.

Experiment 3
Two separate solutions were prepared as in the previous experiments. After the addition of $NaNO_2$, each solution was treated with a small amount of citrate ion and then heated as in Experiment 2. Solution 1 remained a clear, purple liquid. Solution 2 produced a light orange solid that melted at 90° C.

5. The experimental results indicate that Product B is most likely to form when one heats:

   A. a basic solution with added citrate ion.
   B. an acidic solution with added citrate ion.
   C. an acidic solution with no added citrate ion.
   D. a basic solution with no added citrate ion.

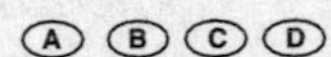

6. Which of the following conclusions is NOT supported by the experimental results?

   F. The formation of Product B is not affected by the presence of citrate ion.
   G. The formation of Product B is not affected by the heating of the solution.
   H. Products A and B form under different conditions.
   J. The formation of Product A is affected by the heating of the solution.

7. Which of the following additional experiments would yield the most useful data concerning the reaction conditions that favor each product?

   A. varying the concentration of the solutions
   B. testing with pH levels of 7.0
   C. heating the solutions to 175° C
   D. freezing the solutions

8. Which of the following hypotheses is supported by the results of Experiment 2 only?

   F. Products A and B can both be formed in solutions heated to 110° C.
   G. Solution 1 must be heated to yield any product.
   H. Citrate ion prevents the formation of Product A.
   J. Product B forms more readily at lower temperatures.

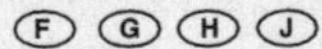

ACT Science Reasoning Quiz: Explanations

Answers
1. A 2. G 3. C 4. D 5. C 6. F 7. B 8. F

Passage 1

The first passage mostly requires an ability to read the two given graphs, each of which traces the rate of decay in a different radioactive isotope. The *y*-axis of each graph represents the proportion of remaining (undecayed) nuclei to original nuclei, while the *x*-axis of each represents time. Notice, though, that the first graph runs from zero days to just six days, while the second graph runs from zero days to 180 days. That's a big difference, indicating that the second isotope—$_{39}Y^{91}$— decays at a much slower rate.

1. **A** In the introduction to the passage, the half-life of an isotope is defined as the amount of time needed for one-half of the isotope's nuclei to decay. To figure out the half-life of $_{39}Y^{90}$, look at the first graph. When half of the nuclei have decayed, the N/N_0 ratio would be 0.5 (since there'd be half as many nuclei after the half-life as there were originally). Draw a horizontal line across the graph at the level of 0.5. The horizontal line will intersect the curve at a specific point; from this point, draw a vertical line down to the *x*-axis. The vertical line intersects the *x*-axis somewhere between 2.5 and 3 days, which means that the amount of time it takes for half of the nuclei to decay is between 2.5 and 3 days. Choice A is the only answer that falls in this range.

2. **G** Since N_0 is the same for both samples, you can use the two graphs to figure out the ratio of $_{39}Y^{90}$ to $_{39}Y^{91}$ after 2.7 days. You know from having done the previous question that after 2.7 days about 0.5 of $_{39}Y^{90}$ still remains. Take a look at the graph for $_{39}Y^{91}$: after 2.7 days, hardly any will have decayed at all. Therefore, the ratio of $_{39}Y^{90}$ to $_{39}Y^{91}$ will be 0.5 to 1, or 1 to 2, choice G.

3. **C** This is a rather strange, convoluted question, but what it means is that one isotope ($_{39}Y^{90}$) will accumulate in the gastrointestinal tract while the other ($_{39}Y^{91}$) will accumulate in the bones. The half-lives of the isotopes will remain the same, so after three days, a little over half of the original $_{39}Y^{90}$ will be left (in the gastrointestinal tract), but just about all of the $_{39}Y^{91}$ will be left (in the bones). With this information in hand, you just have to examine the choices. Choice A is incorrect because $_{39}Y^{91}$ accumulates in the bones, not the gastrointestinal tract. Choice B is incorrect since $_{39}Y^{90}$ accumulates in the gastrointestinal tract, not in the bones. Choice C is correct because, as we said, about half of the nuclei of $_{39}Y^{90}$ decay after three days, so about half of the inhaled amount will be in the gastrointestinal tract after three days. Choice D is out because almost all of the $_{39}Y^{91}$ will be left in the bones.

4. **D** Statement I is true: $_{39}Y^{90}$ is less stable than $_{39}Y^{91}$ because $_{39}Y^{90}$ decays more rapidly (remember that the *x*-axes are scaled differently). This rules out choice B. Statement II is wrong because virtually no $_{39}Y^{90}$ would remain after 116 days. Choice C can thus also be eliminated. Statement III is obviously true, given the fact that they decay in this manner, making choice D the correct answer.

Passage 2

This passage is based around three different experiments, all designed to determine what conditions favor Product A and what conditions favor Product B when a particular cobalt complex reacts with sodium nitrite. Remember to determine what factor is varied in each experiment. In Experiment 1, the varied factor is acidity (one solution is made acidic while the other is made basic). In Experiment 2, the varied factor is heat. And in Experiment 3, the varied factor is the citrate ion.

5. **C** To answer this question, look at the conditions in which Product B was formed. Solution 1 in Experiment 1 and Solution 1 in Experiment 2 both yielded Product B. These solutions were both acidic, so the correct answer must be either choice B or C. The next step is to determine whether Product B was formed when citrate ion was added. The results of Experiment 3 show that there is no yield of Product B with added citrate ion, so choice C is the correct answer.

6. **F** Choice F is the conclusion that is not supported by the experimental results. As you know from the previous question, Product B is not formed when citrate ion is added to the solution. Since it does form in the same solution if no citrate ion is added (Experiment 2), the presence of citrate ion does indeed affect the formation of Product B. All of the other choices are legitimate conclusions based on the experimental data.

7. **B** Varying the pH (choice B) may well show that different degrees of acidity or basicity will have a marked impact on product formation. Heating the solutions (choice C) has been tried already, and freezing the solutions (choice D) should stop the reactions altogether. Varying the concentration (choice A), meanwhile, won't alter the ability of the known compound to react.

8. **F** When you're answering a question that's based on only part of the data, make sure that the answer you choose is based only on the relevant data. In Experiment 2 it was found that when the solutions were heated to 110° C, both Product A and Product B were formed. Therefore, choice F is supported by the results of Experiment 2. All of the other choices are hypotheses that could only be supported or refuted using the results of Experiments 1 and 3 along with the results of Experiment 2.

SAT and ACT Practice Sets

In the following two chapters, you'll find sets of SAT and ACT practice questions subdivided by topic to help you to hone your testing skills. If you're comfortable with the material, try these practice sets under testlike conditions, moving from one question to the next at a rapid pace. If you're not so comfortable, try two or three questions at a time, checking your answers as you go. Complete, strategic explanations to all of these questions follow in Chapters 10 and 11.

8 SAT Practice Sets

SAT Verbal Practice Set 1: Analogies

For each of the following questions, choose the best answer and darken the corresponding oval. Choose the lettered pair of words that is related in the same way as the pair in capital letters.
Example:

FLAKE : SNOW ::

(A) storm : hail
(B) drop : rain
(C) field : wheat
(D) stack : hay
(E) cloud : fog

Ⓐ Ⓑ Ⓒ Ⓓ Ⓔ

---

1. LABORATORY : EXPERIMENT ::

(A) garage : repair
(B) beach : sunbathe
(C) statement : formulate
(D) graveyard : inter
(E) invention : create

Ⓐ Ⓑ Ⓒ Ⓓ Ⓔ

2. EXONERATE : BLAME ::

(A) disinfect : contamination
(B) divert : stream
(C) indict : guilt
(D) obey : order
(E) absolve : ministry

Ⓐ Ⓑ Ⓒ Ⓓ Ⓔ

3. LOOK : SCRUTINIZE ::

(A) amble : scurry
(B) deliberate : propose
(C) read : peruse
(D) importune : plead
(E) flicker : shine

Ⓐ Ⓑ Ⓒ Ⓓ Ⓔ

4. GULLIBLE : DUPE ::

(A) fallible : err
(B) foolhardy : confuse
(C) dejected : dishearten
(D) headstrong : coax
(E) submissive : control

Ⓐ Ⓑ Ⓒ Ⓓ Ⓔ

5. CONVERSATION : INTERLOCUTOR ::

(A) speech : orator
(B) hearing : prosecutor
(C) game : player
(D) novel : publisher
(E) diagnosis : doctor

Ⓐ Ⓑ Ⓒ Ⓓ Ⓔ

6. ENTOMOLOGY : INSECTS ::

(A) agriculture : cows
(B) pedagogy : education
(C) astronomy : telescope
(D) literature : character
(E) evolution : man

Ⓐ Ⓑ Ⓒ Ⓓ Ⓔ

7. SKIRMISH : BATTLE ::

(A) misdemeanor : crime
(B) desertion : divorce
(C) fledgling : expert
(D) faculty : instructor
(E) estimate : measurement

Ⓐ Ⓑ Ⓒ Ⓓ Ⓔ

8. FORENSIC : LITIGATION ::

(A) maritime : sea
(B) euphoria : feeling
(C) conjugal : bliss
(D) exemplary : example
(E) illusory : magic

Ⓐ Ⓑ Ⓒ Ⓓ Ⓔ

9. FEIGN : IMPRESSION ::

(A) adapt : evolution
(B) perjure : testimony
(C) play : role
(D) impersonate : celebrity
(E) slander : reputation

Ⓐ Ⓑ Ⓒ Ⓓ Ⓔ

10. POLEMIC : IMPARTIAL ::

(A) antidote : curative
(B) discipline : harsh
(C) heretic : persecuted
(D) defendant : guilty
(E) extrovert : retiring

Ⓐ Ⓑ Ⓒ Ⓓ Ⓔ

11. SCAR : INJURY ::

(A) monument : marble
(B) fever : illness
(C) dent : collision
(D) exhibition : painting
(E) blood : fistfight

Ⓐ Ⓑ Ⓒ Ⓓ Ⓔ

12. YAWN : BOREDOM ::

(A) react : surprise
(B) pout : displeasure
(C) gasp : breath
(D) repose : sleep
(E) cheer : depression

Ⓐ Ⓑ Ⓒ Ⓓ Ⓔ

13. ACTOR : AUDITION ::

(A) singer : debut
(B) judge : verdict
(C) architect : plan
(D) instrumentalist : solo
(E) gymnast : tryout

Ⓐ Ⓑ Ⓒ Ⓓ Ⓔ

14. INTERESTING : ABSORBING ::

(A) destitute : penniless
(B) enriching : regenerative
(C) mystifying : convoluted
(D) pompous : belligerent
(E) affectionate : doting

Ⓐ Ⓑ Ⓒ Ⓓ Ⓔ

15. SIGNATURE : FORGER ::

(A) account : embezzler
(B) article : plagiarist
(C) novel : author
(D) picture : painter
(E) bill : counterfeiter

Ⓐ Ⓑ Ⓒ Ⓓ Ⓔ

16. LEGEND : MAP ::

(A) translation : story
(B) pawn : chessboard
(C) flag : nation
(D) snapshot : portrait
(E) key : cipher

Ⓐ Ⓑ Ⓒ Ⓓ Ⓔ

17. ALIENATE : ESTRANGEMENT ::

(A) discommode : inconvenience
(B) sequester : monasticism
(C) palliate : boredom
(D) orchestrate : symphony
(E) aspire : enthusiasm

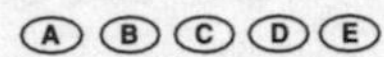

18. PUNGENT : SNIFFED ::

(A) itinerant : traveled
(B) prickly : touched
(C) venomous : bitten
(D) acrid : burned
(E) belligerent : feuded

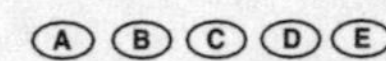

19. ORBIT : SATELLITE ::

(A) course : sailboat
(B) earth : moon
(C) light : insect
(D) target : missile
(E) ring : finger

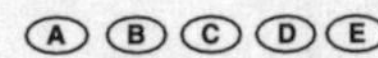

20. DISCONCERT : CONFUSION ::

(A) fear : superstition
(B) daunt : discouragement
(C) spend : extravagance
(D) remonstrate : reward
(E) stabilize : imbalance

21. RINK : SKATE ::

(A) bridge : connect
(B) pipe : smoke
(C) casino : gamble
(D) law : respect
(E) track : compete

22. NIBBLE : BITE ::

(A) dab : paint
(B) chew : swallow
(C) condemn : accuse
(D) grasp : hand
(E) wade : swim

23. THIRSTY : PARCHED ::

(A) dirty : hygenic
(B) unaggressive : lazy
(C) surly : boring
(D) experienced : gullible
(E) scared : terrified

24. DEMONSTRATIVE : EFFUSIVE ::

(A) biased : partisan
(B) generous : lavish
(C) sentimental : pitiable
(D) saccharine : sugary
(E) ethical : devout

25. CREDULOUS : CONVINCE ::

(A) eminent : praise
(B) tortuous : navigate
(C) accessible : reach
(D) hospitable : house
(E) sodden : soak

26. COAGULATE : CLOT ::

(A) prosecute : sentence
(B) inject : needle
(C) obstruct : blockade
(D) freeze : ice
(E) dwindle : hoard

27. RUE : REGRET ::

(A) dive : concealment
(B) ease : apprehension
(C) amaze : familiarity
(D) miss : opportunity
(E) worry : anxiety

Ⓐ Ⓑ Ⓒ Ⓓ Ⓔ

28. PITTANCE : WAGE ::

(A) surrender : defeat
(B) return : investment
(C) scorn : admiration
(D) trickle : stream
(E) rhyme : poem

Ⓐ Ⓑ Ⓒ Ⓓ Ⓔ

29. FEINT : DISTRACT ::

(A) preface : introduce
(B) slumber : stir
(C) chaos : jumble
(D) diversion : ignore
(E) charge : surrender

Ⓐ Ⓑ Ⓒ Ⓓ Ⓔ

30. IDEA : GERMINATE ::

(A) seed : sprout
(B) myth : explode
(C) crop : harvest
(D) argument : persuade
(E) virus : spread

Ⓐ Ⓑ Ⓒ Ⓓ Ⓔ

SAT Verbal Practice Set 2: Sentence Completions

For each of the following questions, choose the best answer and darken the corresponding oval. Select the lettered word or set of words that best completes the sentence. Example:

> Today's small, portable computers contrast markedly with the earliest electronic computers, which were ----.
>
> (A) effective
> (B) invented
> (C) useful
> (D) destructive
> (E) enormous

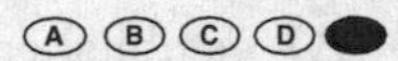

---

1. Finding an old movie poster that is still ---- usually proves difficult because such posters were meant to be used and then ----.

(A) recognizable . . returned
(B) relevant . . discarded
(C) intact . . destroyed
(D) immaculate . . restored
(E) displayed . . maintained

2. The Kemp's Ridley turtle, long considered one of the most ---- creatures of the sea, finally appears to be making some headway in its battle against extinction.

(A) elusive
(B) prevalent
(C) combative
(D) voracious
(E) imperiled

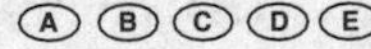

3. Before the invention of the tape recorder, quotes from an interview were rarely ----; journalists usually paraphrased the words of their subject.

(A) verbatim
(B) misconstrued
(C) pragmatic
(D) extensive
(E) plagiarized

4. Batchelor's reputation as ---- novelist encouraged hopes that his political thriller would offer more ---- characterizations than are usually found in the genre.

(A) a serious . . subtle
(B) a maturing . . sweeping
(C) a prolific . . accurate
(D) an accomplished . . fictional
(E) a reclusive . . authentic

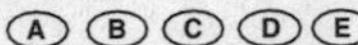

5. The governor commented on the disadvantages of political ----, saying that after his extended tenure in office the voters had grown used to blaming him for everything.

(A) acumen
(B) savvy
(C) longevity
(D) decorum
(E) celebrity

6. Although normally ----, the researcher was ---- by the news that her work had not been accepted for publication.

(A) introverted . . devastated
(B) imperious . . incensed
(C) melodramatic . . electrified
(D) buoyant . . subdued
(E) reserved . . bewildered

7. The agency's failure to ---- policies that it has acknowledged are flawed is a potent demonstration of its ---- approach to correcting its problems.

(A) support . . ambiguous
(B) institute . . earnest
(C) rescind . . lackadaisical
(D) amend . . devoted
(E) chasten . . meticulous

Ⓐ Ⓑ Ⓒ Ⓓ Ⓔ

8. The inconsistency of the educational policies adopted by various schools across the state has been greatly ---- by the rapid turnover of school superintendents.

(A) counteracted
(B) stabilized
(C) criticized
(D) exacerbated
(E) understated

Ⓐ Ⓑ Ⓒ Ⓓ Ⓔ

9. To the ---- of those who in bygone years tiptoed their way past poinsettia displays for fear of causing leaves to fall, breeders have developed more ---- versions of the flower.

(A) consternation . . amorphous
(B) dismay . . fragrant
(C) surprise . . alluring
(D) disappointment . . diversified
(E) relief . . durable

Ⓐ Ⓑ Ⓒ Ⓓ Ⓔ

10. Aristotle espoused a ---- biological model in which all extant species are unchanging and eternal and no new species ever come into existence.

(A) paradoxical
(B) morbid
(C) static
(D) holistic
(E) homogeneous

Ⓐ Ⓑ Ⓒ Ⓓ Ⓔ

11. The journalist's claim of ---- is belied by her record of contributing to the campaign funds of only one party's candidates.

(A) innocence
(B) corruption
(C) impartiality
(D) affluence
(E) loyalty

Ⓐ Ⓑ Ⓒ Ⓓ Ⓔ

12. The repeated breakdown of negotiations only ---- the view that the two sides were not truly committed to the goal of ---- a military confrontation.

(A) established . . escalating
(B) undermined . . avoiding
(C) distorted . . financing
(D) strengthened . . initiating
(E) reinforced . . averting

Ⓐ Ⓑ Ⓒ Ⓓ Ⓔ

13. These are times of national budgetary ---- now that a long era of sustained growth has been succeeded by a period of painful ----.

(A) turmoil . . acquisition
(B) stringency . . decline
(C) expansion . . stagnation
(D) indecision . . renewal
(E) prudence . . development

Ⓐ Ⓑ Ⓒ Ⓓ Ⓔ

14. The prospective actors commented on the ---- of having to audition for a program that ---- to tape real people in everyday situations.

(A) contradiction . . declines
(B) incongruity . . purports
(C) plight . . endeavors
(D) necessity . . prefers
(E) utility . . claims

Ⓐ Ⓑ Ⓒ Ⓓ Ⓔ

15. Elephant distress calls are so low-frequency as to be ---- to humans, who can recognize that an alarm has been sounded only by observing the animals' behavior.

(A) vexatious
(B) inaudible
(C) dormant
(D) indifferent
(E) cacophonous

Ⓐ Ⓑ Ⓒ Ⓓ Ⓔ

16. As the ---- of recovered fossil specimens from the Cretaceous period attests, terrestrial life during that time was not ---- the dinosaurs.

(A) sturdiness . . dominated by
(B) paucity . . eradicated by
(C) variety . . limited to
(D) preservation . . extinguished with
(E) plethora . . advantageous for

Ⓐ Ⓑ Ⓒ Ⓓ Ⓔ

17. Although the president did not publicly ---- the strategy he had been espousing, he ---- its serious pursuit.

(A) explicate . . recognized
(B) acknowledge . . forbade
(C) condemn . . encouraged
(D) recant . . abandoned
(E) endorse . . hindered

Ⓐ Ⓑ Ⓒ Ⓓ Ⓔ

18. As snow crystals descend through the atmosphere, they join up with one another, forming ---- known as snowflakes.

(A) aggregations
(B) junctures
(C) accessories
(D) juggernauts
(E) collages

Ⓐ Ⓑ Ⓒ Ⓓ Ⓔ

19. To cultural anthropologists, what a society ate and drank ---- not just its requirements for ---- but its customs, knowledge, and environment as well.

(A) mirrored . . civility
(B) met . . survival
(C) skirted . . consumption
(D) obviated . . appetite
(E) reflected . . sustenance

Ⓐ Ⓑ Ⓒ Ⓓ Ⓔ

20. Considering ---- necessary for the creative process, the architect ---- the offer to design the airport because no one had set any guidelines for the project.

(A) autonomy . . spurned
(B) preparation . . contemplated
(C) constraints . . declined
(D) inspiration . . waived
(E) solitude . . seized

Ⓐ Ⓑ Ⓒ Ⓓ Ⓔ

21. The band has courted controversy before in order to get attention, and the ---- lyrics on their new album demonstrate that they found the strategy ----.

(A) sedate . . plausible
(B) vacuous . . rewarding
(C) belligerent . . counterproductive
(D) scandalous . . effective
(E) provocative . . comparable

Ⓐ Ⓑ Ⓒ Ⓓ Ⓔ

22. James Joyce regarded ---- as central to the creative process, which is evident in the numerous scribbled edits that cover even his supposedly final drafts.

(A) contrivance
(B) revision
(C) inspiration
(D) obsession
(E) disavowal

Ⓐ Ⓑ Ⓒ Ⓓ Ⓔ

23. Fans who believe that the players' motivations are not ---- would be ---- to learn that they now charge for their signatures.

(A) self-serving . . vindicated
(B) venal . . chagrined
(C) altruistic . . unsurprised
(D) atypical . . disillusioned
(E) tainted . . gratified

Ⓐ Ⓑ Ⓒ Ⓓ Ⓔ

24. Though the film ostensibly deals with the theme of ----, the director seems to have been more interested in its absence—in isolation and the longing for connection.

(A) reliance
(B) fraternity
(C) socialism
(D) privation
(E) levity

Ⓐ Ⓑ Ⓒ Ⓓ Ⓔ

25. Everything the candidate said publicly was ----; he manipulated the media in order to present the image he wanted.

(A) incendiary
(B) calculated
(C) facetious
(D) scrupulous
(E) impromptu

Ⓐ Ⓑ Ⓒ Ⓓ Ⓔ

26. Most young artists struggle, producing works that have but ---- of future greatness, but Walt Whitman's transformation into a genius was ----.

(A) glimmers . . effortless
(B) shadows . . noteworthy
(C) features . . protracted
(D) critiques . . immediate
(E) aspirations . . unforeseeable

Ⓐ Ⓑ Ⓒ Ⓓ Ⓔ

27. Although sub-Saharan Africa encompasses a large number of ---- cultures, its music is often considered an essentially ---- mass.

(A) disparate . . homogeneous
(B) impoverished . . inimitable
(C) warring . . concrete
(D) interwoven . . distinctive
(E) proud . . languid

Ⓐ Ⓑ Ⓒ Ⓓ Ⓔ

28. His face was ----, his features pulled downward by the weight of heavy thoughts.

(A) morose
(B) onerous
(C) contorted
(D) ossified
(E) inscrutable

Ⓐ Ⓑ Ⓒ Ⓓ Ⓔ

29. The unfortunate demise of the protagonist in the final scene of the movie ---- all possibility of a sequel.

(A) entertained
(B) dissembled
(C) raised
(D) exacerbated
(E) precluded

Ⓐ Ⓑ Ⓒ Ⓓ Ⓔ

30. The notion that democracies are naturally ---- is dubious; the British Empire, a parliamentary democracy, often employed force in acquiring and maintaining territorial possessions.

(A) political
(B) expansive
(C) autonomous
(D) venturesome
(E) pacific

Ⓐ Ⓑ Ⓒ Ⓓ Ⓔ

SAT Verbal Practice Set 3: Critical Reading

Answer the questions below based on the information in the accompanying passages.

Passage 1

James Weldon Johnson was a poet, diplomat, composer, and historian of African American culture who wrote around the turn of the century. In this narrative passage Johnson recalls his first experience of hearing ragtime jazz.

When I had somewhat collected my senses, I realized that in a large back room into which the main room opened, there was a young fellow singing a song, accompanied on the piano by a short, thickset black man. After each verse he did some dance steps, which brought forth great applause and a shower of small coins at his feet. After the singer had responded to a rousing encore, the stout man at the piano began to run his fingers up and down the keyboard. This he did in a manner which indicated that he was a master of a good deal of technique. Then he began to play; and such playing! I stopped talking to listen. It was music of a kind I had never heard before. It was music that demanded physical response, patting of the feet, drumming of the fingers, or nodding of the head in time with the beat. The dissonant harmonies, the audacious resolutions, often consisting of an abrupt jump from one key to another, the intricate rhythms in which the accents fell in the most unexpected places, but in which the beat was never lost, produced a most curious effect. . . .

This was ragtime music, then a novelty in New York, and just growing to be a rage, which has not yet subsided. It was originated in the questionable resorts about Memphis and St. Louis by Negro piano players who knew no more of the theory of music than they did of the theory of the universe, but were guided by natural musical instinct and talent. It made its way to Chicago, where it was popular some time before it reached New York. These players often improvised simple and, at times, vulgar words to fit the melodies. This was the beginning of the ragtime song. . . .

American musicians, instead of investigating ragtime, attempt to ignore it, or dismiss it with a contemptuous word. But that has always been the course of scholasticism in every branch of art. Whatever new thing the *people* like is pooh-poohed; whatever is *popular* is spoken of as not worth the while. The fact is, nothing great or enduring, especially in music, has ever sprung full-fledged and unprecedented from the brain of any master; the best that he gives to the world he gathers from the hearts of the people, and runs it through the alembic* of his genius. In spite of the bans which musicians and music teachers have placed upon it, the people still demand and enjoy ragtime. One thing cannot be denied; it is music which possesses at least one strong element of greatness: it appeals universally; not only the American, but the English, the French, and even the German people find delight in it. In fact, there is not a corner of the civilized world in which it is not known, and this proves its originality; for if it were an imitation, the people of Europe, anyhow, would not have found it a novelty. . . .

I became so interested in both the music and the player that I left the table where I was sitting, and made my way through the hall into the back room, where I could see as well as hear. I talked to the piano player between the musical numbers and found out that he was just a natural musician, never having taken a lesson in his life. Not only could he play almost anything he heard, but he could accompany singers in songs he had never heard. He had, by ear alone, composed some pieces, several of which he played over for me; each of them was properly proportioned and balanced. I began to wonder what this man with such a lavish natural endowment would have done had he been trained. Perhaps he wouldn't have done anything at all; he might have become, at best, a mediocre imitator of the great masters in what they have already done to a finish, or one of the modern innovators who strive after originality by seeing how cleverly they can dodge about through the rules of harmony and at the same time avoid melody. It is certain that he would not have been so delightful as he was in ragtime.

*alembic: scientific apparatus used in the process of distillation.

1. In relating his initial impression of ragtime music to the reader, the narrator makes use of

(A) comparison with the improvisations of classical music
(B) reference to the audience's appreciative applause
(C) description of the music's compelling rhythmic effect
(D) evocation of poignant visual images
(E) allusion to several popular contemporary tunes

Ⓐ Ⓑ Ⓒ Ⓓ Ⓔ

2. In the first paragraph, the narrator portrays ragtime as a type of music that

(A) would be a challenge to play for even the most proficient musician
(B) satisfied the narrator's expectations regarding the genre
(C) violated all of the accepted rules governing musical composition
(D) made up for a lack of melody with a seductive rhythm
(E) contained several surprises for the discerning listener

Ⓐ Ⓑ Ⓒ Ⓓ Ⓔ

3. In line 28, *questionable* most nearly means

(A) disreputable
(B) ambiguous
(C) doubtful
(D) approachable
(E) unconfirmed

Ⓐ Ⓑ Ⓒ Ⓓ Ⓔ

4. The narrator's perspective during the second and third paragraphs is that of

(A) an impartial historian of events in the recent past
(B) a mesmerized spectator of a musical spectacle
(C) a knowledgeable critic of the contemporary musical scene
(D) a commentator reflecting on a unique experience
(E) an adult reminiscing fondly about his youth

Ⓐ Ⓑ Ⓒ Ⓓ Ⓔ

5. In line 31, the reference to "the theory of the universe" serves to

(A) emphasize that ragtime at its inception was an unconventional musical form
(B) show that the originators of ragtime were wholly engrossed in their own music
(C) imply that the attainment of musical proficiency should take priority over academic pursuits
(D) suggest that those who founded ragtime could not have imagined the extent of its future influence
(E) demonstrate that level of education is not commensurate with artistic success

Ⓐ Ⓑ Ⓒ Ⓓ Ⓔ

6. The discussion in the third paragraph of the refusal of American musicians to investigate ragtime suggests that they

(A) have little or no interest in pleasing people with their music
(B) need to be made aware of the popularity of ragtime in Europe
(C) are misguided in their conservative and condescending attitude
(D) attack ragtime for being merely an imitation of an existing style
(E) know that it would be difficult to refine ragtime as a musical form

Ⓐ Ⓑ Ⓒ Ⓓ Ⓔ

7. Which statement best summarizes the author's argument in the third paragraph?

(A) Any type of music that is extremely popular should be considered great.
(B) The two criteria for musical greatness are popularity and originality.
(C) Music that has become popular overseas cannot be ignored by American musicians.
(D) Ragtime must be taken up by a musical master and purified to earn critical acclaim.
(E) Mass appeal in music can be a sign of greatness rather than a stigma.

Ⓐ Ⓑ Ⓒ Ⓓ Ⓔ

8. The statement in lines 79–80 ("Perhaps he wouldn't have done anything at all. . . .") is best interpreted as conveying

(A) doubt about the depth of the piano player's skill
(B) understanding that no amount of talent can compensate for a lack of discipline
(C) cynicism about the likelihood that a man can live up to his potential
(D) a recognition that the piano player might have wasted his talent
(E) frustration at the impossibility of knowing what might have been

Ⓐ Ⓑ Ⓒ Ⓓ Ⓔ

9. The author's view (lines 79–88) about the ragtime piano player's lack of formal training can best be summarized as which of the following?

(A) The piano player's natural talent had allowed him to develop technically to the point where formal training would have been superfluous.
(B) Formal lessons would have impaired the piano player's native ability to play and compose by ear alone.
(C) More would have been lost than gained if the piano player had been given formal lessons.
(D) The piano player's potential to be a truly innovative ragtime artist had been squandered because he had not been formally trained.
(E) Although dazzling when improvising ragtime, the piano player could never have been more than mediocre as a classical pianist.

Ⓐ Ⓑ Ⓒ Ⓓ Ⓔ

Passages 1 and 2

These passages present two critics' perspectives on the topic of design museums.

Passage 1

City museums are places where people can learn about various cultures by studying objects of particular historical or artistic value. The increasingly popular "design museums" that are opening today perform quite a different function. Unlike most city museums, the design museum displays and assesses objects that are readily available to the general public. These museums place ignored household appliances under spotlights, breaking down the barriers between commerce and creative invention.

Critics have argued that design museums are often manipulated to serve as advertisements for new industrial technology. But their role is not simply a matter of merchandising—it is the honoring of impressive, innovative products. The difference between the window of a department store and the showcase in a design museum is that the first tries to sell you something, while the second informs you of the success of the attempt.

One advantage that the design museum has over other civic museums is that design museums are places where people feel familiar with the exhibits. Unlike the average art gallery patron, design museum visitors rarely feel intimidated or disoriented. Partly this is because design museums clearly illustrate how and why mass-produced consumer objects work and look as they do, and show how design contributes to the quality of our lives. For example, an exhibit involving a particular design of chair would not simply explain how it functions as a chair. It would also demonstrate how its various features combine to produce an artistic effect or redefine our manner of performing the basic act of being seated. The purpose of such an exhibit would be to present these concepts in ways that challenge, stimulate, and inform the viewer. An art gallery exhibit, on the other hand, would provide very little information about the chair and charge the visitor with understanding the exhibit on some abstract level.

Within the past decade, several new design museums have opened their doors. Each of these museums has responded in totally original ways to the public's growing interest in the field. London's Design Museum, for instance, displays a collection of mass-produced objects ranging from Zippo™ lighters to electric typewriters to a show of Norwegian sardine-tin labels. The options open to curators of design museums seem far less rigorous, conventionalized, and preprogrammed than those applying to curators in charge of public galleries of paintings and sculpture. The humorous aspects of our society are better represented in the display of postmodern playthings or quirky Japanese vacuum cleaners in pastel colors than in an exhibition of Impressionist landscapes.

Passage 2

The short histories of some of the leading technical and design museums make clear an underlying difficulty in this area. The tendency everywhere today is to begin with present machines and technological processes and to show how they operate and the scientific principles on which they are based without paying much attention to their historical development, to say nothing of the society that produced them. Only a few of the oldest, largest, and best-supported museums collect historical industrial objects. Most science centers put more emphasis on mock-ups, graphs, and multimedia devices. This approach of "presentism" often leads the museum to drop all attempts at study and research; if industry is called upon to design and build the exhibits, curators may be entirely dispensed with, so that impartial and scientific study disappears, and emphasis is placed on the idea that progress automatically follows technology.

Industrialization and the machine have, of course, brought much progress; a large portion of humankind no longer works from sunup to sundown to obtain the bare necessities of life. But industrialization also creates problems—harm to the environment and ecology, neglect of social, cultural, and humanistic values, depletion of resources, and even threats of human extinction. Thus progress needs to be considered critically—from a wider social and humanitarian point of view. Unfortunately, most museums of science and technology glorify machines. Displayed in pristine condition, elegantly painted or polished, they can make the observer forget the noise, dirt, danger, and frustration of machine tending. Mines, whether coal, iron, or salt, are a favorite museum display but only infrequently is there even a hint of the dirt, the damp, the smell, the low headroom, or the crippling and destructive accidents that sometimes occur in industry.

Machinery also ought to be operated to be meaningful. Consequently, it should not be shown in sculptured repose but in full, often clattering, action. This kind of operation is difficult to obtain, and few museums can command the imagination, ingenuity, and manual dexterity it requires. Problems also arise in providing adequate safety devices for both the public and the machine operators. These, then, are some of the underlying problems of the technical museum—problems not solved by the usual push buttons, cranks, or multimedia gimmicks. Yet attendance figures show that technical museums outdraw all the others; the public possesses lively curiosity and a real desire to understand science and technology.

10. In line 8, the word *readily* most nearly means

(A) easily
(B) willingly
(C) instantly
(D) cheaply
(E) constantly

Ⓐ Ⓑ Ⓒ Ⓓ Ⓔ

11. In lines 15–22, the author of Passage 1 suggests that design museums are different from store windows in that

(A) design museums display more technologically advanced products
(B) store window displays are not created with as much concern to the visual quality of the display
(C) design museums are not concerned with the commercial aspects of a successful product
(D) design museums focus on highlighting the artistic qualities that help sell products
(E) the objects in store displays are more commercially successful than those in design museums

Ⓐ Ⓑ Ⓒ Ⓓ Ⓔ

12. From lines 23–33, it can be inferred that the author believes that most museum visitors

(A) are hostile towards the concept of abstract art
(B) prefer to have a context in which to understand museum exhibits
(C) are confused when faced with complex technological exhibits
(D) are unfamiliar with the exhibits in design museums
(E) undervalue the artistic worth of household items

Ⓐ Ⓑ Ⓒ Ⓓ Ⓔ

13. The third paragraph of Passage 1 suggests that one important difference between design museums and the art galleries is

(A) the low price of admission at design museums
(B) the amount of information presented with design museum exhibits
(C) the intelligence of the average museum visitor
(D) that art galleries feature exhibits that have artistic merit
(E) the contribution that design museums make to our quality of life

Ⓐ Ⓑ Ⓒ Ⓓ Ⓔ

14. In line 55, the word *options* most likely refers to the ability of curators of design museums to

(A) afford large collections of exhibits
(B) attract a wide range of visitors
(C) put together unconventional collections
(D) feature rare objects that interest the public
(E) satisfy their own personal whims in planning exhibitions

Ⓐ Ⓑ Ⓒ Ⓓ Ⓔ

15. In line 64, the author most likely mentions Impressionist landscapes in order to

(A) provide an example of a typical design museum exhibit
(B) compare postmodern exhibits to nineteenth-century art
(C) point out a decline in the sophistication of the museum-going public
(D) refute the notion that postmodern art is whimsical
(E) emphasize the contrast between two different types of exhibits

Ⓐ Ⓑ Ⓒ Ⓓ Ⓔ

16. Which of the following best describes the "underlying difficulty" mentioned in line 67 of Passage 2?

(A) Design museums rarely mention the historical origin of objects they display.
(B) Industrial involvement often forces curators out of their jobs.
(C) Design museums appropriate technology that is essential for study and research.
(D) Technology almost never leads to progress.
(E) Industry places too much emphasis on impartial research.

Ⓐ Ⓑ Ⓒ Ⓓ Ⓔ

17. The author of Passage 2 most likely mentions "harm to the environment and ecology" (lines 92–93) in order to

(A) encourage a critical response to the technological age
(B) discourage the reader from visiting technology museums
(C) describe the hazardous conditions in coal, iron, and salt mines
(D) dissuade museum visitors from operating the machinery on display
(E) praise museums that present an accurate depiction of technology

Ⓐ Ⓑ Ⓒ Ⓓ Ⓔ

18. The author uses the phrase *sculptured repose* (line 111) in order to

(A) condemn the curators of design museums for poor planning
(B) illustrate the greatest problem inherent in design museums
(C) present an idealized vision of a type of exhibit
(D) describe the unrealistic way in which machinery is generally displayed
(E) compare the shape of a machine to a work of art

Ⓐ Ⓑ Ⓒ Ⓓ Ⓔ

19. The word *command* (line 114) most nearly means

(A) oversee
(B) direct
(C) control
(D) summon
(E) order

Ⓐ Ⓑ Ⓒ Ⓓ Ⓔ

20. The author of Passage 2 would probably object to the statement that design "contributes to the quality of our lives" (lines 32–33) on the grounds that

(A) technical innovation has historically posed threats to our physical and social well-being
(B) the general public would benefit more from visiting art galleries
(C) machinery that is not shown in action is meaningless to the viewer
(D) industry has made a negligible contribution to human progress
(E) few people have a genuine interest in the impact of science and technology

Ⓐ Ⓑ Ⓒ Ⓓ Ⓔ

21. The authors of both passages would probably agree that

(A) machinery is enjoyable to watch only when it is moving
(B) most people are curious about the factors behind the design of everyday objects
(C) the public places a higher value on packaging than it does on quality
(D) the very technology that is displayed in the museums is likely to cost curators their jobs
(E) design museums are flawed because they fail to accurately portray the environmental problems that technology sometimes causes

Ⓐ Ⓑ Ⓒ Ⓓ Ⓔ

SAT Math Practice Set 4: Regular Math

Solve each of the following problems, decide which is the best answer choice, and darken the corresponding oval on the answer sheet. Use available space in the test booklet for scratchwork.*

Notes:

(1) Calculator use is permitted.
(2) All numbers used are real numbers.
(3) Figures are provided for some problems. All figures are drawn to scale and lie in a plane UNLESS otherwise indicated.

Reference Information

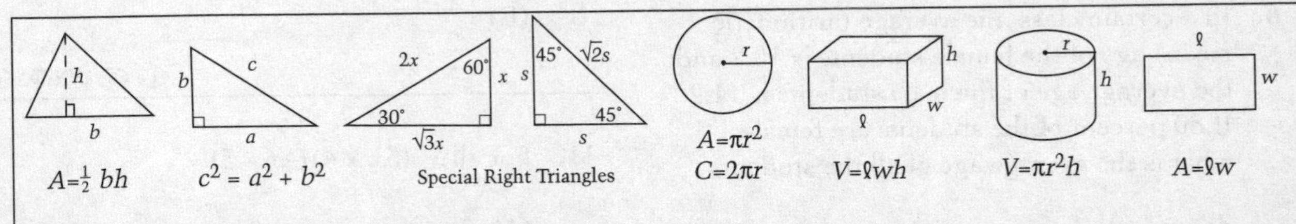

The sum of the degree measures of the angles of a triangle is 180.
The number of degrees of arc in a circle is 360.
A straight angle has a degree measure of 180.

1. If the sum of the integers from 1,001 to 1,100 is A and the sum of the integers from 2,001 to 2,100 is B, what is the value of $B - A$?

(A) 1,000
(B) 2,000
(C) 10,000
(D) 100,000
(E) 200,000

2. If an integer is divisible by 6 and by 9, then the integer must be divisible by which of the following?

I. 12
II. 18
III. 36

(A) I only
(B) II only
(C) I and II only
(D) II and III only
(E) I, II, and III

3. When $\frac{4}{11}$ is written as a decimal, what is the 100th digit after the decimal point?

(A) 3
(B) 4
(C) 5
(D) 6
(E) 7

4. What is the average (arithmetic mean) of $2x + 5$, $5x - 6$, and $-4x + 2$?

(A) $x + \frac{1}{3}$
(B) $x + 1$
(C) $3x + \frac{1}{3}$
(D) $3x + 3$
(E) $3x + 3\frac{1}{3}$

*The directions on the actual SAT will vary slightly.

5. Rachel's average (arithmetic mean) score after six tests is 83. If Rachel earns a score of 97 on the seventh test, what is her new average?

(A) 85
(B) 86
(C) 87
(D) 88
(E) 90

Ⓐ Ⓑ Ⓒ Ⓓ Ⓔ

6. In a certain class, the average (arithmetic mean) age of the female students is 10.2 and the average age of the male students is 11.2. If 80 percent of the students are female, what is the average age of all the students?

(A) 10.4
(B) 10.5
(C) 10.6
(D) 10.7
(E) 11.0

Ⓐ Ⓑ Ⓒ Ⓓ Ⓔ

7. For all x, $3x^2 \times 5x^3 =$

(A) $8x^5$
(B) $8x^6$
(C) $15x^5$
(D) $15x^6$
(E) $15x^8$

Ⓐ Ⓑ Ⓒ Ⓓ Ⓔ

8. $\left(5\sqrt{3}\right)^2 =$

(A) 15
(B) $10\sqrt{3}$
(C) $25\sqrt{3}$
(D) 30
(E) 75

Ⓐ Ⓑ Ⓒ Ⓓ Ⓔ

9. If $x = -5$, then $2x^2 - 6x + 5 =$

(A) -15
(B) 15
(C) 25
(D) 85
(E) 135

Ⓐ Ⓑ Ⓒ Ⓓ Ⓔ

10. For all $x > 0$, $\dfrac{1}{1+\dfrac{1}{x}} =$

(A) $x+1$
(B) $\dfrac{x}{x+1}$
(C) $x+2$
(D) $\dfrac{x}{x+2}$
(E) $\dfrac{x}{2}$

Ⓐ Ⓑ Ⓒ Ⓓ Ⓔ

11. For all x, $(3x + 4)(4x - 3) =$

(A) $7x + 1$
(B) $7x - 12$
(C) $12x^2 - 12$
(D) $12x^2 - 25x - 12$
(E) $12x^2 + 7x - 12$

Ⓐ Ⓑ Ⓒ Ⓓ Ⓔ

12. If $\dfrac{m}{2} = 15$, then $\dfrac{m}{3} =$

(A) 5
(B) 10
(C) 15
(D) 30
(E) 90

Ⓐ Ⓑ Ⓒ Ⓓ Ⓔ

13. If $k - 3 = -\dfrac{5}{3}$, then $3 - k =$

(A) $-\dfrac{5}{3}$
(B) $-\dfrac{3}{5}$
(C) $\dfrac{3}{5}$
(D) $\dfrac{5}{3}$
(E) $\dfrac{7}{3}$

Ⓐ Ⓑ Ⓒ Ⓓ Ⓔ

14. Which of the following is an equation for the graph above?

(A) $y = -2x + 1$
(B) $y = x + 1$
(C) $y = x + 2$
(D) $y = 2x + 1$
(E) $y = 2x + 2$

A B C D E

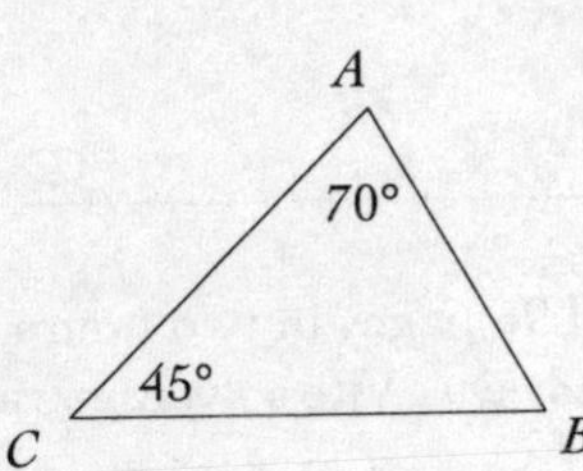

15. In the triangle above, what is the degree measure of angle B ?

(A) 45
(B) 60
(C) 65
(D) 75
(E) 80

A B C D E

16. If the lengths of all three sides of a triangle are integers, and the length of one side is 7, what is the least possible perimeter of the triangle?

(A) 9
(B) 10
(C) 15
(D) 21
(E) 24

A B C D E

17. If the area of a triangle is 36 and its base is 9, what is the length of the altitude to that base?

(A) 2
(B) 4
(C) 6
(D) 8
(E) 12

A B C D E

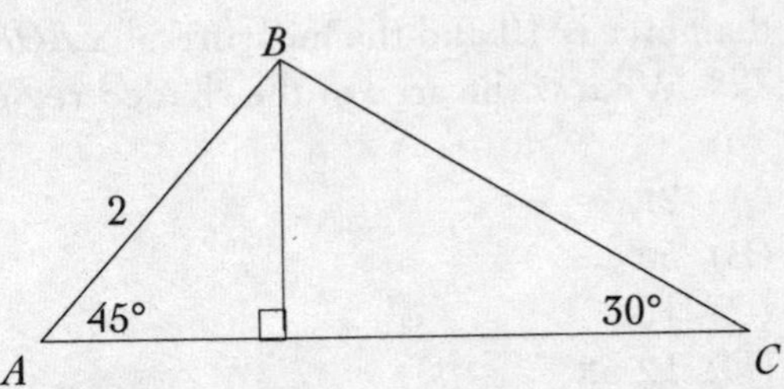

18. In the figure above, $AB = 2$. What is the area of ΔABC ?

(A) $\sqrt{6}$
(B) $1+\sqrt{3}$
(C) $2\sqrt{2}$
(D) $\sqrt{2}+\sqrt{6}$
(E) $2+2\sqrt{3}$

A B C D E

19. What is the area of a circle whose circumference is 2π ?

(A) $\frac{\pi}{2}$
(B) π
(C) 2π
(D) 4π
(E) 8π

A B C D E

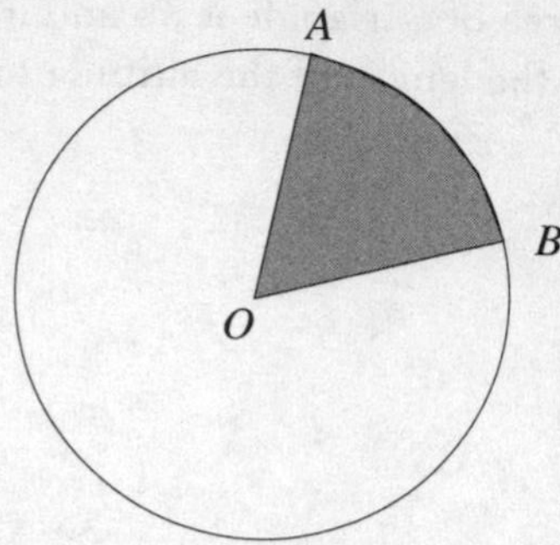

20. In the circle with center O shown above, the diameter is 10 and the measure of $\angle AOB$ is 72°. What is the area of the shaded region?

(A) 2π
(B) 5π
(C) 10π
(D) 12.5π
(E) 25π

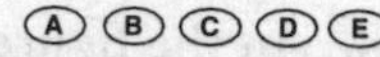

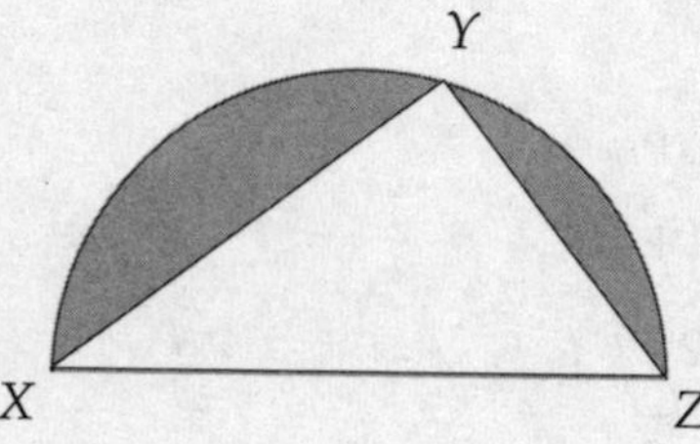

21. Triangle XYZ is inscribed in the semicircle with diameter XZ. If $XY = 16$ and $YZ = 12$, what is the combined area of the shaded regions?

(A) $8(25\pi - 12)$
(B) $4(25\pi - 24)$
(C) $4(25\pi - 48)$
(D) $2(25\pi - 48)$
(E) $2(25\pi - 24)$

22. Erica has eight squares of felt, each with area 16. For a certain craft project she cuts the largest circle possible from each square of felt. What is the combined area of the excess felt left over after cutting out all the circles?

(A) $4(4 - \pi)$
(B) $8(4 - \pi)$
(C) $8(\pi - 2)$
(D) $32(4 - \pi)$
(E) $16(16 - \pi)$

Ⓐ Ⓑ Ⓒ Ⓓ Ⓔ

23. A wooden cube with volume 64 is sliced in half horizontally. The two halves are then glued together to form a rectangular solid that is not a cube. What is the surface area of this new solid?

(A) 128
(B) 112
(C) 96
(D) 56
(E) 48

Ⓐ Ⓑ Ⓒ Ⓓ Ⓔ

24. Vito read 96 pages in two hours and 40 minutes. What was Vito's average rate of pages per hour?

(A) 24
(B) 30
(C) 36
(D) 42
(E) 48

Ⓐ Ⓑ Ⓒ Ⓓ Ⓔ

25. Danielle drives from her home to the store at an average speed of 40 miles per hour. She returns home along the same route at an average speed of 60 miles per hour. What is her average speed, in miles per hour, for her entire trip?

(A) 45
(B) 48
(C) 50
(D) 52
(E) 55

Ⓐ Ⓑ Ⓒ Ⓓ Ⓔ

26. There are three routes from Bay City to Riverville. There are four routes from Riverville to Straitstown. There are three routes from Straitstown to Frog Pond. If a driver must pass through Riverville and Straitstown exactly once, how many possible ways are there to go from Bay City to Frog Pond?

(A) 6
(B) 10
(C) 12
(D) 24
(E) 36

27. Let $a\clubsuit$ be defined for all positive integers a by the equation $a\clubsuit = \frac{a}{4} - \frac{a}{6}$. If $x\clubsuit = 3$, what is the value of x ?

(A) 18
(B) 28
(C) 36
(D) 40
(E) 54

28. Edwina makes a gallons of orange-and-pineapple punch that is 40 percent pineapple juice. She wants to change this punch so that it is 25 percent pineapple juice. How many gallons of orange juice must she add?

(A) $\frac{a}{6}$

(B) $\frac{a}{3}$

(C) $\frac{3a}{5}$

(D) $\frac{5a}{6}$

(E) $\frac{8a}{5}$

29. A drawer contains six blue socks, 12 black socks, and 14 white socks. If one sock is chosen at random, what is the probability that it will be black?

(A) $\frac{1}{4}$

(B) $\frac{1}{3}$

(C) $\frac{3}{8}$

(D) $\frac{1}{2}$

(E) $\frac{5}{8}$

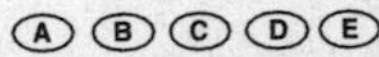

30. If Jim and Bill have less than $15 between them, and Bill has $4, which of the following could be the number of dollars that Jim has?

I. 10
II. 11
III. 15

(A) I only
(B) II only
(C) I and II only
(D) II and III only
(E) I, II, and III

SAT Math Practice Set 5: Quantitative Comparisons

Solve each of the following problems, decide which is the best answer choice, and darken the corresponding oval on the answer sheet. Use available space in the test booklet for scratchwork.*

Notes:
(1) Calculator use is permitted.
(2) All numbers used are real numbers.
(3) Figures are provided for some problems. All figures are drawn to scale and lie in a plane UNLESS otherwise indicated.

Reference Information

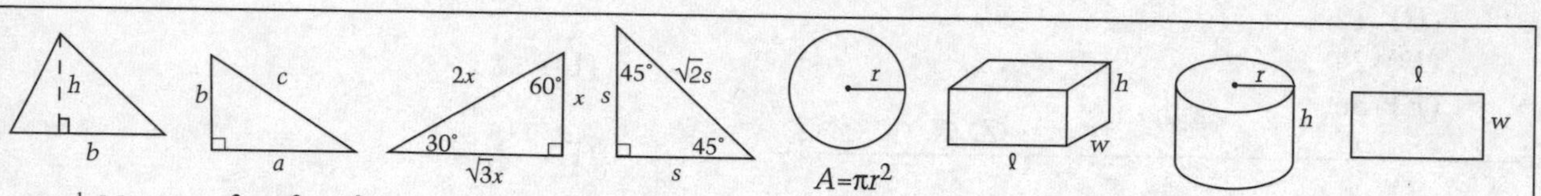

$A=\frac{1}{2}bh$ $c^2 = a^2 + b^2$ Special Right Triangles $A=\pi r^2$ $C=2\pi r$ $V=\ell wh$ $V=\pi r^2 h$ $A=\ell w$

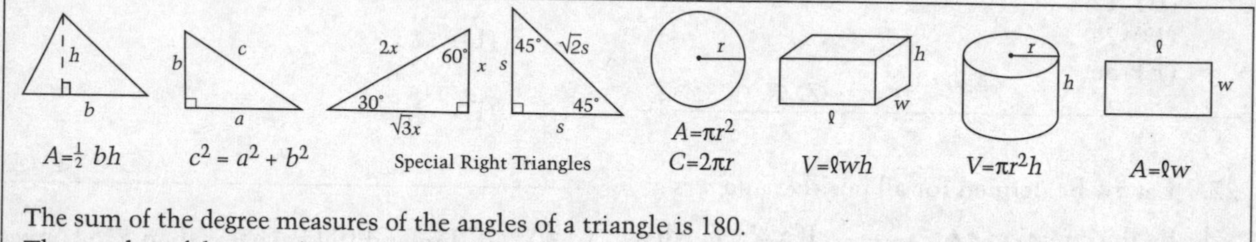

The sum of the degree measures of the angles of a triangle is 180.
The number of degrees of arc in a circle is 360.
A straight angle has a degree measure of 180.

Directions for Quantitative Comparison Questions

Compare the boxed quantity in Column A with the boxed quantity in Column B. Select answer choice

A if Column A is greater;
B if Column B is greater;
C if the columns are equal; or
D if more information is needed to determine the relationship.

An E response will be treated as an omission.

Notes:

1. Some questions include information about one or both quantities. That information is centered and unboxed.
2. A symbol that appears in both Column A and Column B stands for the same thing in both columns.
3. All numbers used are real numbers.

EXAMPLES

	Column A	Column B	Answers
E1	3×4	$3 + 4$	● Ⓑ Ⓒ Ⓓ Ⓔ
	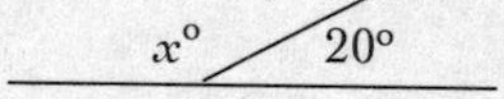		
E2	x	160	Ⓐ Ⓑ ● Ⓓ Ⓔ
	x and y are positive		
E3	$x + 1$	$y - 1$	Ⓐ Ⓑ Ⓒ ● Ⓔ

*The directions on the actual SAT will vary slightly.

Column A	Column B
1. $\frac{1}{8} + \frac{1}{10}$	$\frac{1}{9} + \frac{1}{11}$

(A) (B) (C) (D) (E)

2. 52% of 34	17

(A) (B) (C) (D) (E)

Wilfredo's math test scores are the following: 88, 82, 94, 93, 85, 90, 93, 98

3. Wilfredo's mode test score	Wilfredo's median test score

(A) (B) (C) (D) (E)

$$a^2 = b^3$$

4. a^4	b^5

(A) (B) (C) (D) (E)

$$x > 0$$

5. $4\sqrt{x} + 4\sqrt{x}$	$8\sqrt{x}$

(A) (B) (C) (D) (E)

6. $3(x - 2)$	$3x - 4$

(A) (B) (C) (D) (E)

7. $(n + 3)(n - 3)$	$n^2 + 9$

(A) (B) (C) (D) (E)

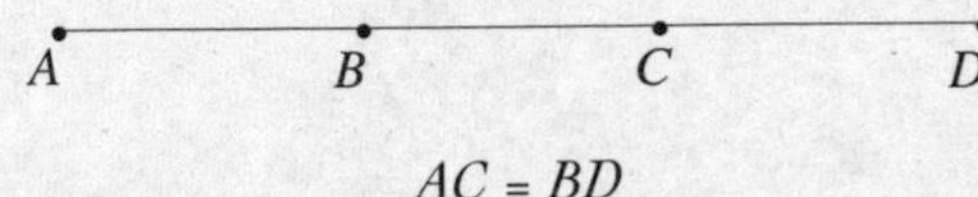

$$AC = BD$$

8. AB	BC

(A) (B) (C) (D) (E)

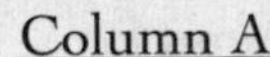

Column B

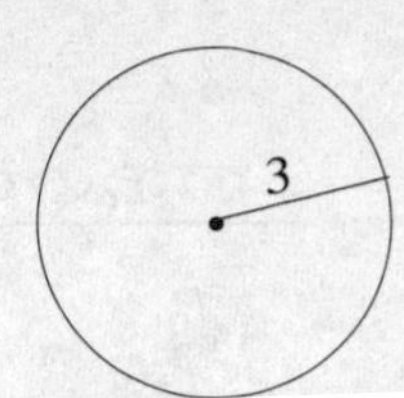

9. The area of the circle	The area of the rectangle

(A) (B) (C) (D) (E)

Four distinct points, *A*, *B*, *C*, and *D*, all lie on the same circle. Line segment *AB* passes through the center of the circle and is parallel to line segment *CD*.

10. The length of *AB*	The length of *CD*

(A) (B) (C) (D) (E)

Line segments *AB* and *XY* are parallel and equal in length. *F* is the midpoint of *AB*, and *S* is the midpoint of *XY*. The perpendicular distance from *AB* to *XY* is 3.

11. The length of *FS*	3

(A) (B) (C) (D) (E)

12. The number of square units in the area of a square with side 6	The number of units in the perimeter of a square with side 9

(A) (B) (C) (D) (E)

13. 19(56) + 44(19)	1,901

(A) (B) (C) (D) (E)

14. 50×8.01	$\frac{801}{2}$

(A) (B) (C) (D) (E)

15. $\frac{(-2)(-4)}{(-6)(-8)}$	$\frac{(-6)(-8)}{(-4)(-10)(-12)}$

(A) (B) (C) (D) (E)

	Column A	Column B
16.	$\sqrt{5\times 4}$	3
17.	$\sqrt{48}$	$4\sqrt{2}$
18.	–2	–1
19.	x	$x - 1$

$x < -1$

	Column A	Column B
20.	x	$\frac{1}{x}$

$x > x^2$

	Column A	Column B
21.	x	0

$x < 1$

	Column A	Column B
22.	x	$\frac{1}{x}$
23.	$\frac{-3}{2}$	$\frac{-1}{2}$
24.	8×3.4	34×0.8

$x > 0$

	Column A	Column B
25.	$\frac{99x}{100}$	$\frac{100}{99x}$

$xyz > 0$

	Column A	Column B
26.	$50x \times 14y \times 23z$	$100x \times 7y \times 23z$

$a > b > c > 0$

	Column A	Column B
27.	$a - c$	$b - c$

$y > 0$

	Column A	Column B
28.	$1-\frac{y}{1+y}$	$1-\frac{1}{1+y}$

$14 < x < 16$
$18 < y < 20$

	Column A	Column B
29.	34	$x + y$

$a + b \neq 0$
$ab \neq 0$

	Column A	Column B
30.	$\frac{1}{a}+\frac{1}{b}$	$\frac{1}{a+b}$

Each item: Ⓐ Ⓑ Ⓒ Ⓓ Ⓔ

SAT Math Practice Set 6: Grid-Ins

For each of the questions below, solve the problem and indicate your answer by darkening the ovals in the special grid. For example:

Answer: 1.25 or $\frac{5}{4}$ or 5/4

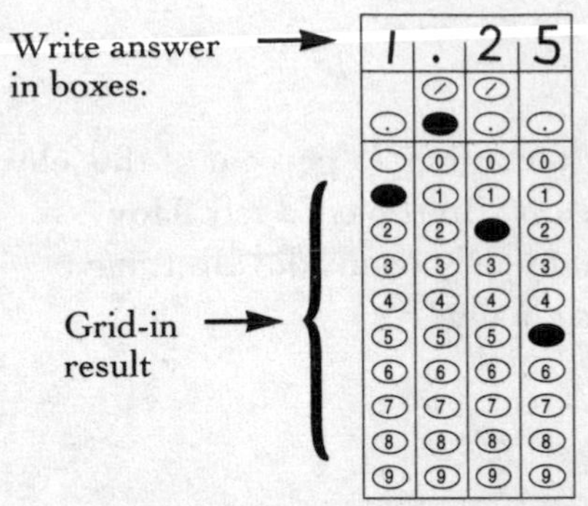

Fraction line

Decimal point

You may start your answers in any column, space permitting. Columns not needed should be left blank.

Either position is correct.

- It is recommended, though not required, that you write your answer in the boxes at the top of the columns. However, you will receive credit only for darkening the ovals correctly.
- Grid only one answer to a question, even though some problems have more than one correct answer.
- Darken no more than one oval in a column.
- No answers are negative.
- Mixed numbers cannot be gridded. For example: the number $1\frac{1}{4}$ must be gridded as 1.25 or 5/4.

  (If 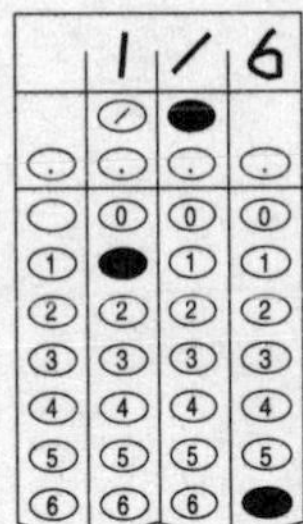 is gridded, it will be interpreted as $\frac{11}{4}$, not $1\frac{1}{4}$.)

- Decimal Accuracy: Decimal answers must be entered as accurately as possible. For example, if you obtain an answer such as 0.1666 . . ., you should record the result as .166 or .167. **Less accurate values such as .16 or .17 are not acceptable.**

  Acceptable ways to grid $\frac{1}{6}$ = .1666. . .

1. If a traffic light's cycle flashes red, green, and yellow lights in that order, how many of the first 143 flashes will be red?

$$\frac{3}{a}, \frac{5}{a}, \frac{14}{a}$$

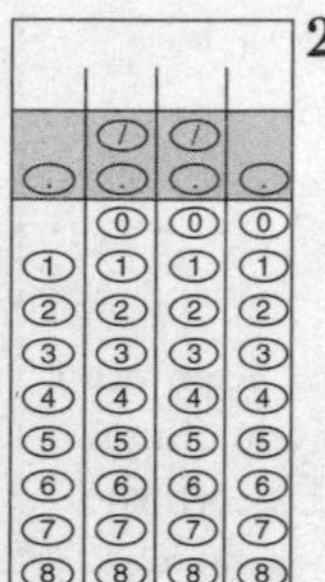

2. Each of the fractions above is in its simplest reduced form and a is an integer greater than 1 and less than 50. Grid in one possible value of a.

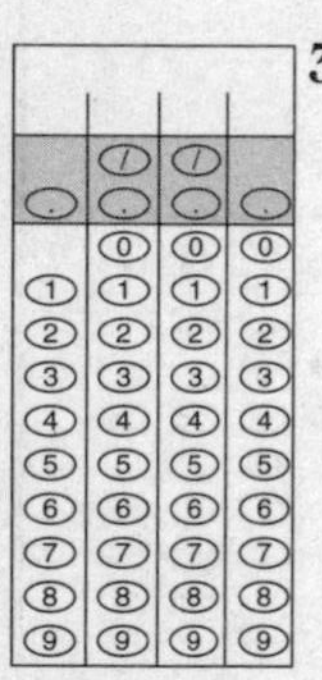

3. What is the sum of $\frac{2}{3}$ and $\frac{1}{12}$?

4. What is the value of:

$$2+\left(\frac{3}{2}-\frac{4}{3}\right)+\left(\frac{4}{3}-\frac{5}{4}\right)+\left(\frac{5}{4}-\frac{6}{5}\right)+\left(\frac{6}{5}-\frac{7}{6}\right)?$$

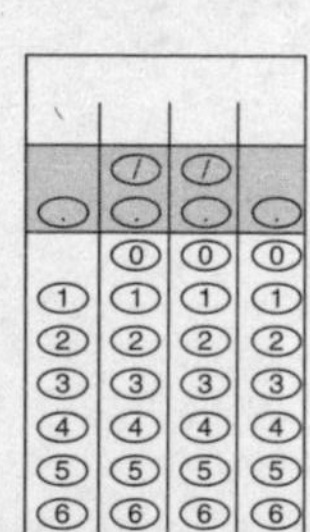

5. If there are 36 men and 24 women in a group, women make up what fraction of the entire group?

6. Pat deposited 15 percent of last week's take-home pay into a savings account. If she deposited \$37.50, what was last week's take-home pay?

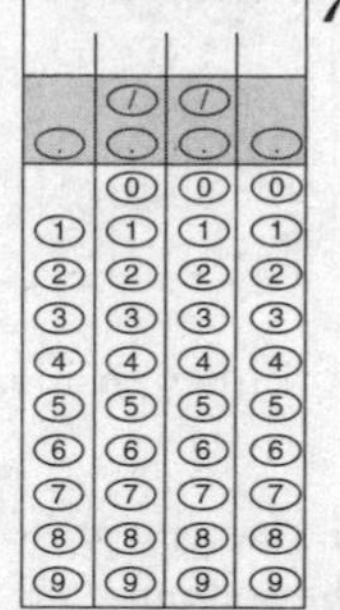

7. After eating 25 percent of the jelly beans, Brett has 72 left. How many jelly beans did Brett have originally?

8. What is the average (arithmetic mean) of all the even integers from 42 through 88, inclusive?

9. If the average (arithmetic mean) number of raffle tickets sold per person by a group of eight people is 12, how many tickets did the group sell?

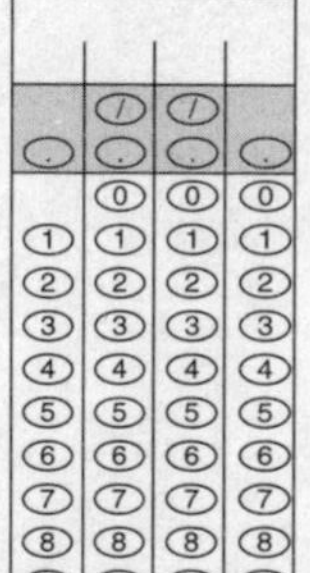

10. What is the value of $\frac{3s+5}{4}$ when $s = 9$?

11. What is the value of x if

$$\frac{x}{3}+\frac{x}{4}=1?$$

12. If $(x + 4)(5 - 2) = 18$, then $x =$

$$3x+4y=31$$
$$3x-4y=-1$$

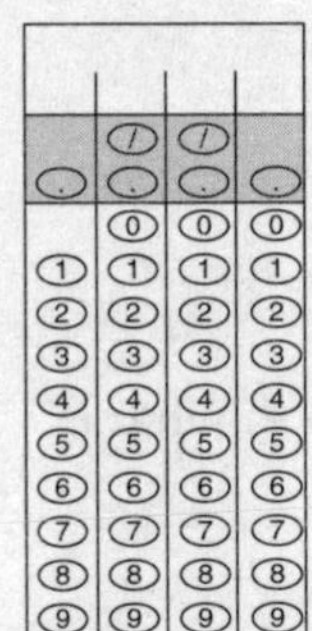

13. What is the solution for x in the system of equations above?

14. Grid in the positive value of x for which $3x^2=8x+3$.

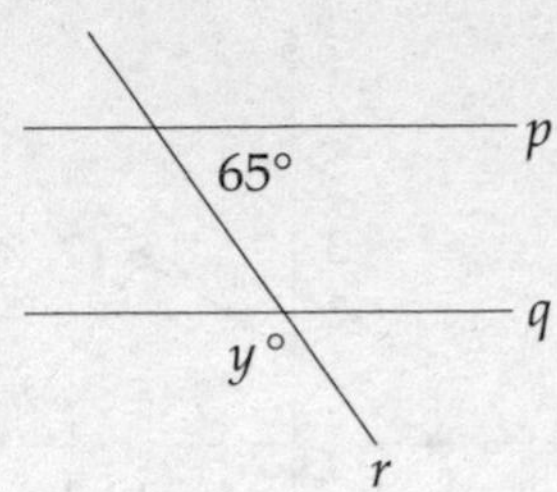

15. In the figure above, if line p is parallel to line q, what is the value of y ?

16. If triangle ABC is drawn so that angle A measures 30 degrees and angle B measures 40 degrees, what is the degree measure of an exterior angle formed at point C ?

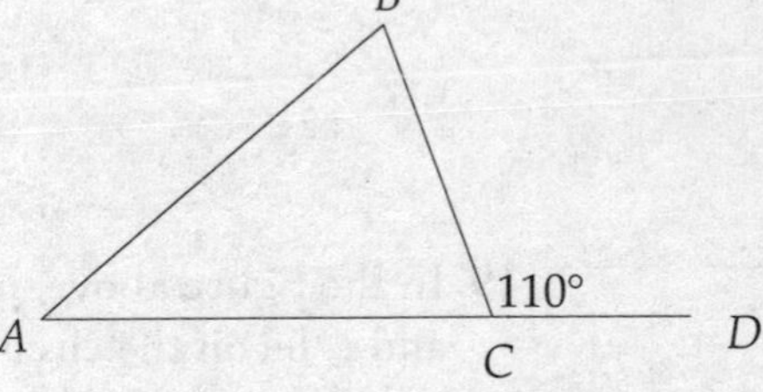

17. In the figure above, ΔABC is isosceles with $AB = AC$. If the measure of $\angle BCD$ is 110°, what is the degree measure of $\angle BAC$?

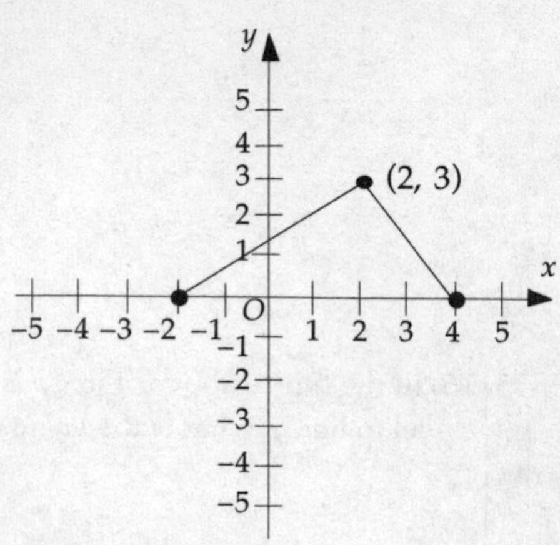

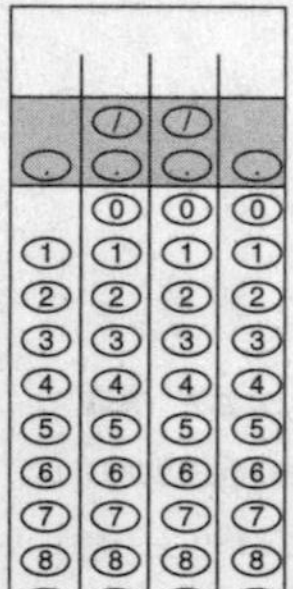

18. What is the area of the triangle in the figure above?

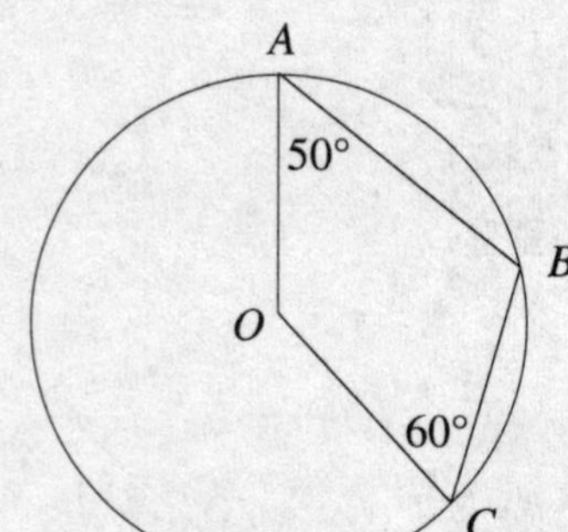

19. In the figure above, points A, B, and C lie on the circumference of the circle centered at O. If $\angle OAB$ measures 50° and $\angle BCO$ measures 60°, what is the degree measure of $\angle AOC$?

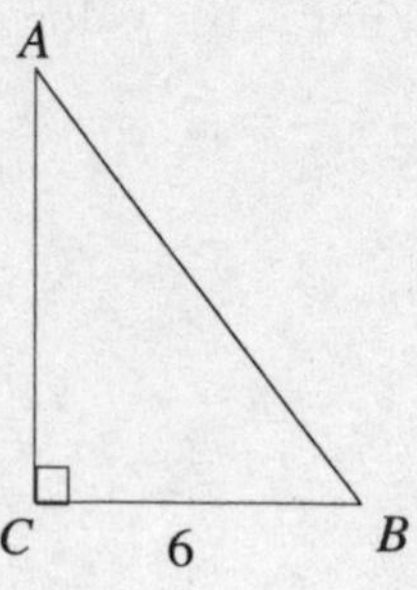

20. If the area of ΔABC in the figure above is 24, what is the perimeter?

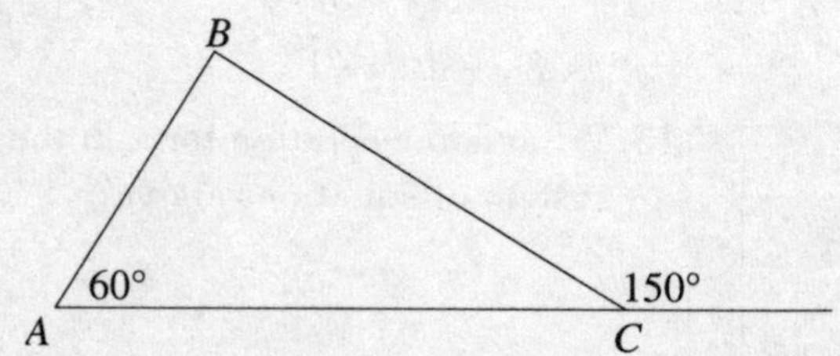

21. In ΔABC above, if $AB = 4$, what is the length of AC ?

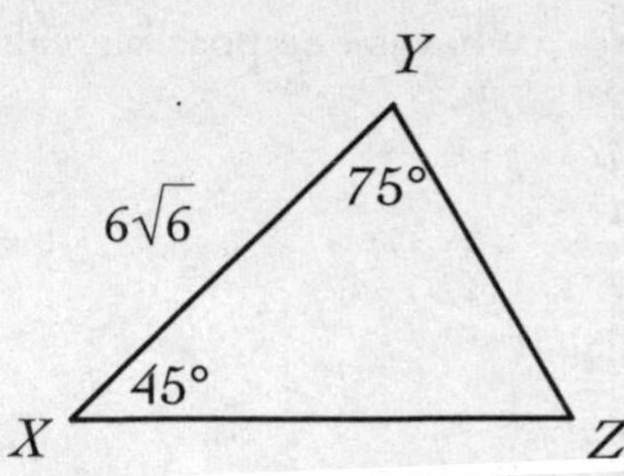

22. In ΔXYZ above, what is the length of YZ ?

23. The radius of circle A is half the radius of circle B. The radius of circle C is one and a half times the radius of circle B. The radius of circle C is what percent of the radius of circle A ? (Disregard the % sign when gridding your answer.)

24. A ladder 20 feet long is placed against a wall such that the foot of the ladder is 12 feet from the wall. How many feet above the ground is the top of the ladder?

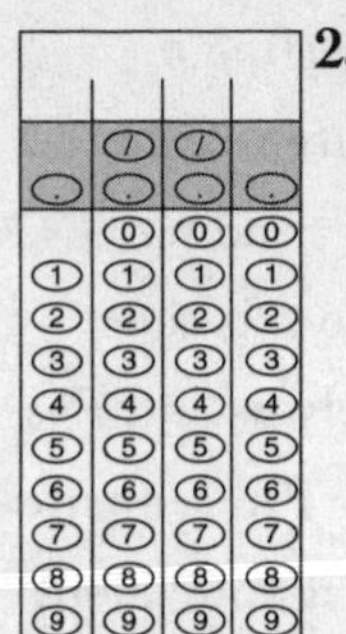

25. What is the area of a right isosceles triangle with a hypotenuse of length 10?

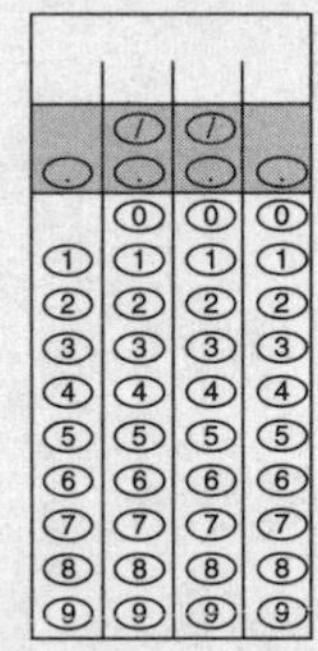

26. When water is poured into rectangular box A, which has a base that measures 4 inches by 9 inches, the water comes to a height of 10 inches. If the same amount of water is poured into box B, which has a base that measures 5 inches by 6 inches, the water will come to a height of how many inches? (Assume that both boxes are tall enough to contain the water without overflow.)

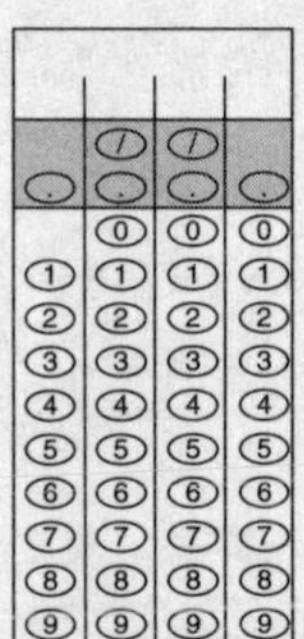

27. A school cafeteria has to order 240 cartons of milk to feed 600 students daily. If the student population rises to 700 students and they buy milk at the same rate, how many cartons of milk will need to be ordered every day?

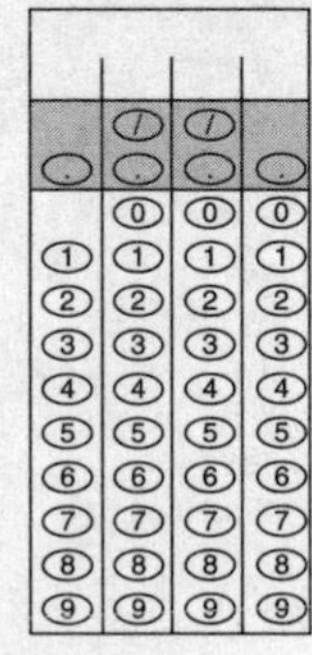

28. A cyclist rode up a hill at 12 miles per hour. He rode down the same route at 24 miles per hour. What was his average speed, in miles per hour, for the entire trip?

29. The formula for converting a Fahrenheit temperature reading to a Celsius temperature reading is $C = \frac{5}{9}(F - 32)$, where C is the reading in degrees Celsius and F is the reading in degrees Fahrenheit. What is the Fahrenheit equivalent to a reading of 95° Celsius?

30. If $-5 - 4n < -25$ and $-2n + 12 > 0$, what is one possible value of n ?

SAT Practice Set Answer Key

Analogies	Sentence Completions	Critical Reading	Regular Math
1. D	1. C	1. C	1. D
2. A	2. E	2. E	2. B
3. C	3. A	3. A	3. D
4. E	4. A	4. C	4. A
5. C	5. C	5. A	5. A
6. B	6. D	6. C	6. A
7. A	7. C	7. E	7. C
8. A	8. D	8. D	8. E
9. B	9. E	9. C	9. D
10. E	10. C	10. A	10. B
11. C	11. C	11. D	11. E
12. B	12. E	12. B	12. B
13. E	13. B	13. B	13. D
14. E	14. B	14. C	14. E
15. E	15. B	15. E	15. C
16. E	16. C	16. A	16. C
17. A	17. D	17. A	17. D
18. B	18. A	18. D	18. B
19. A	19. E	19. D	19. B
20. B	20. C	20. A	20. B
21. C	21. D	21. B	21. D
22. A	22. B		22. D
23. E	23. B		23. B
24. B	24. B		24. C
25. C	25. B		25. B
26. D	26. A		26. E
27. E	27. A		27. C
28. D	28. A		28. C
29. A	29. E		29. C
30. A	30. E		30. A

Quantitative Comparisons

1. A
2. A
3. A
4. D
5. A
6. B
7. B
8 D
9. A
10. A
11. D
12. C
13. B
14. C
15. A
16. A
17. A
18. B
19. A
20. B
21. A
22. D
23. B
24. C
25. D
26. C
27. A
28. D
29. D
30. D

Grid-Ins

1. 48
2. 11, 13, 17, 19, 23, 29, 31, 37, 41, 43 or 47
3. .75
4. $\frac{14}{6}$, $\frac{7}{3}$ or 2.33
5. $\frac{2}{5}$ or .4
6. 250
7. 96
8. 65
9. 96
10. 8
11. $\frac{12}{7}$
12. 2
13. 5
14. 3
15. 115
16. 70
17. 40
18. 9
19. 140
20. 24
21. 8
22. 12
23. 300
24. 16
25. 25
26. 12
27. 280
28. 16
29. 203
30. $5 < n < 6$

See Chapter 10 for strategic explanations of each of these practice questions.

9 ACT Practice Sets

ACT Practice Set 1: English

DIRECTIONS: In the passages that follow, certain words and phrases have been underlined and numbered. You will find alternatives for each underlined portion in the right-hand column. Select the one that best expresses the idea, that makes the statement acceptable in standard written English, or that is phrased most consistently with the style and tone of the entire passage. If you feel that the original version is best, select "NO CHANGE." You will also find questions asking about a section of the passage or about the entire passage. For these questions, decide which choice gives the most appropriate response to the given question. For each question in the test, select the best choice and fill in the corresponding space on the answer line. You may wish to read each passage through before you begin to answer the questions associated with it. Most answers cannot be determined without reading several sentences around the phrases in question. Make sure to read far enough ahead each time you choose an alternative.

Passage 1

[1]

If you are like most visitors to Athens, you will make your way to the Acropolis, the hill$_{1}$ that once served as a fortified, strategic position overlooking the Aegean Sea—to see the Parthenon. This celebrated temple was dedicated in the fifth century B.C. to the goddess Athena. There is no more famous building in all of Greece; to climb up its marble steps is to have beheld$_{2}$ a human creation that has attained the stature of a natural phenomenon like the Grand Canyon. You should also make an attempt to sample Athenian cuisine while you're there.$_{3}$

1. A. NO CHANGE
   B. Acropolis. The hill
   C. Acropolis—the hill
   D. Acropolis

   Ⓐ Ⓑ Ⓒ Ⓓ

2. F. NO CHANGE
   G. to behold
   H. beholding
   J. to be holding

   Ⓕ Ⓖ Ⓗ Ⓙ

3. A. NO CHANGE
   B. Also make an attempt to sample Athenian cuisine while you're there.
   C. While you're there, you should also make an attempt to sample Athenian cuisine.
   D. OMIT the underlined portion.

   Ⓐ Ⓑ Ⓒ Ⓓ

[2]

Generations of architects have proclaimed[4] the Parthenon to be the most brilliantly conceived structure in the Western world. The genius of its construction is subtle for example[5] the temple's columns were made to bulge outward slightly in order to compensate for the fact, viewed from a distance, that straight columns appear concave.[6] Using this and other techniques, the architects strove to create an optical illusion of: uprightness,[7] solidity, and permanence.

4. F. NO CHANGE
   G. has proclaimed
   H. proclaims
   J. are proclaiming

5. A. NO CHANGE
   B. subtle; for example
   C. subtle. For example
   D. subtle. For example,

6. F. NO CHANGE
   G. fact that straight columns, viewed from a distance, appear concave.
   H. view from a distance: straight columns appearing concave.
   J. fact, when viewed from far away, that straight columns appear concave.

7. A. NO CHANGE
   B. illusion of: uprightness,
   C. illusion of, uprightness,
   D. illusion of uprightness,

[3]

Because of this,[8] the overall impression you'll get of the Parthenon will be far different from the one the ancient Athenians had. Only by standing on the marble steps of the Parthenon and allowing your imagination to transport you back to the Golden Age of Athens. You will[9] be able to see the temple's main attraction, the legendary statue of Athena Parthenos. It was 38 feet high and made of ivory and over a ton of pure gold. Removed from the temple in the fifth century A.D.,[10] all that remains is the slight rectangular depression on the floor where it stood.

8. F. NO CHANGE
   G. Thus,
   H. Rather,
   J. Of course,

9. A. NO CHANGE
   B. Athens; you will
   C. Athens will you
   D. Athens. You may

10. F. NO CHANGE
    G. Having been removed from the temple in the fifth century A.D.,
    H. Given its removal from the temple in the fifth century A.D.,
    J. The statue was removed from the temple in the fifth century A.D.;

[4]

Many of the ornate carvings and sculptures that adorned the walls of the Acropolis <u>is</u> [11] no longer there, either. In the early nineteenth century, the British diplomat Lord <u>Elgins' decision to</u> [12] "protect" the ones that survived by removing them from the Parthenon and carrying them back to Britain (he had the permission of the Ottoman Turks, who controlled Greece at the time, to do so).

11. A. NO CHANGE
    B. will be
    C. have been
    D. are

Ⓐ Ⓑ Ⓒ Ⓓ

12. F. NO CHANGE
    G. Elgin's deciding that
    H. Elgin decided to
    J. Elgin's decision to

Ⓕ Ⓖ Ⓗ Ⓙ

[5]

After they gained independence from the Turks, <u>they</u> [13] began to demand the sculptures and carvings back from the British, to no avail. Thus, if you want to gain a complete picture of what the Parthenon once looked like, you'll have to visit not only the Acropolis of Athens, but the British Museum in London as well.

13. A. NO CHANGE
    B. the Turks
    C. the Greeks
    D. who

Ⓐ Ⓑ Ⓒ Ⓓ

Items 14 and 15 pose questions about the passage as a whole.

14. The writer wishes to insert the following material into the essay:

"Some of them were destroyed in 1687 when attacking Venetians bombarded the Acropolis, setting off explosives that had been stored in the Parthenon."

The new material best supports, and therefore would most logically be placed in, paragraph:

F. 1
G. 2
H. 3
J. 4

15. Suppose the editor of an architecture journal had requested that the writer focus primarily on the techniques the ancient Greek architects used in constructing the Parthenon. Does the essay fulfill this request?

A. Yes, because the essay makes it clear that the Parthenon was an amazing architectural achievement.
B. Yes, because the essay explains in the second paragraph the reason the temple's columns bulge outward slightly.
C. No, because the Parthenon's construction is only one of several topics covered in the essay.
D. No, because the author never explains what the architects who designed the Parthenon were trying to accomplish.

Ⓐ Ⓑ Ⓒ Ⓓ

Passage 2

Although there is no conclusive evidence that a man named Robin Hood ever actually existed, the story of Robin Hood and his band of merry men has become one of the most popular traditional tales in English literature.

Robin is the hero in a series of ballads dating from at least the fourteenth century. These ballads are telling [16] of discontent among the lower classes in the north of England during a turbulent era culminating in the Peasants' Revolt of 1381. A good deal of the rebellion against authority stemmed from restriction of hunting rights. These early ballads reveal the cruelty that was a part of medieval life. Robin Hood was a rebel, and many of the most striking episodes depict him and his companions robbing and killing representatives of authority, and they gave [17] the gains to the poor.

16. **F.** NO CHANGE
G. telling
H. tell
J. they are telling

(F) (G) (H) (J)

17. **A.** NO CHANGE
B. they were giving
C. giving
D. gave

(A) (B) (C) (D)

Their most frequent [18] enemy was the Sheriff of Nottingham, a local agent of the central government. Other enemies included wealthy ecclesiastical landowners.

18. **F.** NO CHANGE
G. even more frequenter
H. frequent
J. frequently

(F) (G) (H) (J)

While Robin could be ruthless with those who abused their power, he was kind to the oppressed. He was a people's hero as King Arthur was a noble's. <u>(The Broadway musical *Camelot* and Walt Disney's *The Sword in the Stone* are based on the legend of King Arthur.)</u> 19

Some scholars have sought to prove that there was an actual Robin Hood. However, references to the Robin Hood legends by medieval writers make it clear that the ballads were the only evidence for Robin's existence available to <u>them.</u> 20 A popular modern belief that Robin was of the time of Richard I probably stems from the antiquary Richard <u>Stukely's fabrication</u> 21 of a "pedigree." [22]

19. A. NO CHANGE
B. (The Broadway musical and the movie, respectively, *Camelot* and Walt Disney's *The Sword in the Stone,* are based on the legend of King Arthur.)
C. (Movies and musicals, including *The Sword in the Stone* and *Camelot,* are derived from the legend of King Arthur.)
D. OMIT the underlined portion.

Ⓐ Ⓑ Ⓒ Ⓓ

20. F. NO CHANGE
G. him.
H. it.
J. those writing ballads about him.

Ⓕ Ⓖ Ⓗ Ⓙ

21. A. NO CHANGE
B. Stukelys fabrication
C. Stukelys fabrication,
D. Stukely's, fabrication

Ⓐ Ⓑ Ⓒ Ⓓ

22. Suppose that at this point in the passage the writer wanted to add more information about Richard Stukely. Which of the following additions would be most relevant to the passage as a whole?

F. a discussion of relevant books on England during the realm of Richard I
G. a definition of the term *antiquary*
H. an example of Stukely's interest in King Arthur
J. a description of the influence Stukely's fabricated pedigree has had on later versions of the Robin Hood tale

Ⓕ Ⓖ Ⓗ Ⓙ

In the eighteenth century, the nature of the legend was distorted by the suggestion that Robin <u>was as a</u> [23] fallen nobleman. Writers adopted this new element <u>as eagerly as puppies.</u> [24] Robin was also given a love <u>interest; Maid</u> [25] Marian. Some critics say that these ballads lost much of their vitality and poetic value by losing the social impulse that prompted their creation.

<u>Consequently, in the twentieth century,</u> [26] the legend of Robin Hood has inspired several movies and a television series. Even a Broadway musical <u>basing</u> [27] on the tale. So, whether or not a Robin Hood actually lived in ancient <u>Britain, and</u> [28] the legendary Robin has lived in the popular imagination for more than 600 years.

23. **A.** NO CHANGE
B. was like as if he was
C. was a
D. is as a

(A) (B) (C) (D)

24. **F.** NO CHANGE
G. eagerly.
H. eagerly, like a puppy.
J. like a puppy's eagerness.

(F) (G) (H) (J)

25. **A.** NO CHANGE
B. interests—Maid
C. interest: Maid,
D. interest—Maid

(A) (B) (C) (D)

26. **F.** NO CHANGE
G. (Do NOT begin new paragraph) In the twentieth century, on the one hand,
H. (Begin new paragraph) In the twentieth century,
J. (Begin new paragraph) In the twentieth century, therefore,

(F) (G) (H) (J)

27. **A.** NO CHANGE
B. has been based
C. to base
D. OMIT the underlined portion.

(A) (B) (C) (D)

28. **F.** NO CHANGE
G. Britain,
H. Britain, therefore
J. Britain;

(F) (G) (H) (J)

Items 29 and 30 pose questions about the passage as a whole.

29. Suppose this passage were written for an audience that was unfamiliar with the legend of Robin Hood. The writer could most effectively strengthen the passage by:

A. citing examples of legendary rebels from Spanish and French literature.
B. including further evidence of Robin Hood's actual existence.
C. quoting a few lines from a Broadway musical about ancient Britain.
D. including a brief summary of the Robin Hood legend.

Ⓐ Ⓑ Ⓒ Ⓓ

30. This passage was probably written for readers who:

F. are experts on how legends are handed down.
G. are authorities on ancient British civilization and culture.
H. are convinced that Robin Hood was an actual historical personage.
J. have some familiarity with the Robin Hood legends.

Ⓕ Ⓖ Ⓗ Ⓙ

ACT Practice Set 2: Reading

DIRECTIONS: After reading each passage, select the best answer to each question and fill in the corresponding oval on your answer sheet. You are allowed to refer to the passages while answering the questions.

Passage 1

Enlightenment ideas were put forth by a variety of intellectuals who in France came to be known as the *philosophes*. *Philosophes* is French for philosophers, and in a sense these thinkers were rightly considered philosophers, for the questions they dealt with were philosophical: How do we discover truth? How should life be lived? What is the nature of God? But on the whole the term has a meaning different from the usual meaning of *philosopher.* The *philosophes* were intellectuals, often not formally trained or associated with a university. They were usually more literary than scientific. They generally extended, applied, popularized, or propagandized ideas of others rather than originating those ideas themselves. The *philosophes* were more likely to write plays, satires, pamphlets, or simply participate in verbal exchanges at select gatherings than to write formal philosophical books.

It was the *philosophes* who developed the philosophy of the Enlightenment and spread it to much of the educated elite in Western Europe (and the American colonies). Although the sources for their philosophy can be traced to the Scientific Revolution in general, the *philosophes* were most influenced by their understanding of Newton, Locke, and English institutions.

The *philosophes* saw Newton as the great synthesizer of the Scientific Revolution who rightly described the universe as ordered, mechanical, material, and only originally set in motion by God, who since then has remained relatively inactive. Newton's synthesis showed to the *philosophes* that reason and nature were compatible: Nature functioned logically and discernibly, and what was natural was also reasonable. Newton exemplified the value of reasoning based on concrete experience. The *philosophes* felt that his empirical methodology was the correct path to discovering truth.

John Locke (1632–1704) agreed with Newton but went further. This English thinker would not exempt even the mind from the mechanical laws of the material universe. In his *Essay Concerning Human Understanding* (1691), Locke pictured the human brain at birth as a blank sheet of paper on which nothing would ever be written except sense perception and reason. What human beings become depends on their experiences—on the information received through the senses. Schools and social institutions could therefore play a great role in molding the individual from childhood to adulthood. Human beings were thus by nature far more malleable than had been assumed. This empirical psychology of Locke rejected the notion that human beings were born with innate ideas or that revelation was a reliable source of truth. Locke also enunciated liberal and reformist political ideas in his *Second Treatise of Civil Government* (1690), which influenced the *philosophes*. On the whole Locke's empiricism, psychology, and politics were appealing to the *philosophes*.

England, not coincidentally the country of Newton and Locke, became the admired model for many of the *philosophes*. They tended to idealize it, but England did seem to allow greater individual freedom, tolerate religious differences, and evidence greater political reform than other countries, especially France. England seemed to have gone furthest in freeing itself from traditional institutions and accepting the new science of the seventeenth century. Moreover, England's approach seemed to work, for England was experiencing relative political stability and prosperity. The *philosophes* wanted to see in their own countries much of what England already seemed to have.

Many *philosophes* reflected the influence of Newton, Locke, and English institutions, but perhaps the most representative in his views was Voltaire (1778). Of all leading figures of the Enlightenment, he was the most influential. Voltaire, the son of a Paris lawyer, became the idol of the French intelligentsia while still in his early twenties. His versatile mind was sparkling; his wit was mordant. An outspoken critic, he soon ran afoul of both church and state authorities. First he was imprisoned in the Bastille; later he was exiled to England. There he encountered the ideas of Newton and Locke and came to admire English parliamentary government and tolerance. In *Letters on the English* (1732), *Elements of the Philosophy of Newton* (1738), and other writings, he popularized the ideas of Newton and Locke, extolled the virtues of English society, and indirectly criticized French society. Slipping back into France, he was hidden for a time and protected by a wealthy woman who became his mistress. Voltaire's facile mind and pen were never idle. He wrote poetry, drama, history, essays, letters, and scientific treatises—ninety volumes in all. The special targets of his cynical wit were the Catholic church and Christian institutions. Few people in history have dominated their age intellectually as did Voltaire.

1. The *philosophes* can best be described as:

   A. writers swept up by their mutual admiration of John Locke.
   B. professors who lecture in philosophy at French universities.
   C. intellectuals responsible for popularizing Enlightenment ideas.
   D. scientists who furthered the work of the Scientific Revolution.

   Ⓐ Ⓑ Ⓒ Ⓓ

2. Which of the following would most likely have been written by Voltaire?

   F. a treatise criticizing basic concepts of the Scientific Revolution
   G. a play satirizing religious institutions in France
   H. a collection of letters mocking the English Parliament
   J. a sentimental poem expounding the virtues of courtly love

   Ⓕ Ⓖ Ⓗ Ⓙ

3. According to the passage, Locke felt that schools and social institutions could "play a great role in molding the individual" (lines 52–53) primarily because:

   A. human beings were born with certain innate ideas.
   B. human nature becomes more malleable with age.
   C. society owes each individual the right to an education.
   D. the human mind is chiefly influenced by experience.

   Ⓐ Ⓑ Ⓒ Ⓓ

4. Based on the information in the passage, which of the following best describes Newton's view of the universe?

   I. The universe was initially set in motion by God.
   II. Human reason is insufficient to understand the laws of nature.
   III. The universe operates in a mechanical and orderly fashion.

   F. I only
   G. I and II only
   H. I and III only
   J. II and III only

   Ⓕ Ⓖ Ⓗ Ⓙ

5. According to the passage, which of the following works questioned the idea that revelation was a reliable source of truth?

   A. *Letters on the English*
   B. *Second Treatise of Civil Government*
   C. *Elements of the Philosophy of Newton*
   D. *Essay Concerning Human Understanding*

   Ⓐ Ⓑ Ⓒ Ⓓ

6. The passage supports which of the following statements concerning the relationship between Newton and Locke?

F. Locke's psychology contradicted Newton's belief in an orderly universe.
G. Locke maintained that Newton's laws of the material universe also applied to the human mind.
H. Newton eventually came to accept Locke's revolutionary ideas about the human mind.
J. Newton's political ideas were the basis of Locke's liberal and reformist politics.

Ⓕ Ⓖ Ⓗ Ⓙ

7. According to the passage, the *philosophes* believed that society should:
I. allow individuals greater freedom.
II. free itself from traditional institutions.
III. tolerate religious differences.

A. I only
B. I and II only
C. II and III only
D. I, II, and III

Ⓐ Ⓑ Ⓒ Ⓓ

8. It can be inferred from the passage that the author regards England's political stability and economic prosperity as:

F. the reason the *philosophes* did not idealize England's achievement.
G. evidence that political reforms could bring about a better way of life.
H. the result of Voltaire's activities after he was exiled to England.
J. an indication that the Scientific Revolution had not yet started there.

Ⓕ Ⓖ Ⓗ Ⓙ

9. The passage suggests that the French political and religious authorities during the time of Voltaire:

A. allowed little in the way of free speech.
B. overreacted to Voltaire's mild satires.
C. regarded the *philosophes* with indifference.
D. accepted the model of English parliamentary government.

Ⓐ Ⓑ Ⓒ Ⓓ

10. How does the passage support the point that the *philosophes* were "more literary than scientific" (lines 12–13)?

F. It demonstrates how the *philosophes'* writings contributed to the political change.
G. It compares the number of works that Voltaire authored to Newton's output.
H. It traces the influences of English literary works on French scientists.
J. It describes the kinds of literary activities the *philosophes* commonly engaged in.

Ⓕ Ⓖ Ⓗ Ⓙ

Passage 2

The ozone layer, the tenuous layer of gas that surrounds our planet between 12 and 45 kilometers above our surface, is being rapidly depleted. Seasonally occurring holes have appeared in it over the Poles, and, more recently, over the temperate regions of the northern hemisphere. The threat is a serious one since the ozone layer traps almost all in-coming ultraviolet radiation, which is harmful to all living organisms—humans, animals, and plants.

Even though the ozone layer is 25 kilometers thick, the atmosphere in it is very tenuous and the total amount of ozone, compared with other atmospheric gases, is quite small. If all of the ozone in a vertical column reaching up through the atmosphere were to be compressed to sea-level pressure, it would form a layer only a few millimeters thick. . . .

Detailed study of the ozone layer began comparatively recently, in 1930, the earliest observations being made by the English scientist Sydney Chapman. These initial observations were taken up by the World Meteorological Organization (WMO), which established the Dobson network consisting of one hundred observation stations. Since 1983, on the initiative of WMO and the United Nations Environment Programme (UNEP), seven of these stations have been entrusted with the task of making long-term forecasts of the likely evolution of our precious shield.

In 1958, the researchers who permanently monitor the ozone content of the layer above the South Pole began to observe several seasonal variations. From June there was a slight reduction in ozone content, which reached a minimum in October. In November there was a sudden increase in the ozone content. The fluctuations appeared to result from the natural phenomena of wind effects and temperature change.

However, although the October minimum remained constant until 1979, the total ozone content over the Pole was steadily diminishing until, in 1985, public opinion was finally roused by reports of a "hole" in the ozone layer and observations were intensified.

The culprits responsible for the hole had already been identified as being supersonic aircraft, such as the Concorde (although these have now been exonerated), and the notorious compounds known as chlorofluorocarbons, or CFCs. Synthesized in 1928 by chemists working at General Motors in the United States, CFCs are compounds of atoms of chlorine and fluorine. Having the advantage of being nonflammable, nontoxic, and noncorrosive, they came into widespread use in the 1950s. They are widely used in refrigerators, air conditioners, and to make the "bubbles" in the foam plastic used, for example, in car seats and as insulation in buildings. . . .

In 1989 they represented a market valued at over $1.5 billion and a labor force of 1.6 million. Of the 25 countries producing CFCs, the United States, France, the United Kingdom, Japan, and Germany account for three-quarters of the total world production of some 1.2 million tons.

These figures give some idea of the importance of the economic interests that are at stake in any decision to ban the industrial use of CFCs. But, with CFCs incriminated by scientists, the question arose as to whether we were prepared to take the risk of seeing an increase in the number of cases of skin cancer, eye ailments such as cataracts, or even a lowering of the human immune defense system, all effects that would follow further depletion of the ozone layer. . . .

In 1987, 24 industrialized countries signed the Montreal Protocol on Substances that Deplete the Ozone Layer, the first world agreement aimed at halting the production of CFCs. As more evidence emerged concerning the seriousness of the threat, it became apparent that the protocol was not stringent enough and, year by year, its severity was increased until in 1990 in London, 70 countries agreed to stop all production of CFCs by the year 2000. . . .

Unfortunately, even if the entire world were to agree today to halt all production and use of CFCs, this would not provide an immediate solution to the problem. A single molecule of chlorine can destroy from 10,000 to 100,000 molecules of ozone. Furthermore, CFCs have a lifespan of between 75 and 400 years and they take ten years to reach the ozone layer. In other words, what we are experiencing now results from CFCs emitted ten years ago.

Industrialists are now urgently searching for substitute products. Some, such as propane, are too dangerous because they are inflammable;

others, the HCFCs, might prove to be toxic and to contribute to the greenhouse effect, i.e., to the process of global warming. Nevertheless, nobody can say that the situation will not right itself, whether in the short term or long term, if we ourselves lend a hand.

From "Earth's Ozone Shield Under Threat," by France Bequette, *UNESCO Courier* (June 1990).

11. As it is used in the passage, the term *tenuous* most likely means:

A. thin.
B. dangerous.
C. substantial.
D. fragile.

Ⓐ Ⓑ Ⓒ Ⓓ

12. According to the passage, the public first became aware of the depletion of ozone layer in:

F. 1930
G. 1958
H. 1979
J. 1985

Ⓕ Ⓖ Ⓗ Ⓙ

13. According to the passage, all of the following contribute to fluctuations in the content of the ozone layer EXCEPT:

A. supersonic aircraft.
B. chlorofluorocarbons.
C. temperature changes.
D. wind effects.

Ⓐ Ⓑ Ⓒ Ⓓ

14. The main point of the seventh paragraph (lines 62–67) is to:

F. highlight the amount of CFCs produced every year.
G. criticize the countries responsible for producing CFCs.
H. indicate the economic interests at stake in the CFC debate.
J. list the most important members of the Montreal Protocol.

Ⓕ Ⓖ Ⓗ Ⓙ

15. According to the passage, alternatives to using CFCs may be difficult to find because substitute products:

I. may prove to be toxic.
II. are too dangerous to use.
III. contribute to global warming.

A. II only
B. II and III only
C. I and II only
D. I, II, and III

Ⓐ Ⓑ Ⓒ Ⓓ

16. According to the passage, forecasts about the future of the ozone layer are made by:

F. the WMO.
G. the Dobson network.
H. the Montreal Protocol.
J. the UNEP.

Ⓕ Ⓖ Ⓗ Ⓙ

17. Which of the following would be the most likely result if all production of CFCs were to end today?

A. Scientists would have to replace the quantities of ozone already lost.
B. The ozone layer would only return to normal levels after 75 years.
C. Scientists would also have to destroy all chlorine molecules in the atmosphere.
D. The benefits would not be experienced for another ten years.

Ⓐ Ⓑ Ⓒ Ⓓ

18. According the passage, the ozone layer is:

F. a few millimeters thick.
G. 12 kilometers thick.
H. 25 kilometers thick.
J. over 25 kilometers thick.

Ⓕ Ⓖ Ⓗ Ⓙ

19. Which of the following statements is best supported by the fourth paragraph (lines 32–40)?

A. The ozone layer undergoes seasonal variations in density.
B. The number of CFCs in the atmosphere increases from June to October.
C. The ozone layer over the South Pole is more at risk than in other areas.
D. The first studies of ozone layer depletion underestimated its severity.

Ⓐ Ⓑ Ⓒ Ⓓ

20. The main conclusion reached in the passage about the threat to the ozone layer is that:

F. the cost of banning CFCs altogether may make it an impractical answer.
G. finding alternative products to CFCs may provide a long-term remedy to the situation.
H. halting production of CFCs is unlikely to produce a solution to the problem.
J. agreements between CFC-producing countries need to be more strictly enforced.

Ⓕ Ⓖ Ⓗ Ⓙ

ACT Practice Set 3: Math

DIRECTIONS: Solve each of the following problems, select the correct answer, and then fill in the corresponding space. Don't linger over problems that are too time-consuming. Do as many as you can, then come back to the others in the time you have remaining.

Note: Unless otherwise noted, all of the following should be assumed.

1. Illustrative figures are not necessarily drawn to scale.
2. All geometric figures lie in a plane.
3. The term *line* indicates a straight line.
4. The term *average* indicates arithmetic mean.

1. If $\left(\frac{1}{2}+\frac{1}{6}\right)-\left(\frac{1}{12}+\frac{1}{3}\right)$ is calculated and the result is reduced to simplest terms, what is the numerator of this fraction?

A. 1
B. 2
C. 3
D. 4
E. 5

Ⓐ Ⓑ Ⓒ Ⓓ Ⓔ

2. A jar contains four green marbles, five red marbles, and 11 white marbles. If one marble is chosen at random, what is the probability that it will be green?

F. $\frac{1}{3}$
G. $\frac{1}{4}$
H. $\frac{1}{5}$
J. $\frac{1}{16}$
K. $\frac{1}{55}$

Ⓕ Ⓖ Ⓗ Ⓙ Ⓚ

3. What is $\frac{1}{4}$ percent of 16?

A. 0.004
B. 0.04
C. 0.4
D. 4
E. 64

Ⓐ Ⓑ Ⓒ Ⓓ Ⓔ

4. Which of the following is equal to $\frac{(3.0\times10^4)(8.0\times10^9)}{1.2\times10^6}$?

F. 2.0×10^6
G. 2.0×10^7
H. 2.0×10^8
J. 2.0×10^{30}
K. 2.0×10^{31}

Ⓕ Ⓖ Ⓗ Ⓙ Ⓚ

5. Jan types at an average rate of 12 pages per hour. At that rate, how long will it take Jan to type 100 pages?

A. 8 hours and 3 minutes
B. 8 hours and 15 minutes
C. 8 hours and 20 minutes
D. 8 hours and 30 minutes
E. 8 hours and $33\frac{1}{3}$ minutes

Ⓐ Ⓑ Ⓒ Ⓓ Ⓔ

6. $\left[\left(5^{-2}\right)^2\right]^{-1} =$

F. 5^{-5}
G. 5^{-4}
H. 5^{-1}
J. 5^1
K. 5^4

Ⓕ Ⓖ Ⓗ Ⓙ Ⓚ

7. $\frac{1}{2-\sqrt{2}} = ?$

A. $\frac{1+\sqrt{2}}{2}$

B. $\frac{-1+\sqrt{2}}{2}$

C. $\frac{2+\sqrt{2}}{2}$

D. $\frac{2-\sqrt{2}}{2}$

E. $\frac{-2+\sqrt{2}}{2}$

(A) (B) (C) (D) (E)

8. The formula for the lateral surface area S of a right circular cone is $S = \pi r\sqrt{r^2 + h^2}$, where r is the radius of the base and h is the altitude. What is the lateral surface area, in square feet, of a right circular cone with base radius 3 feet and altitude 4 feet?

F. $3\pi\sqrt{5}$

G. $3\pi\sqrt{7}$

H. 15π

J. 21π

K. $\frac{75\pi}{2}$

(F) (G) (H) (J) (K)

9. If $\sqrt[6]{x} = 5^{\frac{1}{3}}$, then $x =$

A. $\frac{1}{10}$

B. $\sqrt{5}$

C. $2\sqrt{5}$

D. 10

E. 25

(A) (B) (C) (D) (E)

10. If $x^2 + 6x + 7 = 0$, what are the possible values of x ?

F. $2 \pm \sqrt{3}$

G. $-2 \pm \sqrt{3}$

H. $3 \pm \sqrt{2}$

J. $-3 \pm \sqrt{2}$

K. $-3 \pm \sqrt{3}$

(F) (G) (H) (J) (K)

11. What is the value of a if $\frac{1}{a} + \frac{2}{a} + \frac{3}{a} + \frac{4}{a} = 5$?

A. $\frac{1}{2}$

B. 2

C. 4

D. $12\frac{1}{2}$

E. 50

(A) (B) (C) (D) (E)

12. Which graph below represents the solutions for x of the inequality $-3(x-2) \leq 15$?

F.

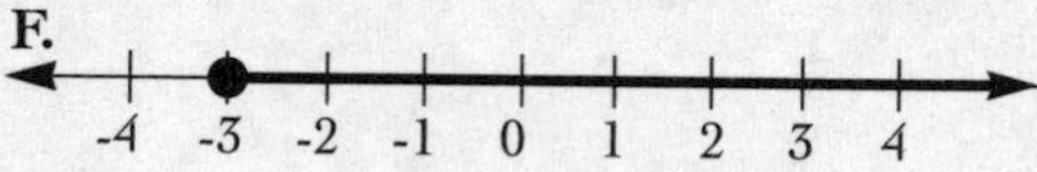

G.

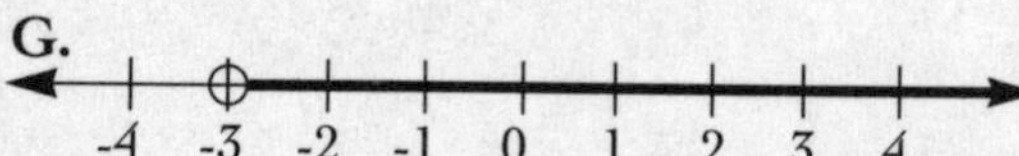

H.

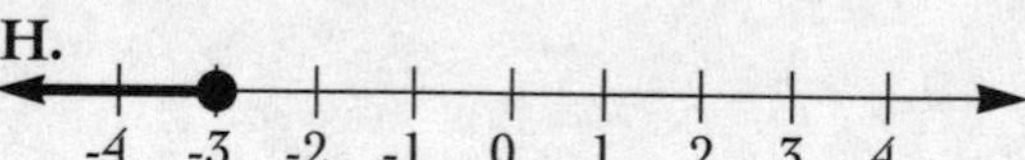

J.

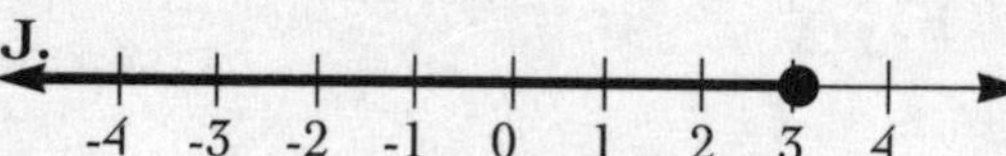

K.

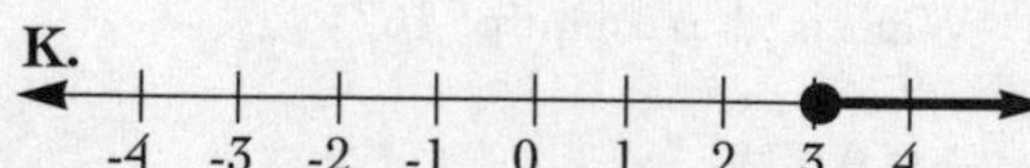

(F) (G) (H) (J) (K)

13. Joan has q quarters, ∂ dimes, n nickels, and no other coins in her pocket. Which of the following represents the total number of coins in Joan's pocket?

A. $q + \partial + n$
B. $5q + 2\partial + n$
C. $.25q + .10\partial + .05n$
D. $(25 + 10 + 5)(q + \partial + n)$
E. $25q + 10\partial + 5n$

Ⓐ Ⓑ Ⓒ Ⓓ Ⓔ

14. Which of the following inequalities is represented by the shaded region below?

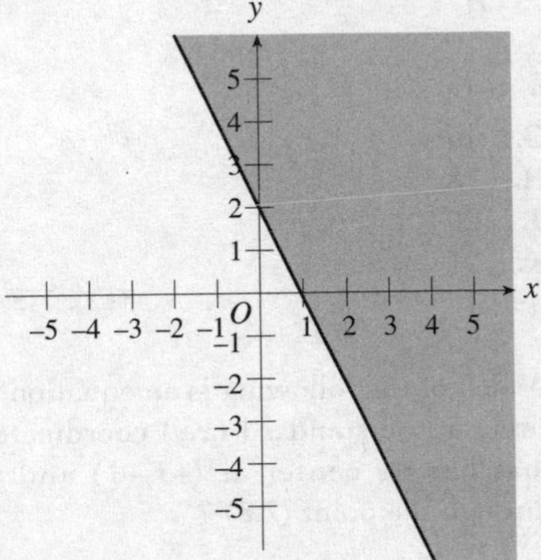

F. $y \geq -\frac{1}{2}x + 2$

G. $y \leq -\frac{1}{2}x + 2$

H. $y \geq -\frac{1}{2}x + \frac{1}{2}$

J. $y \geq -2x + 2$

K. $y \leq -2x + 2$

Ⓕ Ⓖ Ⓗ Ⓙ Ⓚ

15. In the standard (x, y) coordinate plane, line m represents the equation $5x + 2y = 29$ and line n represents the equation $y - x = -3$. What are the coordinates of the point of intersection of lines m and n ?

A. (2, 5)
B. (3, 6)
C. (5, 2)
D. (6, 3)
E. (10, 7)

Ⓐ Ⓑ Ⓒ Ⓓ Ⓔ

16. Which of the following is an equation of the parabola graphed in the (x, y) coordinate plane below?

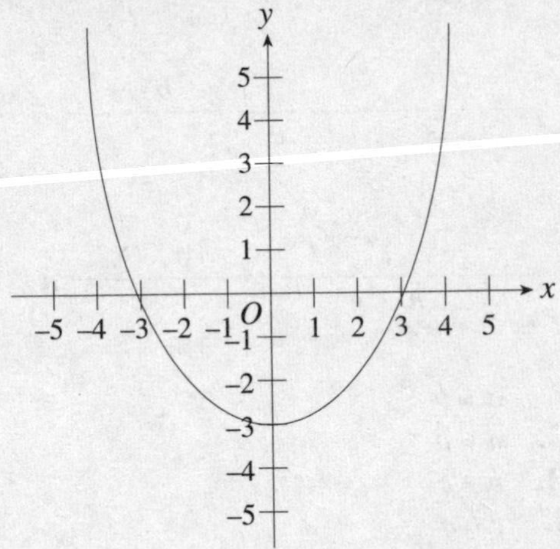

F. $y = \frac{x^2}{3} - 3$

G. $y = \frac{x^2 - 3}{3}$

H. $y = \frac{x^2}{3} + 3$

J. $y = \frac{x^2 + 3}{3}$

K. $y = 3x^2 - 3$

Ⓕ Ⓖ Ⓗ Ⓙ Ⓚ

17. What is the length, in units, of the line segment with endpoints (3, 4) and (5, 12) in the standard (x, y) coordinate plane?

A. 6
B. 8
C. $2\sqrt{17}$
D. $6\sqrt{2}$
E. 10

Ⓐ Ⓑ Ⓒ Ⓓ Ⓔ

18. In the figure below, line t crosses parallel lines m and n. Which of the following statements must be true?

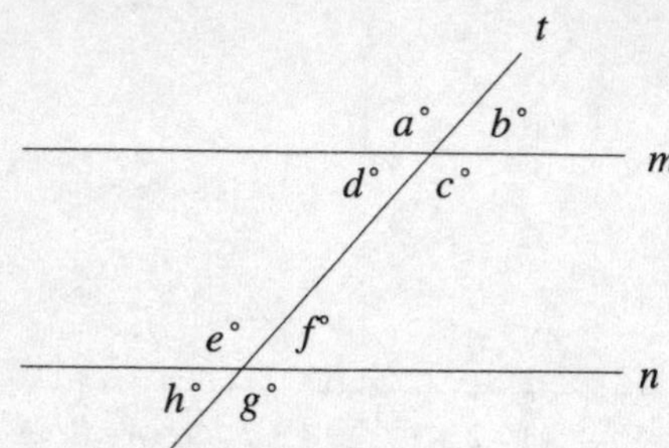

F. $a = b$
G. $a = d$
H. $b = e$
J. $c = g$
K. $d = g$

Ⓕ Ⓖ Ⓗ Ⓙ Ⓚ

19. In the standard (x, y) coordinate plane, line m is perpendicular to the line containing the points (5, 6) and (6, 10). What is the slope of line m ?

A. -4

B. $-\frac{1}{4}$

C. $\frac{1}{4}$

D. 4

E. 8

Ⓐ Ⓑ Ⓒ Ⓓ Ⓔ

20. In the figure below, $\overline{EF}$ is perpendicular to $\overline{FG}$, and $\overline{FH}$ is perpendicular to $\overline{EG}$. If $\overline{EF}$ is 10 inches long and $\overline{EG}$ is 25 inches long, how many inches long is $\overline{HG}$?

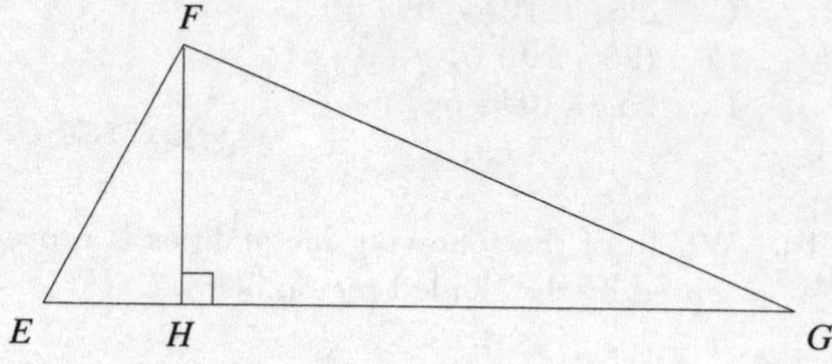

F. 15
G. 16
H. 18
J. 20
K. 21

Ⓕ Ⓖ Ⓗ Ⓙ Ⓚ

21. Which of the following is an equation for the circle in the standard (x,y) coordinate plane that has its center at $(-1,-1)$ and passes through the point $(7,5)$?

A. $(x-1)^2+(y-1)^2=10$

B. $(x+1)^2+(y+1)^2=10$

C. $(x-1)^2+(y-1)^2=12$

D. $(x-1)^2+(y-1)^2=100$

E. $(x+1)^2+(y+1)^2=100$

Ⓐ Ⓑ Ⓒ Ⓓ Ⓔ

22. The figure shown below belongs in which of the following classifications?

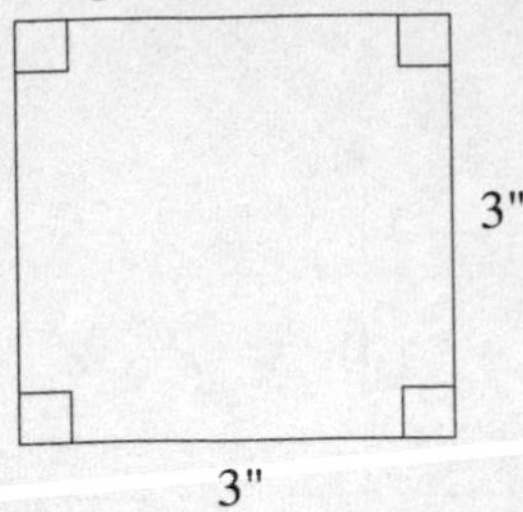

I. square
II. rectangle
III. parallelogram
IV. trapezoid

F. I only
G. II only
H. I and II only
J. I, II, and III only
K. I, II, III, and IV

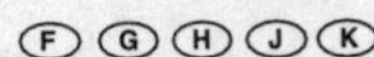

23. In the figure below, $\overline{BD}$ bisects $\angle ABC$. The measure of $\angle ABC$ is 100° and the measure of $\angle BAD$ is 60°. What is the measure of $\angle BDC$?

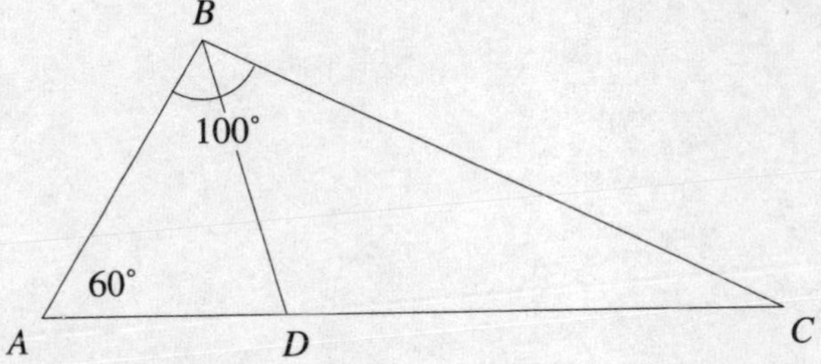

A. 80°
B. 90°
C. 100°
D. 110°
E. 120°

A B C D E

24. How many feet long is the diameter of a circle whose circumference is 36π feet?

F. 12
G. 18
H. 6π
J. 36
K. 18π

F G H J K

25. In the figure below, $\sin a = \frac{4}{5}$. What is $\cos \beta$?

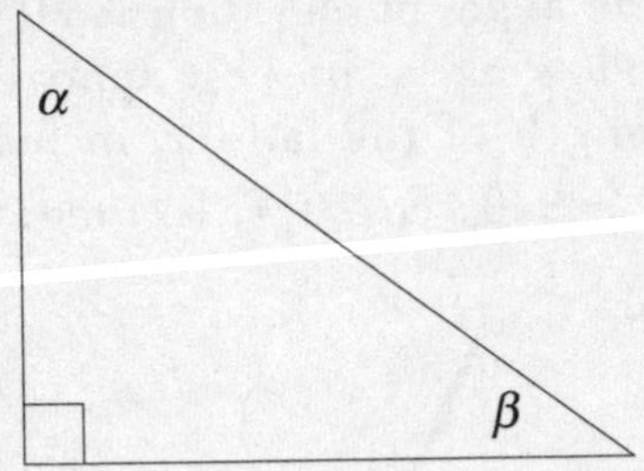

A. $\frac{3}{4}$
B. $\frac{3}{5}$
C. $\frac{4}{5}$
D. $\frac{5}{4}$
E. $\frac{4}{3}$

26. In the figure below, the radius of the circle centered at O is 9 units and the length of minor arc PQ is 2π units. What is the degree measure of $\angle POQ$?

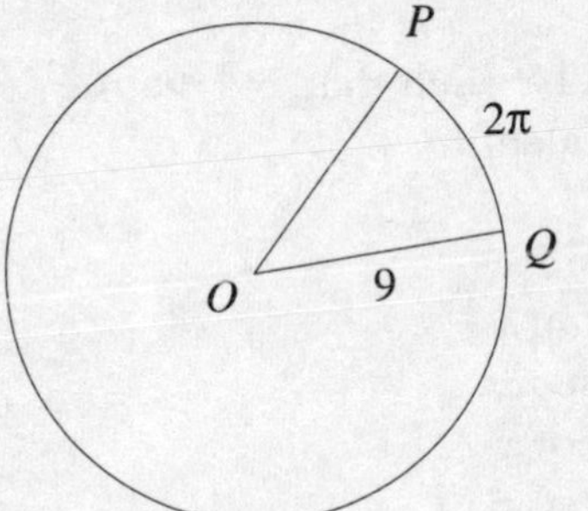

F. 10°
G. 18°
H. 20°
J. 36°
K. 40°

27. A ladder is leaning against the side of a building as shown in the figure below. If the base of the ladder is 4.0 feet from the wall and the angle of elevation is 70°, which of the following is the best approximation of the length of the ladder, in feet? (Note: $\sin 70° \approx .940$; $\cos 70° \approx .342$; $\tan 70° \approx 2.75$)

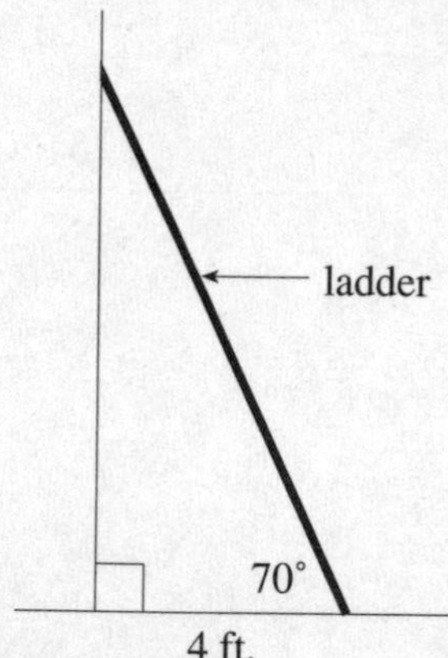

A. 11.0
B. 11.7
C. 12.0
D. 13.7
E. 28.0

Ⓐ Ⓑ Ⓒ Ⓓ Ⓔ

28. For all x such that $-\frac{\pi}{2} < x < \frac{\pi}{2}$, $\frac{\sin^2 x + \cos^2 x}{\cos x}$ is equivalent to:

F. $\sin x$
G. $\tan x$
H. $\sec x$
J. $\cot x$
K. $\csc x$

Ⓕ Ⓖ Ⓗ Ⓙ Ⓚ

29. $\cos 240° = ?$

A. $-\frac{\sqrt{3}}{2}$
B. $-\frac{\sqrt{3}}{3}$
C. $-\frac{1}{2}$
D. $\frac{\sqrt{3}}{3}$
E. $\frac{\sqrt{3}}{2}$

Ⓐ Ⓑ Ⓒ Ⓓ Ⓔ

30. Which of the following is an equation of the graph shown below?

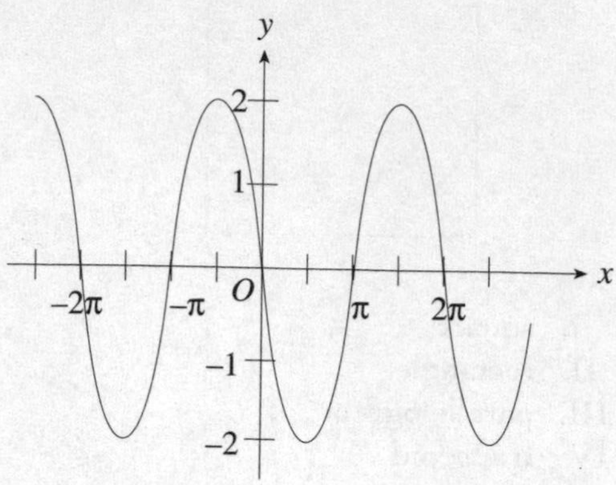

F. $y = -\sin 2x$
G. $y = \sin 2x$
H. $y = -2 \sin x$
J. $y = 2 \sin x$
K. $y = -2 \sin 2x$

Ⓕ Ⓖ Ⓗ Ⓙ Ⓚ

ACT PRACTICE SET 4: SCIENCE REASONING

DIRECTIONS: Each of the passages is followed by several questions. After reading each passage, decide on the best answer to each question and fill in the corresponding answer oval. You are allowed to refer to the passages while answering the questions.

Passage 1

The utilization and replenishing of the earth's carbon supply is a cyclic process involving all living matter. This cycle is shown in the figure below.

1. What effect would a sudden drop in the amount of the earth's decay bacteria have on the amount of carbon dioxide in the atmosphere?

   A. The CO_2 level will drop to a life-threatening level since the bacteria is the sole source of CO_2.
   B. The CO_2 level will rise because the bacteria usually consume CO_2.
   C. The CO_2 level may decrease slightly, but there are other sources of CO_2.
   D. The CO_2 level will increase slightly due to an imbalance in the carbon cycle.

   Ⓐ Ⓑ Ⓒ Ⓓ

2. Which of the following statements are consistent with the carbon cycle as presented in the diagram?

   I. A non-plant-eating animal does not participate in the carbon cycle.
   II. Both plant and animal respiration contribute CO_2 to the earth's atmosphere.
   III. All CO_2 is released into the air by respiration.

   F. I only
   G. II only
   H. I and II only
   J. II and III only

   Ⓕ Ⓖ Ⓗ Ⓙ

3. A direct source of CO_2 in the atmosphere is:

   A. the fermentation of green-plant carbohydrates.
   B. the photosynthesis of tropical plants.
   C. the digestion of plant matter by animals.
   D. the respiration of animal parasites.

   Ⓐ Ⓑ Ⓒ Ⓓ

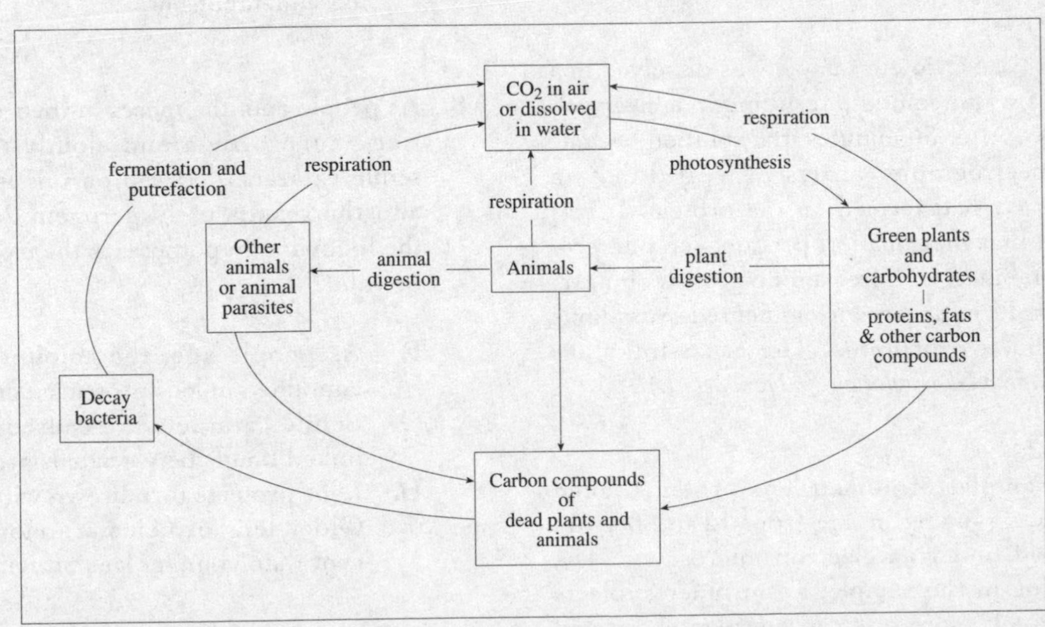

4. Which of the following best describes the relationship between animal respiration and photosynthesis?

   F. Respiration and photosynthesis serve the same function in the carbon cycle.
   G. Animal respiration provides vital gases for green plants.
   H. Animal respiration prohibits photosynthesis.
   J. There is no relationship between respiration and photosynthesis.

   Ⓕ Ⓖ Ⓗ Ⓙ

5. The elimination of which of the following would cause the earth's carbon cycle to grind to a complete halt?

   A. green plants
   B. animals
   C. animal predation
   D. decay bacteria

   Ⓐ Ⓑ Ⓒ Ⓓ

Passage 2

Preliminary research indicates that dietary sugar may react with proteins in the body, damaging the proteins and perhaps contributing to the aging process. The chemical effects of glucose on lens proteins in the eye were investigated in the following experiments.

Experiment 1

A human tissue protein sample was dissolved in a glucose-and-water solution, resulting in a clear yellow solution. After 30 minutes, the solution became opaque. Spectrographic analysis revealed that an *Amadori product* had formed on the protein. It was determined that the Amadori products on one protein had combined with free amino groups on nearby proteins, forming brown pigmented cross-links between the two proteins. The cross-links are termed *Advanced Glycosylation End products (AGE)*.

Experiment 2

Forty-six samples of human lens proteins taken from subjects ranging in age from 12 to 80 years were studied under an electron microscope. The lens proteins in the samples from older subjects occurred much more often in aggregates formed by cross-linked bonds than did the lens proteins in the samples from younger subjects. Fluorescent characteristics revealed the cross-links to be of two types: di-sulfide bonds and an indeterminate formation with brownish pigmentation.

Experiment 3

Two solutions containing lens proteins from cow lenses were prepared, one with glucose and one without. Only the glucose solution turned opaque. Analysis revealed that the lens proteins in the glucose solution had formed pigmented cross-links with the brownish color and fluorescence characteristics of those observed in Experiment 2.

6. It was assumed in the design of Experiment 3 that cow-lens proteins:

   F. have a brownish pigment.
   G. react with sulfides.
   H. remain insoluble in water.
   J. react similarly to human lens proteins.

   Ⓕ Ⓖ Ⓗ Ⓙ

7. Based on the results in Experiment 1 only, it can be concluded that:

   A. proteins can form di-sulfide cross-links.
   B. glucose dissolved in water forms AGE.
   C. glucose can react with proteins to form cross-links.
   D. Amadori products are a result of glucose metabolism.

   Ⓐ Ⓑ Ⓒ Ⓓ

8. As people age, the lenses in their eyes sometimes turn brown and cloudy (known as senile cataracts). Based on this information and the results of Experiment 2, which of the following hypotheses is the most likely to be valid?

   F. As people age, the amount of sulfur contained in lens proteins increases.
   G. Senile cataracts are caused by cross-linked bonds between lens proteins.
   H. Lens proteins turn brown with age.
   J. Older lens proteins are more fluorescent than younger lens proteins.

   Ⓕ Ⓖ Ⓗ Ⓙ

9. Which of the following hypotheses about the brown pigmented cross-links observed in Experiment 2 is best supported by the results of the three experiments?

A. Their brownish color is caused by di-sulfide bonds.
B. They are a natural formation that can be found at birth.
C. They are caused by glucose in the diet reacting with lens proteins.
D. They form when proteins are dissolved in water.

Ⓐ Ⓑ Ⓒ Ⓓ

10. Based on the experimental results, lens proteins from a 32-year-old man would most likely have:

F. more cross-links than lens proteins from a 32-year-old woman.
G. more cross-links than lens proteins from an 18-year-old cow.
H. more cross-links than lens proteins from an 18-year-old man.
J. more cross-links than lens proteins from an 80-year-old man.

Ⓕ Ⓖ Ⓗ Ⓙ

11. People with uncontrolled diabetes have excess levels of blood glucose. Based on this information and the results of the experiments, a likely symptom of advanced diabetes would be:

A. senile cataracts, due to an increase of free amino groups in the urine.
B. senile cataracts, due to glucose interacting with di-sulfide cross-links on lens proteins.
C. senile cataracts, due to AGE cross-links of lens proteins.
D. kidney failure, due to high levels of free amino groups in the urine.

Ⓐ Ⓑ Ⓒ Ⓓ

Passage 3

Two scientists discuss their views about the Quark Model.

Scientist 1

According to the Quark Model, each proton consists of three quarks: two up quarks, which carry a charge of +2/3 each, and one down quark, which carries a charge of –1/3. All mesons, one of which is the π^+ particle, are composed of one quark and one antiquark, and all baryons, one of which is the proton, are composed of three quarks. The Quark Model explains the numerous different types of mesons that have been observed. It also successfully predicted the essential properties of the Ψ meson. Individual quarks have not been observed because they are absolutely confined within baryons and mesons. However, the results of deep inelastic scattering experiments indicate that the proton has a substructure. In these experiments, high-energy electron beams were fired into protons. While most of the electrons incident on the proton passed right through, a few bounced back. The number of electrons scattered through large angles indicated that there are three distinct lumps within the proton.

Scientist 2

The Quark Model is seriously flawed. Conventional scattering experiments should be able to split the proton into its constituent quarks, if they existed. Once the quarks were free, it would be easy to distinguish quarks from other particles using something as simple as the Millikan oil drop experiment, because they would be the only particles that carry fractional charge. Furthermore, the lightest quark would be stable because there is no lighter particle for it to decay into. Quarks would be so easy to produce, identify, and store that they would have been detected if they truly existed. In addition, the Quark Model violates the Pauli exclusion principle, which originally was believed to hold for electrons but was found to hold for all particles of half-integer spin. The Pauli exclusion principle states that no two particles of half-integer spin can occupy the same state. The Δ^{++} baryon, which supposedly has three up quarks, violates the Pauli exclusion principle because two of those quarks would be in the same state. Therefore, the Quark Model must be replaced.

12. Which of the following would most clearly strengthen Scientist 1's hypothesis?

F. detection of the Δ^{++} baryon
G. detection of a particle with fractional charge
H. detection of mesons
J. detection of baryons

Ⓕ Ⓖ Ⓗ Ⓙ

13. Which of the following are reasons why Scientist 2 claims quarks should have been detected, if they existed?

I. They have a unique charge.
II. They are confined within mesons and baryons.
III. They are supposedly fundamental particles, and therefore could not decay into any other particle.

A. I only
B. II only
C. I and III only
D. I, II, and III

Ⓐ Ⓑ Ⓒ Ⓓ

14. Which of the following could Scientist 1 use to counter Scientist 2's point about the Pauli exclusion principle?

F. evidence that quarks do not have half-integer spin
G. evidence that the Δ^{++} baryon exists
H. evidence that quarks have fractional charge
J. evidence that quarks have the same spin as electrons

Ⓕ Ⓖ Ⓗ Ⓙ

15. If Scientist 1's hypothesis is correct, the Δ^{++} baryon should have a charge of:

A. –1
B. 0
C. 1
D. 2

Ⓐ Ⓑ Ⓒ Ⓓ

16. According to Scientist 2, the Quark Model is flawed:

F. because the existence of individual baryons cannot be experimentally verified.
G. because the existence of individual quarks cannot be experimentally verified.
H. because particles cannot have fractional charge.
J. because it doesn't include electrons as elementary particles.

Ⓕ Ⓖ Ⓗ Ⓙ

17. Scientist 1 believes that some of the high-energy electrons that were aimed into the proton in the deep inelastic scattering experiments bounced back because:

A. they hit quarks.
B. they hit other electrons.
C. they were repelled by the positive charge on the proton.
D. they hit baryons.

Ⓐ Ⓑ Ⓒ Ⓓ

18. The fact that deep inelastic scattering experiments revealed a proton substructure of three lumps supports the Quark Model because:

F. protons are mesons, and meson supposedly consist of three quarks.
G. protons are mesons, and mesons supposedly consist of a quark and an antiquark.
H. protons are baryons, and baryons supposedly consist of three quarks.
J. protons are baryons, and baryons supposedly consist of one quark and one antiquark.

Ⓕ Ⓖ Ⓗ Ⓙ

ACT Practice Set Answer Key

English	Reading	Math	Science Reasoning
1. C	1. C	1. A	1. C
2. G	2. G	2. H	2. G
3. D	3. D	3. B	3. D
4. F	4. H	4. H	4. G
5. D	5. D	5. C	5. A
6. G	6. G	6. K	6. J
7. D	7. D	7. C	7. C
8. J	8. G	8. H	8. G
9. C	9. A	9. E	9. C
10. J	10. J	10. J	10. J
11. D	11. A	11. B	11. C
12. H	12. J	12. F	12. G
13. C	13. A	13. A	13. C
14. J	14. H	14. J	14. F
15. C	15. D	15. C	15. D
16. H	16. G	16. F	16. G
17. C	17. D	17. C	17. A
18. H	18. H	18. J	18. H
19. D	19. A	19. B	
20. F	20. G	20. K	
21. A		21. E	
22. J		22. J	
23. C		23. D	
24. G		24. J	
25. D		25. C	
26. H		26. K	
27. B		27. B	
28. G		28. H	
29. D		29. C	
30. J		30. H	

See Chapter 11 for strategic explanations of each of these practice questions.

10 SAT Practice Sets: Explanations

SAT Verbal Practice Set 1: Analogies

1. D A **LABORATORY** is by definition a place where you **EXPERIMENT**. A **graveyard** is by definition a place where you **inter**, or bury, people. Choices (A) and (B) are wrong because you can do things in a garage besides repair things, and you can do things on a beach besides sunbathe.

2. A To **EXONERATE** someone is to remove **BLAME** from that person. To **disinfect** something is to remove **contamination** from it. To divert a stream (B) is to change its course; to indict (C) someone is to assert that person's guilt. Choice (E) is a bridgeless pair.

3. C To **SCRUTINIZE** something is to **LOOK** at it very carefully. To **peruse** something is to **read** it very carefully. In (D), the word *importune* means the same thing as the word *plead*.

4. E A **GULLIBLE** person is easy to **DUPE** or fool. A **submissive** person is easy to **control**. In (A), a fallible person has a tendency to err; this is a different bridge. Choice (B) is a bridgeless pair. In (C), a dejected person is already disheartened. In (D), a headstrong person is difficult to coax.

5. C A **CONVERSATION** is carried on by two or more **INTERLOCUTORs**, the people who participate in a conversation. A **game** is carried on by two or more **players**. The other choices have different bridges. An orator (A) makes a speech and a doctor (E) makes a diagnosis. Choices (B) and (D) have weak bridges: a prosecutor can take part in a hearing, and a publisher can publish a novel.

6. B **ENTOMOLOGY** is the study of **INSECTS**. **Pedagogy** is the study of **education.** In each of the other choices, there is a connection between the two words, but not the same connection as in the stem pair.

7. A A **SKIRMISH** is a minor **BATTLE**. A **misdemeanor** is a minor **crime**.

8. A **FORENSIC** means "having to do with **LITIGATION**," or legal procedure (you've probably heard of "forensic medicine," medical procedure used in the investigation of a crime). **Maritime** means "having to do with the **sea**." Choice (D) may be tempting. But to be exemplary means to be ideal; it has nothing to do with an example. Choice (C) simply combines two words that are often paired, but have no necessary relation. In (B), euphoria is an example of a feeling. In (E), something illusory does not necessarily have to do with magic.

9. B To **FEIGN** is to give a false **IMPRESSION**. To **perjure** is to give false **testimony**. In (C), (D), and (E), the first word has connotations of falsehood, but it does not specifically mean falsifying the second word.

10. E A **POLEMIC** is a speech or piece of writing that advocates a particular point of view; by definition, it is not **IMPARTIAL**. Similarly, an **extrovert**, a sociable, outgoing person, is not **retiring** or shy and withdrawn. In (A), an antidote is curative. As for the other choices, discipline may or may not be harsh, a heretic may or may not be persecuted, and a defendant may or may not be guilty.

11. C A **SCAR** is the mark left by an **INJURY**. A **dent** is the mark left by a **collision**. In (E), blood is not a permanent mark, and it is not always the result of a fistfight.

12. B To **YAWN** is to display **BOREDOM**. To **pout** is to display **displeasure**. As for (A), one can react to any number of things; to react is not necessarily to show surprise.

13. E An **ACTOR**'s tryout is called an **AUDITION**. A **gymnast**'s audition is called a **tryout**. In each of the other choices, there is a valid bridge, but not the stem bridge. In (A), a debut is a singer's first performance.

14. E Something extremely **INTERESTING** is said to be **ABSORBING**. Someone extremely **affectionate** is said to be **doting**. In (A), the words *destitute* and *penniless* are roughly equal in intensity.

15. E A **FORGER** produces a false **SIGNATURE**. A **counterfeiter** produces a false **bill** or piece of currency. In (A), an embezzler might produce a false account, but to say so doesn't give a clear definition of what an embezzler is, whereas the bridge provides a precise definition of the stem and the correct answer. A plagiarist (B) steals material, but doesn't necessarily produce a false article. Choices (C) and (D) convey no sense of fraud.

16. E A **LEGEND** is the table of symbols and their meanings that you need to read a **MAP** (it might tell you, for example, that a star represents a capital city). A **key** is similarly used to interpret a **cipher** or code. In (A), you don't necessarily need a translation to read a story; you might already know the language in which the story is written.

17. A To **ALIENATE** is to impose **ESTRANGEMENT**, making people aliens or strangers. To **discommode** is to impose **inconvenience**. In (B), monks and nuns live a life of monasticism; these people are usually sequestered or separated from other people. But not everyone who is sequestered enters a life of monasticism (for example, juries are often sequestered). In (C), to palliate is to relieve boredom.

18. B Something **PUNGENT** or foul smelling is unpleasant to be **SNIFFED**. Something **prickly** is unpleasant to be **touched**. As for (C), something venomous does not necessarily work by being bitten.

19. A The path followed by a **SATELLITE** is its **ORBIT**. The path followed by a **sailboat** is its **course**. Most of the wrong answer choices provide words that may remind you of the stem words.

20. B To **DISCONCERT** is to cause **CONFUSION**. To **daunt** is to cause **discouragement**. Note that (D) is a bridgeless pair.

21. C A **RINK** is a place you go to **SKATE**. A **casino** is a place you go to **gamble**. You can compete at a track (E), but the bridge is a little vague.

22. A To **NIBBLE** is to **BITE** in little bits at a time. To **dab** is to **paint** in little bits at a time. As for (E), wading is quite different from swimming.

23. E Someone **PARCHED** is extremely **THIRSTY**. Someone **terrified** is extremely **scared**. Choice (C), *surly*, means "nasty, irritable"—so a surly person isn't necessarily boring.

24. B Something extremely or excessively **DEMONSTRATIVE** is described as **EFFUSIVE**. Something extremely or excessively **generous** is described as **lavish**. In (A), the words *biased* and *partisan* are at about the same level of intensity. As for (E), being devout doesn't necessarily mean being ethical.

25. C Someone **CREDULOUS** is easy to **CONVINCE**. Someone or something **accessible** is easy to **reach**. Something tortuous or twisted is hard to navigate (B). Something sodden is already soaked (E).

26. D When a liquid (such as blood) **COAGULATE**s, it forms a **CLOT**. When a liquid **freezes**, it forms **ice**. People can obstruct something by forming a blockade (C), but these words don't refer to changes that a liquid undergoes.

27. E To **RUE** is to feel **REGRET**. To **worry** is to feel **anxiety**.

28. D A **PITTANCE** is a small **WAGE**. A **trickle** is a small **stream**. As for (C), scorn is the opposite of admiration.

29. A A **FEINT** is a motion or gesture used to **DISTRACT** (think of a "fake" in basketball). A **preface** is used to **introduce**.

30. A As an **IDEA** develops, it's said to **GERMINATE**. As a **seed** develops, it's said to **sprout**. In (E), the spread of a virus does not refer to the development of an individual virus.

SAT Verbal Practice Set 2: Sentence Completions

1. C The phrase *proves difficult* is a clue: the two missing words have to be nearly opposite in meaning. Choice (C) is correct, because few posters would be **intact** if they were meant to be **destroyed**. None of the other choices makes sense: being returned would not stop something from being recognizable (A), being discarded would not necessarily stop something from being relevant (B), and so on.

2. E The words *long considered* and *finally* suggest contrast. The missing word is probably the opposite of "making some headway in its battle against extinction." Choice (E) **imperiled**, meaning "in danger," is the best answer. To be elusive (A) is to be hard to find; something that is prevalent (B) is common; to be combative (C) is to be eager to fight; and to be voracious (D) is to have a huge appetite.

3. A The sentence sets up a contrast between the situation before the invention of the tape recorder, and the situation after. We need a word that's the opposite of the word *paraphrased,* which means "expressed in different words." The answer is **verbatim**, which means "word for word."

4. A The phrase *encouraged hopes* suggests that the two missing words will be somewhat related in meaning. Choice (A) is the best answer, because we expect **a serious** novelist to use **subtle** characterizations. The other choices make less sense; in fact, it's not clear what accurate (C) or fictional (D) or authentic (E) characterizations would be. To be prolific (C) means to be highly productive; to be accomplished (D) means to be skillful or experienced; and to be reclusive (E) means to be unsociable.

5. C The missing word has to be related in meaning to *extended tenure.* **Longevity** (C) is the best choice. The words *acumen* (A) and *savvy* (B) both refer to having skill or knowledge. Decorum (D) is proper behavior, and celebrity (E) is fame.

6. D The word *although* indicates contrast: the two missing words have to be opposite in meaning. This is the case with **buoyant** (light hearted, cheerful) and **subdued** (quiet.) In (A), to be introverted is to be reserved, not outgoing. In (B), to be imperious is to be commanding, and to be incensed is to be angry.

7. C The phrase *failure to* establishes the negative tone of the sentence. An agency ought to fix or get rid of flawed policies. Possible answers for the first blank are (C) (to **rescind** is to remove, cancel) and (D) (to amend is to fix). Failure to do this is a bad thing, so we need a negative word for the second blank. The best choice is in (C); to be **lackadaisical** is to be careless or sloppy.

8. **D** Rapid turnover would tend to increase inconsistency, so we need a word that means *increased* or *worsened*. Something that is **exacerbated** is made worse, so (D) is the right choice.

9. **E** The word in the second blank has to relate in some logical way to "fear of causing leaves to fall," and the only word that does so is **durable**, which means "tough, not fragile." If the plant has become more **durable**, that should be a **relief** to those who were afraid of damaging it. In (A), consternation is concern or worry, and something that is amorphous is shapeless.

10. **C** Words such as *unchanging* and *eternal* provide a definition of the missing word, **static** (C). Something that is holistic (D) is functioning as a whole, and something that is homogeneous (E) is all of one kind. Neither of these words implies species being unchanging and no new species coming into existence.

11. **C** What claim would be belied or contradicted by a record of contributing to only one party? A claim of **impartiality**, of not favoring one side over the other.

12. **E** "Repeated breakdown of negotiations" would tend to support or **reinforce** the view that the sides "were not truly committed to" preventing or **averting** a military confrontation. In (A) and (D), the words *established* and *strengthened* fit the first blank, but the words *escalating* and *initiating* are wrong for the second blank. In (B), the word *avoiding* fits the second blank, but the word *undermined* is wrong for the first.

13. **B** The phrase *now that* suggests a similarity of tone between the two missing words, and the word *painful* tells us that the words will be negative. Only (B) provides a negative word for both blanks. A painful **decline** would indeed tend to cause budgetary **stringency** or tightness.

14. **B** Here you have to figure out the logic of the sentence. It doesn't make sense to have actors audition for a show that supposedly doesn't use actors, that tapes "real people in everyday situations." This is a contradiction (A) or **incongruity** (B). And if the show uses actors, then it doesn't really tape real people in everyday situations; it only **purports** (B) or claims (E) to do so. Choice (B) provides fitting answers for both blanks.

15. **B** Humans "can recognize that an alarm has been sounded only by observing the animals' behavior." In other words, humans can't hear the alarm themselves. It is **inaudible** to them.

16. **C** The word *not* indicates that the blanks have to contrast each other. **Variety** and **limited to** make sense in the sentence. Choice (D) also provides a contrast. But in the first place, it's unlikely that anyone has seriously believed that terrestrial life was extinguished with the dinosaurs (that would make it hard to explain where we came from); in the second place, the destruction of life has nothing directly to do with the preservation of fossils.

17. **D** The words *although* and *did not* indicate that the two missing words have to be similar in meaning. That is the case with **recant**, which is to renounce, and **abandoned**. Choices (C) and (E) provide pairs of near-opposites. The words in (A) are hardly related at all. In (B), *did not publicly acknowledge* contradicts *had been espousing*.

18. **A** Remember that the missing word has to relate logically to the rest of the sentence. The only thing we're told about snowflakes is that they're formed by snow crystals joining up with one another. The missing word probably therefore means "things made by things joining up with one another," and that's basically what **aggregations** means. Collages (E) are also compound structures, but they're artificial assemblies of things, not natural structures such as snowflakes. Junctures (B) are meetings, not things formed by meeting. Juggernauts (D) are things that crush whatever gets in front of them; snowflakes could hardly be described as juggernauts.

19. **E** The contrast here is between the most basic needs for food and drink and the "customs, knowledge, and environment" that relate to food. Thus we need a word such as *survival* (B) or ***sustenance*** (E) for the second blank. The words *mirrored* (A) and ***reflected*** (E) fit in the first blank. Only (E) works for both blanks. Something that is obviated (D) is made unnecessary.

20. **C** The word in the first blank has to relate in some logical way to the word *guidelines*. Either the architect considered guidelines necessary, and therefore refused the offer, or the architect considered the absence of guidelines necessary, and therefore agreed to the offer. Choice (C) fits the first of these predictions. In (A), *autonomy* would fit the second prediction, but *spurned* is the opposite of what we would need.

21. **D** The word in the first blank has to be similar in meaning to *controversy*: *belligerent* (C), ***scandalous*** (D), and *provocative* (E) would fit. The band wouldn't do this if they didn't find that the strategy worked, so *rewarding* (B) and ***effective*** (D) fit for the second blank. Only (D) fits for both blanks.

22. **B** The correct answer is implied by "numerous scribbled edits that cover even his supposed final drafts." In other words, Joyce attached great importance to **revision**.

23. **B** The key is that the players "now charge for their signatures." Either the fans who believe that the players are not greedy would be surprised or disappointed, or the fans who believe that the players are not "ungreedy" would have their belief confirmed. Choice (B) fits the former prediction.

24. **B** The words *though* and *absence* indicate contrast, so the missing word has to be nearly opposite in meaning to "isolation and the longing for connection." Choice (B), **fraternity** (brotherhood or fellowship), is the best choice. Choice (C) may be tempting, but the term *socialism* refers to a specific set of political and economic doctrines, not just to any sort of society.

25. **B** The part of the sentence after the semicolon pretty basically defines the missing word. The word is ***calculated***, meaning consciously planned. Something that is incendiary (A) is inflaming; if someone is being facetious (C), he is joking; a scrupulous (D) person is very upstanding and honest; and something that is impromptu (E) is unplanned.

26. **A** The word *but* after the comma indicates that the word in the second blank contrasts with *struggle*. ***Effortless*** (A) and *immediate* (D) are possibilities. The word *but* before the first blank means something like *mere*, so the word in the first blank has to suggest something small, a faint possibility of future greatness. ***Glimmers*** (A) fits the meaning.

27. **A** The word *although* indicates contrast, and the words *large number* and *mass* provide a clue to what's missing. We need something that means "different" for the first blank, and something that means "the same" for the second blank. This is basically what ***disparate*** and ***homogeneous*** mean.

28. **A** We need something here that goes with *heavy thoughts*. The word ***morose*** (A), meaning "gloomy," is the best choice.

29. **E** The demise, or death, of the protagonist presumably eliminated all possibility of a sequel. That's what ***precluded*** means.

30. **E** The phrase *is dubious* indicates contrast; the missing word has to contrast in meaning with *employed force*. The best answer is ***pacific*** (E), which means "peaceful."

SAT Verbal Practice Set 3: Critical Reading

Passage 1: Questions 1–9

James Weldon Johnson, the author of this autobiographical piece, does not just describe the experience he had watching the piano player playing ragtime; he also uses the scene as a jumping-off point from which to comment on the origin of ragtime (second paragraph), to disparage American musicians for refusing to accept ragtime (third paragraph), and to speculate on what the piano player could have amounted to under different circumstances (fourth paragraph).

1. C The author's initial impression of ragtime can be found in the first paragraph. He emphasizes how the beat demanded a physical response and meshed with the "dissonant harmonies," etcetera, to produce a "curious effect." Choice (C) is the correct answer. The only other choice that has anything to do with the first paragraph is (B). (B) is wrong because the audience is said to have applauded the singer's dance steps, not the ragtime music.

2. E Let's go through the choices one by one, keeping in mind that we're focusing exclusively on the first paragraph. Although the piano player is "master of a good deal of technique," choice (A) is too extreme to be correct. We know nothing in the first paragraph of the author's expectations of ragtime, so (B) is out, too. Choices (C), (D), and (E) are different interpretations of the author's description of the piano player's playing. While it is certainly true that ragtime has dissonant harmonies and jumps from one key to another, you cannot infer from this that ragtime violates every rule of musical composition (C) or that it has no melody at all (D). Choice (E) is correct since the narrator notes that "the accents fell in the most unexpected places."

3. A In the context of the phrase *questionable resorts about Memphis and St. Louis,* the word *questionable* means "disreputable" (A).

4. C Choice (B) might have jumped right out at you since the narrator's perspective in the first paragraph is that of a mesmerized spectator. But his perspective in the second and third paragraphs changes. He steps back from the description of his first encounter with ragtime and begins to discuss ragtime's history, appeal, and impact on the contemporary musical scene. Therefore, (C) is the correct answer.
Choice (A) is wrong because the author is not impartial; he thinks highly of ragtime. Watching ragtime being played is not a "unique experience," which eliminates (D). As for (E), the narrator says nothing about his youth in the second and third paragraphs.

5. A Put the reference to the "theory of the universe" in the context of the second paragraph. The author says that the players who first developed ragtime knew "no more of the theory of music than they did of the theory of the universe"—in other words, they had no formal music education—but their natural talent guided them. Since they had no conventional schooling in music, you can infer that their invention, ragtime, was "an unconventional musical form" (A).
Choices (B) and (E) are the close wrong answers. Choice (B) is out because the originators of ragtime could have been interested in other people's music even though they had no formal music education. Choice (E) is wrong since it misunderstands the overall point of the paragraph; the author is not interested in making general statements about the relationship between education and artistic success. Choice (C) is the sort of choice you can rule out by common sense; no SAT question is going to have a correct answer that downplays the importance of academics. Finally, there is no evidence that indicates (D) could be true.

6. C The narrator argues in the third paragraph that ragtime should not be ignored or dismissed by American musicians just because it is popular. All great music, he states, comes from the hearts of the people. In other words, he is saying that the "conservative and condescending attitude" of the American musicians is misguided (C).
There is no evidence in the third paragraph to support any of the other choices. Choice (B) is perhaps the most tempting, since the author talks in the third paragraph about ragtime's popularity in Europe, but it seems as though American musicians *do* know about ragtime's popularity and find it distasteful.

7. E This question is a follow-up to the previous one. As we've said, the author's argument in the third paragraph is that music should not be dismissed by serious musicians just

because it happens to be popular. Choice (E) paraphrases this idea.

Choice (A) stretches the author's argument way too far. Choice (B) is wrong because the author does not try to establish criteria for musical greatness. Choice (C) focuses too narrowly on the author's mention of the fact that ragtime was popular abroad. Choice (D) is clearly wrong, since ragtime gained popularity even though it had not been "taken up by a musical master."

8. **D** The narrator poses to himself the question about what might have become of the piano player had he been properly trained, and then answers himself by saying "perhaps he wouldn't have done anything at all." The narrator goes on to say that even if the piano player achieved some success as an imitator of the greats or as an innovator, he still would not have been as "delightful" as he was playing ragtime. Thus the statement that "perhaps he wouldn't have done anything at all" can best be interpreted as a "recognition that the piano player might have wasted his talent" (D) had he been formally trained.

Choices (A) and (B) are wrong because the narrator thinks highly of the piano player's skill even if that skill is not at the level of genius or particularly disciplined. Choices (C) and (E) are both far too broad and too negative to be the correct answer.

9. **C** The correct answer here is going to be a paraphrase of the idea that no matter how far the piano player would have gone if trained, he would not have been as delightful as he was as a ragtime player. Choice (C) is the choice you're looking for.

Choice (E) is the most tempting wrong answer, since the author's statements at the end of the passage can easily be misconstrued to mean that the piano player could never have been more than mediocre as a classical artist. However, *never* is too strong a word here; the narrator is not, and cannot be, as sure as that. So this choice is wrong.

Paired Passages 1 and 2: Questions 10–21

Passage 1

The position of the author of this passage starts to become clear in the second paragraph: she likes design museums and is willing to defend them against critics. She thinks design museums are not just advertisements for new technology but places where new products can be honored. Design museums, she asserts, are comfortable for visitors because the exhibits provide a lot of information about the objects displayed—information you wouldn't get in an art gallery. Another advantage of design museums, she says, is that their curators have more freedom than do the curators of public art galleries.

Passage 2

The second author does not hold technical and design museums in the same high regard as the first author does, as you soon find out in this passage. The second author complains about several things:

- Technical museums concentrate on present technology and ignore historical study and research.
- They glorify machines and industrialization when these things do harm as well as good.
- They do not (and cannot safely and imaginatively) show machinery in action.

The second author does admit at the very end, however, that the public has shown a healthy curiosity about science and technology.

10. **A** To say that something is readily available is to say that it is easily available. Choice (A) is the correct answer.

11. **D** The first author says that department store windows try to sell the public something, whereas design exhibits try to give the public an appreciation of the aesthetic value of something. Choice (D) paraphrases this idea. Choices (A), (B), and (E) can be readily eliminated. Be careful with (C), though. Even though design museums focus on the artistic qualities of products, it does not automatically follow from this that design museums are not concerned at all with the commercial aspects of a successful product. Choice (C) is wrong.

12. **B** In the third paragraph of Passage 1, the author argues that design museums make visitors feel comfortable because the exhibits illustrate the purpose behind the look and function of the displayed object; art gallery exhibits, by contrast, provide no such information. From this argument you can infer that the first author thinks that visitors want to be informed about the object they are viewing. This makes (B) correct.

There is no evidence to support any of the other choices, all of which are misreadings of the third paragraph. Choice (A) can be eliminated as soon as you see "hostile towards . . . abstract art." Choices (C) and (D) contradict the author, who says that visitors are not confused by technological exhibits since they are familiar and informative. Choice (E) is an unwarranted inference based on the author's statement that design exhibits point out the artistic qualities of the displayed items; you cannot conclude from this that most museum visitors undervalue the artistic worth of household items.

13. **B** Since you just reviewed the third paragraph for the last question, the answer to this one should jump right out at you. The difference between a design museum exhibit and an art gallery exhibit is that a design museum exhibit provides you with information about the object being displayed, whereas the art gallery exhibit does not. Choice (B) is correct. None of the other choices has any basis in the passage.

14. **C** After mentioning the collection of Zippo lighters, etcetera, in London's Design Museum, the first author says that curators of design museums have options that are far less rigorous, conventionalized, and preprogrammed than those open to curators of art galleries. This is a fancy way of saying that the curators of design museums have more freedom to put together unconventional collections, choice (C).

Choice (E) is the tempting wrong answer to this question. It's wrong because it goes too far; the design curators have freedom, but not, as far as we know, the freedom to satisfy "their own personal whims."

15. **E** In the very last sentence of Passage 1, the author says that design museums ("the display of postmodern playthings or quirky . . . vacuum cleaners. . . .") are better able to represent humor than art galleries ("an exhibition of Impressionist landscapes"). The author is emphasizing the contrast between design museum and art gallery exhibits (E).

Choice (B) is the trickiest wrong answer. It misses the point of the last sentence because the author is not comparing "postmodern playthings" with Impressionist art; she is comparing the different ways these two things are exhibited.

16. **A** The answer to this question will be the choice that summarizes the first paragraph of Passage 2. Since the author spends the first paragraph complaining that design museums ignore the historical aspect of technology, choice (A) is the best answer.

Choice (B) focuses too narrowly on the last part of the paragraph, where the author says that since industry builds the exhibits, curators may be dispensed with. This is not the underlying difficulty referred to at the beginning of the paragraph. The other choices have nothing to do with the first paragraph.

17. **A** The second author's point in the second paragraph of Passage 2 is that industrialization and "progress" have not been all good and should be considered critically, but technology museums just glorify them. He mentions industrialization's harm to the environment and ecology to support this point and to encourage "a critical response" to technology, so (A) is correct.

Choice (B) is wrong because it's too negative even for this author. Choice (C) is a distortion of a detail at the end of the second paragraph, while (D) is a distorted idea from the third paragraph. Choice (E) is out because the second author doesn't do any praising in the second paragraph.

18. **D** Put the phrase in context. The second author says that displayed machinery should be in action, not in "sculptured repose," as is the case with the machinery in technology museums. To the second author,

you can infer, the "sculptured repose" is meaningless and unrealistic, choice (D).

Choice (A) is out because the author is not condemning the curators for poor planning; in fact, the author admits that displaying operating machinery would be extremely difficult. Choice (B) can be eliminated because it's too extreme. The author never says which—if any—of the problems he discusses is the "greatest problem." Choices (C) and (E) miss the author's point and the context in which the phrase *sculptured repose* is found.

19. D Choices (A), (B), (C), and (E) are common synonyms for *command,* but none of them works in the context of the phrase *command the imagination, ingenuity, and manual dexterity it requires.* Only choice (D) can do the job.

20. A Predict the answer to the question before you go looking through the choices. You know that the second author thinks that technology has had a lot of negative consequences, so you can assume that he would point this out in response to the first author's optimistic statement. This makes (A) the best answer.

We don't know what the second author's position on art galleries is, so (B) is out. Choice (C) comes from Passage 2 but is irrelevant to the question asked in the stem. Choices (D) and (E) contradict specific things the second author says in the course of Passage 2.

21. B In questions like this one, wrong answer choices are often statements that one author, but not both, would agree with. For example, the second author would probably agree with choice (A) and would definitely agree with (D) and (E), but the first author would most likely not agree with any of these three. That narrows the field to (B) and (C). Choice (C) is a very general statement that really has no basis in either passage. Choice (B), on the other hand, is an idea that can be found in both passages, so it is the correct answer.

SAT Math Practice Set 4: Regular Math

1. D The key to this problem is to recognize the relationship between the two sums. Take it step-by-step and write out the first few terms of each sum:

$A = 1{,}001 + 1{,}002 + 1{,}003 + \ldots + 1{,}100$

$B = 2{,}001 + 2{,}002 + 2{,}003 + \ldots + 2{,}100$

Note that each of the 100 terms in A has a counterpart in B that is 1,000 greater. So $B = A + 100(1{,}000)$. Therefore $B - A = 100(1{,}000) = 100{,}000$.

2. B An integer that's divisible by 6 has at least one 2 and one 3 in its prime factorization. An integer that's divisible by 9 has at least two 3s in its prime factorization. Therefore, an integer that's divisible by both 6 and 9 has at least one 2 and two 3s in its prime factorization. That means it's divisible by 2, 3, $2 \times 3 = 6$, $3 \times 3 = 9$, and $2 \times 3 \times 3 = 18$. It's *not* necessarily divisible by 12 or 36, each of which includes *two* 2s in its prime factorization.

You could also do this one by picking numbers. Think of a common multiple of 6 and 9 and use it to eliminate some options. $6 \times 9 = 54$ is an obvious common multiple—and it's not divisible by 12 or 36, but it is divisible by 18. The *least* common multiple of 6 and 9 is 18, which is also divisible by 18. It looks like every common multiple of 6 and 9 is also a multiple of 18.

3. D To convert a fraction to a decimal, you divide the denominator into the numerator. Clearly you don't have time to take the division out to 100 places after the decimal point. There must be a pattern you can take advantage of. Start dividing and continue just until you see what the pattern is:

$$11\overline{)4.000000\ldots} = .363636\ldots$$

The first, third, fifth, etcetera, digits are 3; and the second, fourth, etcetera, digits are 6. In other words, every digit in an odd-numbered position is a 3 and every digit in an even-numbered position is a 6. The 100th position is an even-numbered one, so the 100th digit is a 6.

4. A To find the average of three numbers—even if they're algebraic expressions—add them up and divide by 3:

$$\text{Average} = \frac{(2x+5)+(5x-6)+(-4x+2)}{3}$$
$$= \frac{3x+1}{3}$$
$$= x + \frac{1}{3}$$

5. A Don't just average the old average and the last test score—that would give the last score as much weight as all the other scores combined. The best way to deal with changing averages is to use the sums. Use the old average to figure out the total of the first six scores:

Sum of first six scores = (6)(83) = 498

Then add the seventh score and divide:

$$\frac{498+97}{7} = \frac{595}{7} = 85$$

6. A The overall average is not simply the average of the two average ages. Because there are a lot more females than males, the average age of the females carries a lot more weight than the average age of the males, and the overall average will be closer to 10.2 than to 11.2.

This problem's easiest to deal with if you pick particular numbers for females and males. You could just say that there are 80 females and 20 males. The sum of the ages of the females would then be 80 times 10.2, or 816. The sum of the ages of the males would be 20 times 11.2, or 224. The sum of the ages of all the students, female and male, is 816 + 224 = 1,040. The average age is 1,040 divided by 100, or 10.4.

7. C Multiply the coefficients and add the exponents:

$$3x^2 \cdot 5x^3 = 3 \cdot 5 \cdot x^{2+3} = 15x^5$$

8. E Square the coefficient and square the radical:

$$\left(5\sqrt{3}\right)^2 = 5^2 \cdot \left(\sqrt{3}\right)^2 = 25 \cdot 3 = 75$$

9. D Plug in $x = -5$ and see what you get:

$$2x^2 - 6x + 5 = 2(-5)^2 - 6(-5) + 5$$
$$= 2 \cdot 25 - (-30) + 5$$
$$= 50 + 30 + 5$$
$$= 85$$

10. B Turn the denominator into a simple fraction, and then flip it:

$$\frac{1}{1+\frac{1}{x}} = \frac{1}{\frac{x}{x}+\frac{1}{x}} = \frac{1}{\frac{x+1}{x}} = \frac{x}{x+1}$$

11. E Use FOIL:

$$(3x+4)(4x-3)$$
$$= (3x \cdot 4x) + \left(3x \cdot -3\right) + (4 \cdot 4x) + \left(4 \cdot -3\right)$$
$$= 12x^2 - 9x + 16x - 12$$
$$= 12x^2 + 7x - 12$$

12. B First solve for m, and then divide by 3:

$$\frac{m}{2} = 15$$
$$m = 15 \cdot 2 = 30$$
$$\frac{m}{3} = \frac{30}{3} = 10$$

13. D You could solve for k and then subtract the result from 3, but it's far easier—and quicker—if you recognize that the $3 - k$ you're looking for is the negative of the $k - 3$ that appears on the left side of the equation. All you really have to do is multiply both sides of the equation by –1:

$$k - 3 = -\frac{5}{3}$$
$$-1(k-3) = -1\left(-\frac{5}{3}\right)$$
$$3 - k = \frac{5}{3}$$

14. E Use the points where the line crosses the axes—(–1, 0) and (0, 2)—to find the slope:

$$\text{Slope} = \frac{y_2 - y_1}{x_2 - x_1} = \frac{2-0}{0-(-1)} = 2$$

The y-intercept is 2. Now plug m = 2 and b = 2 into the slope-intercept equation form:

$$y = mx + b$$
$$y = 2x + 2$$

15. C The measures of the interior angles of a triangle add up to 180, so add the two given measures and subtract the sum from 180. The difference will be the measure of the third angle:

$$45 + 70 = 115$$
$$180 - 115 = 65$$

16. C If the two unknown side lengths are integers, and the sum of the two lengths has to be greater than 7, then the least amount the two unknown sides could add up to would be 8, which would make the perimeter 7 + 8 = 15.

17. D The area of a triangle is equal to one-half the base times the height:

$$\text{Area} = \frac{1}{2}(\text{base})(\text{height})$$
$$36 = \frac{1}{2}(9)(\text{height})$$
$$36 = \frac{9}{2}h$$
$$h = \frac{2}{9} \cdot 36 = 8$$

18. B Find the lengths of BC and the indicated altitude, and you'll have what you need to calculate the area. BC is composed of one leg of a 45-45-90 triangle and one leg of a 30-60-90 triangle. The altitude is the leg that the two right triangles share. Use the given length of AB to find the legs of the 45-45-90, and then use the leg that the two triangles share to find the other leg of the 30-60-90.

$$\text{leg of } 45\text{-}45\text{-}90 = \frac{\text{hypotenuse}}{\sqrt{2}} = \frac{2}{\sqrt{2}} = \sqrt{2}$$

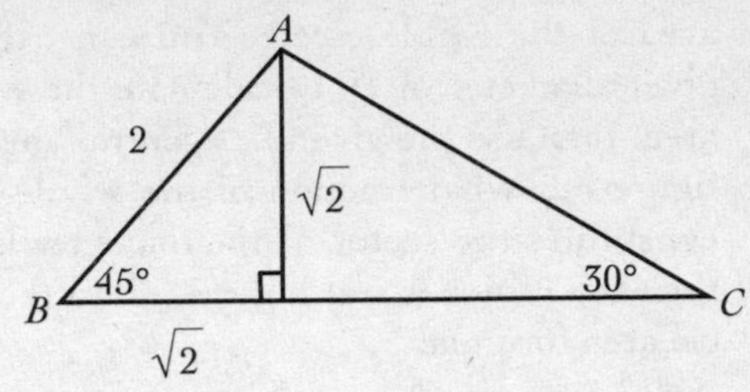

$$\text{Longer leg of } 30\text{-}60\text{-}90 = (\text{shorter leg}) \times \sqrt{3}$$
$$= \sqrt{2} \times \sqrt{3} = \sqrt{6}$$

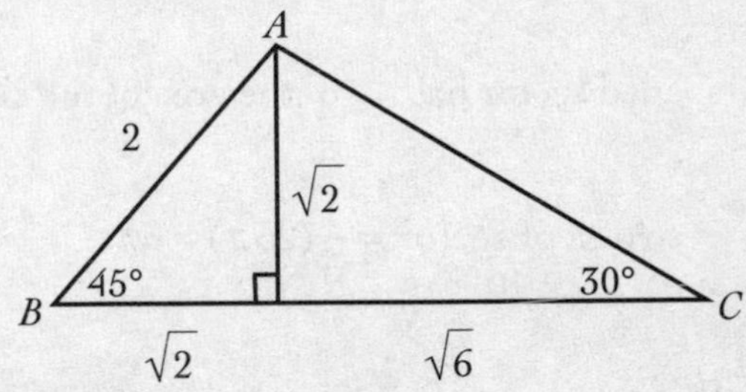

Now you know that the length of base AC is $\sqrt{2} + \sqrt{6}$ and the height is $\sqrt{2}$. Plug those lengths into the triangle area formula:

$$\text{Area} = \frac{1}{2}(\text{base})(\text{height})$$
$$= \frac{1}{2}\left(\sqrt{2} + \sqrt{6}\right)\left(\sqrt{2}\right)$$
$$= \frac{\left(\sqrt{2} \times \sqrt{2}\right) + \left(\sqrt{6} \times \sqrt{2}\right)}{2}$$
$$= \frac{2 + \sqrt{12}}{2}$$
$$= \frac{2 + 2\sqrt{3}}{2} = 1 + \sqrt{3}$$

19. B Use the circumference to find the radius, then use the radius to find the area:

$$\text{Circumference} = 2\pi r$$
$$2\pi = 2\pi r$$
$$1 = r$$
$$\text{Area} = \pi r^2$$
$$\text{Area} = \pi$$

20. **B** Think of the area of a sector as part of the area of the whole circle. You can use the given diameter of 10 to calculate the whole area, then use the given 72° central angle to figure out what fraction of the whole area constitutes the sector. If the diameter is 10, then the radius is 5. Plug $r = 5$ into the circle area formula:

$$\text{Area} = \pi r^2 = \pi(5)^2 = 25\pi$$

The whole area is 25π. The 72° central angle is $\frac{1}{5}$ of a complete 360° rotation, so the shaded sector has $\frac{1}{5}$ of the area of the circle:

$$\text{Area of sector} = \frac{1}{5}(25\pi) = 5\pi$$

21. **D** Don't try to calculate the areas of these two oddly shaped regions. Look for the familiar. If you find the area of the semicircle and subtract from it the area of the triangle, you will be left with the area of the shaded regions. You are given the lengths of two sides of the triangle, but side *XZ*, which is also the diameter of the circle, is unknown. Because *XZ* is a diameter, triangle *XYZ* is a right triangle—a multiple of the 3-4-5 Pythagorean triple, in fact. *YZ* is 4 × 3, and *XY* is 4 × 4, so side *XZ* must be 4 × 5 or 20. Since the diameter of the circle is 20, its radius is 10, making its area 100π. So the area of the semicircle is half this, or 50π. The area of the triangle is $\frac{12 \times 16}{2}$ = 96. So the area of the shaded regions is 50π – 96. This doesn't match any of the choices, so rearrange it. Factoring a 2 out of each term the expression becomes 2(25π – 48), choice (D).

22. **D** A square with area 16 has sides of length 4. Therefore the largest circle that could possibly be cut from such a square would have a diameter of 4.

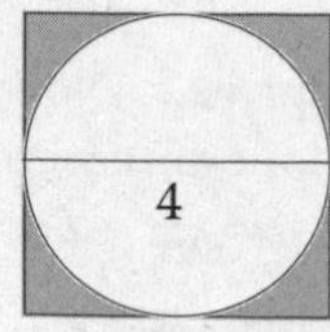

Such a circle would have a radius of 2, making its area 4π. So the amount of felt left after cutting such a circle from one of the squares of felt would be 16 – 4π, or 4(4 – π). There are eight such squares, so the total area of the left over felt is 8 × 4 (4 – π) = 32(4 – π).

23. **B** The volume of a cube is equal to an edge cubed, so $e^3 = 64$ and each edge of the cube has length 4. If the cube is sliced horizontally in two, each of the resulting solids will have two sides of length 4, and one of length 2. So when they are glued together, the resulting figure will have one edge of length 2, one of length 4, and one of length 4 + 4 or 8.

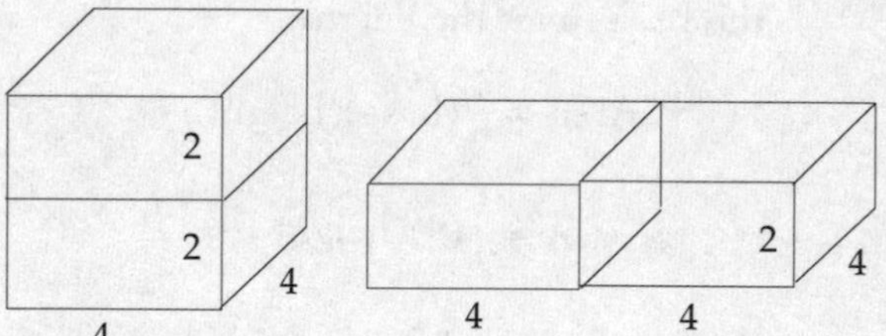

The surface area is the sum of the areas of the solid's six faces. The top and bottom each have area 8 × 4 = 32, the front and back each have area 8 × 2 = 16, and each side has area 4 × 2 = 8. So the surface area of the new solid is 2(32) + 2(16) + 2(8) = 64 + 32 + 16 = 112.

24. **C** To get Vito's rate in pages per hour, take the 96 pages and divide by the time in hours. The time is given as "2 hours and 40 minutes." Forty minutes is $\frac{2}{3}$ of an hour, so

you can express Vito's time as $2\frac{2}{3}$ hours, or $\frac{8}{3}$ hours:

$$\text{Pages per hour} = \frac{96 \text{ pages}}{\frac{8}{3} \text{ hours}}$$

$$= 96 \times \frac{3}{8} = 36$$

25. B This is an average rate problem, so don't just average the two rates. Instead, you have to use total distance and total time to find the average rate. First, pick a distance that is easy to use. For instance, since the speeds for the two halves of the trip are 40 and 60 miles per hour, 120 is an easy number to work with. Using 120 miles as the distance to the store, it would take $\frac{120}{40}$, or three hours to go to the store and $\frac{120}{60}$, or two hours to return. Thus, it takes five hours to complete a round trip of 240 miles. Now find the rate:

$$\text{Average rate} = \frac{\text{distance}}{\text{time}} = \frac{240}{5} = 48$$

26. E In order to find the number of possibilities, multiply the number of possibilities in each step. In other words, there are three routes from Bay City to Riverville and four routes from Riverville to Straitstown. Therefore, there are 3 × 4 = 12 different routes from Bay City to Straitstown. There are three more routes from Straitstown to Frog Pond, so there are 12 × 3 = 36 total routes from Bay City to Frog Pond.

27. C According to the definition, $x ♣ = \frac{x}{4} - \frac{x}{6}$. Set that equal to 3 and solve for x:

$$\frac{x}{4} - \frac{x}{6} = 3$$

$$12\left(\frac{x}{4} - \frac{x}{6}\right) = 12(3)$$

$$3x - 2x = 36$$

$$x = 36$$

28. C Pick numbers. If you let a = 100 gallons, then there are 40 gallons of pineapple juice and 60 gallons of orange juice. You must add enough orange juice so that the 40 gallons of pineapple juice is 25 percent of the total, so there must be 160 gallons of punch total. This means you must add 60 gallons of orange juice to the punch. Now plug a = 100 into the each of the answer choices and eliminate any answer choice that does not equal 60. The only choice that equals 60 is (C):

$$\frac{3 \times 100}{5} = 60$$

29. C Probability equals the number of favorable outcomes over the number of total outcomes. In this case, the favorable outcome is that the chosen sock will be black. Since there are 12 black socks, there are 12 favorable outcomes. The number of total outcomes is the total number of socks; 6 + 12 + 14 = 32, so there are 32 total outcomes. The probability is $\frac{12}{32}$, which can be reduced to $\frac{3}{8}$.

30. A The easiest way to do this problem is to subtract Bill's money from the total of the money that Jim and Bill have. Doing this gives you $15 - 4 = 11$. However, the problem states that they have LESS THAN 15 dollars. Therefore, Jim must have less than 11 dollars. Of I, II, and III, the only value that is less than 11 is I, so the answer must be (A).

To solve this problem algebraically, set up an inequality where J is Jim's money and B is Bill's money:

$$J + B < 15 \text{ where } B = 4$$
$$J + 4 < 15$$
$$J < 11$$

Again, be wary of the fact that this is an inequality, *not* an equation.

SAT Math Practice Set 5: Quantitative Comparisons

1 A Don't calculate. Compare piece by piece. The first fraction in Column A is greater than the first fraction in Column B, and the second fraction in Column A is greater than the second fraction in Column B. Therefore the sum in Column A is also greater.

2. A Don't calculate. Compare Column A to a percent of 34 that's easy to find. Think of 52 percent as just a bit more than 50 percent, or $\frac{1}{2}$. Fifty-two percent of 34, then, is just a bit more than half of 34, so it's more than 17.

3. A The key to this problem is knowing how to find the median and mode of the scores. The mode is the value occurring most often, which is 93 for this set of scores. The median is the middle value, so the first thing you have to do is to rearrange the scores into numerical order:

82, 85, 88, 90, 93, 93, 94, 98

Now take the middle value. Since there is an even number of scores, you'll have to take the average of the two middle scores for the median. In this case, the two middle scores are 90 and 93. $90 + 93 = 183$, which when divided by 2 is 91.5. Therefore, the mode, 93, is greater than the median, 91.5, and Column A is greater than Column B.

4. D This problem features a couple of pitfalls that you must be aware of. The first of these comes when you are calculating the value of a^4 in terms of b. Just because the power of a increases by two from the centered information to Column A, it does not mean that the power of b will increase by 2 as well. In fact, since $a^4 = (a^2)^2$, it is equal to $(b^3)^2 = b^6$. Therefore, the columns are not necessarily equal. Knowing that $a^4 = b^6$ allows you to compare the two columns in terms of b, making things much easier. The second pitfall is that, on the surface, it appears that Column A must be larger because $b^6 > b^5$, and if b is greater than 1 you would be right. But what if $b = 1$? The two columns would be equal. What if $b = .25$? Column B would be greater. Since there is more than one possible relationship, the answer is (D).

5. A Make the columns look more alike. First, add the terms in Column A, giving you $8\sqrt{x}$. Then break Column B into parts. $\sqrt{8x}$ is the same as $\sqrt{8} \times \sqrt{x}$. Now it's easier to compare the two columns. They both have $\sqrt{x}$, so it's the coefficients that make the difference. Since 8 is greater than $\sqrt{8}$, Column A is greater than Column B.

6. B Expand Column A to make it look more like Column B. Distribute the 3 and you get $3x - 6$. No matter what x is, subtracting 6 from $3x$ will leave you with less than subtracting 4 from $3x$.

7. B If you recognize the expression in Column A as the factorization of $n^2 - 9$, you'll quickly realize that Column B is greater. If you didn't recognize the difference of squares, you could have used FOIL to multiply out Column A and make the comparison.

8. D It looks at first glance like B and C divide the segment into three equal pieces. But check the mathematics of the situation to be sure. You're given that $AC = BD$:

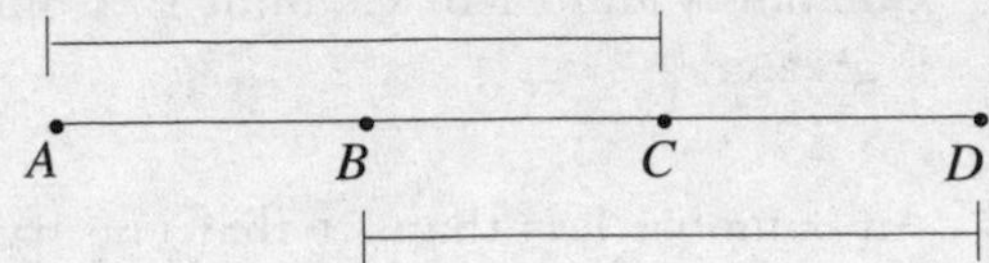

What can you deduce from that? You can subtract BC from both equal lengths and you'll end up with another equality: $AB = CD$. But what about BC? Does it have to be the same as AB and CD? No. The diagram could be resketched like this:

Now you can see that it's possible for AC and BD to be equal but for BC to be longer than AB. It's also possible for BC to be shorter:

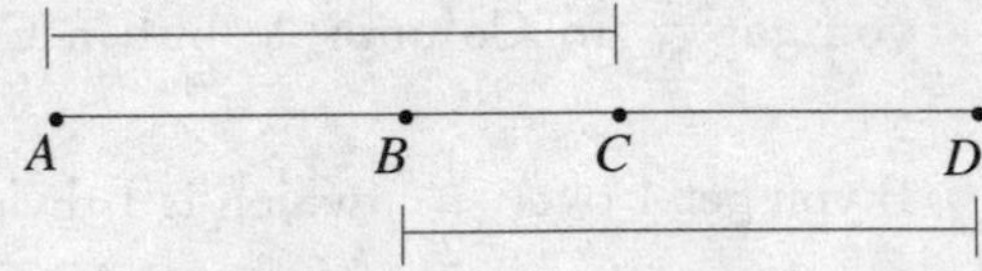

More than one relationship is possible, so the answer is (D).

9. A The area of the circle is $\pi r^2 = \pi(3)^2 = 9\pi$. The area of the rectangle is 9×3. Don't think of it as 27; it's easier to compare in the form 9×3. π is more than 3, so 9π is more than 9×3.

10. A This is a diagramless geometry problem. The key is to sketch a diagram. Draw a circle and segment AB. AB is a chord that passes through the center, so it's a diameter:

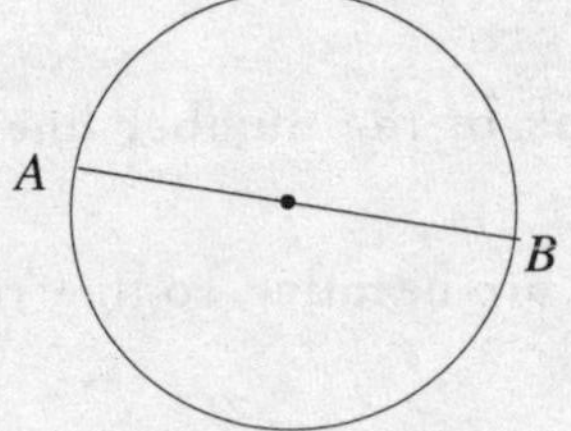

Now think about where to put segment CD. It's another chord, and because it's parallel to AB, it cannot be a diameter:

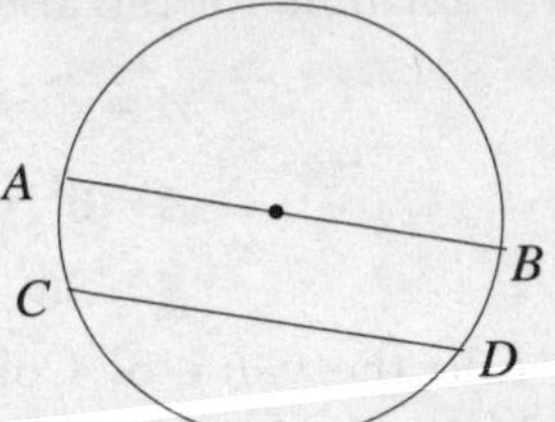

A diameter is the longest possible chord of a circle, so $AB > CD$.

11. D This is a diagramless geometry problem. The key is to sketch a diagram, but remember that there may be more than one way to sketch it. It's tempting to think of the segments as aligned like this:

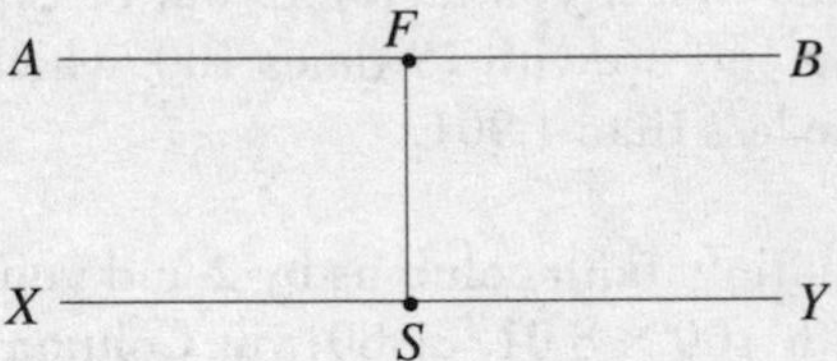

In this case the length of FS is the same as the perpendicular distance 3. Nothing in the given information, however, precludes a more skewed arrangement, like this:

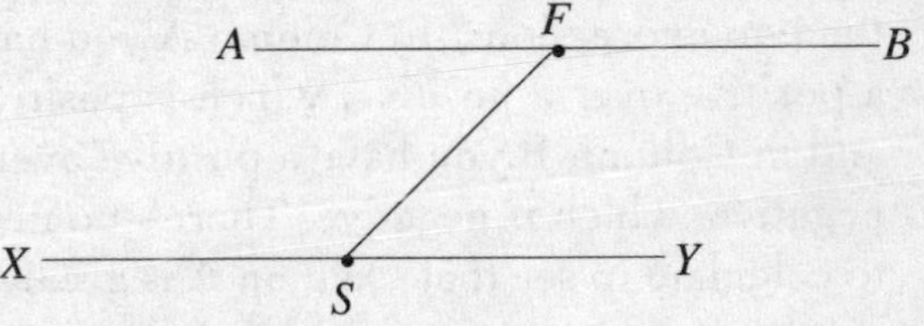

This time the length of FS is *greater* than the perpendicular distance. Therefore, the columns could be equal, or Column A could be greater, so the answer is (D).

12. **C** The first step in this problem is finding the values you must compare. Column A equals the area of a square with side 6, so plug 6 into the formula for the area of a square:

$$A = s^2$$
$$A = 6^2$$
$$A = 36$$

Now find the value of Column B by plugging 9 into the formula for the perimeter of a square:

$$P = 4s$$
$$P = 4(9)$$
$$P = 36$$

Since the columns are equal, the answer is (C).

13. **B** Note that if you factor 19 out of Column A you end up with 19 times 100, which is just one less than 1,901.

14. **C** Multiply both columns by 2 and you end up with 100×8.01, or 801, in Column A, and you also end up with 801 in Column B.

15. **A** Just look at the number of negative signs in each column, use what you know about numbers, and you won't have to evaluate the two expressions. In Column A you have a positive over a positive, which is positive, and in Column B you have a positive over a negative, which is negative. There's no need to calculate to see that Column A is greater.

16. **A** As long as you remember that $\sqrt{5 \times 4} = 20$, you should be fine. Since $3 = \sqrt{9}$, and 20 is greater than 9, clearly Column A is greater.

17. **A** You can square both columns since they're both positive. Column A becomes $\left(\sqrt{48}\right)^2 = 48$. Column B becomes $\left(4\sqrt{2}\right)^2 = \left(4^2\right)\left(\sqrt{2}\right)^2 = (16)(2) = 32$. Since 48 > 32, Column A is greater than Column B.

18. **B** Since –1 is further to the right on the number line than –2, –1 is greater.

19. **A** Subtract x from both columns to get 0 in Column A and –1 in Column B. Column A is greater.

20. **B** Any number less than –1 that you try for x will give you a value between –1 and 0 for $\frac{1}{x}$ in Column B.

21. **A** The question is simply asking: "If a number is greater than its square, does that number have to be positive?" Clearly the number cannot be negative, because any negative number squared will yield a positive result. In fact, the only numbers that are greater than their squares are the numbers between 0 and 1, all of which are positive.

22. **D** Try a few numbers. Plugging in $\frac{1}{2}$ for x, you get $\frac{1}{2}$ in Column A, but in Column B you get 1 over $\frac{1}{2}$, which is 1 divided by $\frac{1}{2}$, which is 2. Here Column B is greater. But when you plug in a negative number, things change. Plugging in $-\frac{1}{2}$ gives you $-\frac{1}{2}$ in Column A, and 1 over $-\frac{1}{2}$, which is the same as –2, in Column B. More than one relationship exists, so the answer is (D).

23. **B** Think of the number line. Both $\frac{-3}{2}$ and $\frac{-1}{2}$ are negative, so they're both to the left of zero. But $\frac{-3}{2}$ is further to the left (between –1 and –2), so it's smaller.

24. **C** It wouldn't take terribly long to calculate this one, but it's even faster just to note that the numbers are the same except for the placement of the decimal points, but that the two products have the same number of decimal places.

25. **D** These two quantities are reciprocals, so when Column A is greater than 1, Column B is less than 1, and vice versa. Column A will be greater than 1, and consequently greater than Column B, when $99x$ is greater than 100—in other words, when x is greater than $\frac{100}{99}$. On the other hand, Column A will be less than 1, and consequently less than Column B, when x is *less* than $\frac{100}{99}$. And of course the columns will be equal when $x = \frac{100}{99}$. More than one relationship is possible, so the answer is (D).

26. **C** Do the same thing to both columns. Divide by $23xyz$ (which is allowable because $23xyz$ is positive) and you're left with $50 \times 14 = 700$ in Column A and $100 \times 7 = 700$ in Column B.

27. **A** Add c to both columns and you end up comparing a and b. The centered information tells you straight out that a is greater.

28. **D** Reexpress both columns. In each case you can turn 1 into $\frac{1+y}{1+y}$. Column A, then, becomes $\frac{1+y}{1+y} - \frac{y}{1+y}$, which is equal to $\frac{1+y-y}{1+y}$, or $\frac{1}{1+y}$. Column B becomes $\frac{1+y}{1+y} - \frac{1}{1+y}$, which is equal to $\frac{1+y-1}{1+y}$, or $\frac{y}{1+y}$. Now both columns have the same positive denominator, so the larger quantity will be the one with the larger numerator. (You could think of it as multiplying both columns by the positive quantity $1 + y$.) All you have to do now is compare 1 to y. Which is bigger? You don't know. All you know is that y is positive, but because it could be less than, more than, or even equal to 1, the answer is (D).

29. **D** Use what you know about x and y to figure out how big and how small the value of $x + y$ can be. Don't assume that x and y are integers. That would make $x = 15$ and $y = 19$, and then the columns would be equal. But x might be less than 15, perhaps 14.5, and y might less than 19, perhaps 18.5. In that case Column A would be greater. (It's also possible for $x + y$ to be *greater* than 34.) More than one relationship is possible, so the answer is (D).

30. D Pick numbers. Try 1 for a and 2 for b. That would give you $\frac{1}{1}+\frac{1}{2}=1\frac{1}{2}$ in Column A and $\frac{1}{1+2}=\frac{1}{3}$ in Column B. In this case Column A is greater. Now try numbers from a different category, such as negatives. If you take $a = -1$ and $b = -2$, you get $\frac{1}{-1}+\frac{1}{-2}=-1\frac{1}{2}$ in Column A and $\frac{1}{(-1)+(-2)}=-\frac{1}{3}$ in Column B. This time Column B is greater, so the answer is (D).

SAT Math Practice Set 6: Grid-Ins

1. **48**
To solve this problem, you have to figure out how many cycles are completed after 143 flashes. This is done by dividing the total number of flashes (143) by the number of flashes in one cycle (3). 143 ÷ 3 = 47 with a remainder of 2. Since the red light is the first to flash in each cycle, there is a 48th red flash, the 142nd flash overall, so the number of red flashes in the first 143 flashes is 48.

2. **11, 13, 17, 19, 23, 29, 31, 37, 41, 43, or 47**
In order for each of these fractions to be in its simplest form, a would have to be a number that has no prime factors in common with 3, 5, or 14 . So just find a value between 2 and 50 that fits that description. Your best bet is to use a prime number, such as 11. That's one of 11 acceptable answers.

3.. **3/4 or 75**
Find common denominators and add:

$$\frac{2}{3}+\frac{1}{12}=\frac{8}{12}+\frac{1}{12}=\frac{9}{12}=\frac{3}{4}=0.75$$

4. **14/6, 7/3, or 2.33**
At first, this problem looks like one that is really involved with finding common denominators and adding fractions. However, if you take a closer look, you'll see that there's a much easier way to do it. First, since all the operations in the problem are addition or subtraction, you can remove the parentheses, leaving

$$2+\frac{3}{2}-\frac{4}{3}+\frac{4}{3}-\frac{5}{4}+\frac{5}{4}-\frac{6}{5}+\frac{6}{5}-\frac{7}{6}$$

Now you can combine fractions that have the same denominator. When you do, you're left with:

$$2+\frac{3}{2}-\frac{7}{6}=\frac{12}{6}+\frac{9}{6}-\frac{7}{6}=\frac{12+9-7}{6}=\frac{14}{6}$$

By eliminating terms, this problem became much easier and quicker to do.

5. **2/5 or .4**
If there are 36 men and 24 women in the group, then the total number of group members is 60. The women make up $\frac{24}{60}$ of the group. Since this fraction cannot be gridded, reduce it or turn it into a decimal. To reduce it, divide both the numerator and denominator by 12, and you end up with $\frac{2}{5}$. To turn it into a decimal, divide 60 into 24, and you end up with .4.

6. **250**
Percent × Whole = Part:
(15%) × (take-home pay) = \$37.50
(0.15) × (take-home pay) = \$37.50
take-home pay = $\frac{\$37.50}{0.15}$ = \$250.00

7. **96**

Be careful with a question like this one. You're given the percent decrease (25 percent) and the *new* number (72), and you're asked to reconstruct the original number. Don't just take 25 percent of 72 and add it on. That 25 percent is based not on the new number, 72, but on the original number—the number you're looking for. The best way to do a problem like this is to set up an equation: (Original #) – (25% of Original #) = New #

$$x - .25x = 72$$
$$.75x = 72$$
$$x = 96$$

8. **65**

To find the average of evenly spaced integers, all you have to do is take the average of the two outside terms. The sum of 42 and 88 is 130, and there are two terms, so the average is 130 divided by 2, or 65.

9. **96**

If you are asked to find the sum when given the average and the number of terms, all you have to do is multiply the two given quantities together. In this question, the average is 12 and the number of terms is 8, so the total number of raffle tickets sold is 12 times 8, or 96.

10. **8**

To evaluate this expression when $s = 9$, simply plug 9 in for s. Substituting 9 into the expression yields:

$$\frac{3(9)+5}{4} = \frac{27+5}{4} = \frac{32}{4} = 8$$

11. **12/7 or 1.71**

First clear the denominators by multiplying both sides of the equation by 12:

$$\frac{x}{3} + \frac{x}{4} = 1$$
$$12\left(\frac{x}{3} + \frac{x}{4}\right) = 12 \cdot 1$$
$$4x + 3x = 12$$
$$7x = 12$$
$$x = \frac{12}{7}$$

12. **2**

First get rid of the parentheses in the last term by subtracting 2 from 5. The equation is now $(x + 4)(3) = 18$. Dividing each side by 3 leaves $x + 4 = 6$, which simplifies to $x = 2$ when you subtract 4 from both sides.

13. **5**

Since it's x you're looking for, eliminate y. Fortunately, the equations are all ready for you—just add them and the $+4y$ cancels with the $-4y$. You're left with $6x = 30$, so $x = 5$.

14. **3**

Solve the quadratic equation:

$$3x^2 - 8x - 3 = 0$$
$$(3x + 1)(x - 3) = 0$$
$$3x + 1 = 0 \text{ or } x - 3 = 0$$
$$x = -\frac{1}{3} \text{ or } 3$$

You're asked for the positive value of x, so grid in 3.

15. **115**

Since lines p and q are parallel, we can use the rule about alternate interior angles to fill in the following:

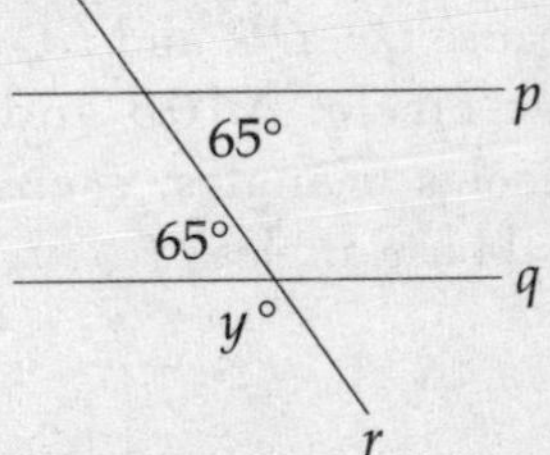

Since the angle marked $y°$ is adjacent and supplementary to a 65° angle, $y = 180 - 65 = 115$.

16. **70**

An exterior angle of a triangle is equal to the sum of the two remote interior angles. In this case, that means that an exterior angle formed at point C would equal the sum of the measures of interior angles A and B:

$$30 + 40 = 70$$

17. **40**

The angle adjacent to the 110° angle measures 180° – 110° = 70°. Because $AB = AC$, angle B also measures 70°. The two base angles have 70 + 70 = 140 of the whole triangle's 180 degrees, which leaves 40 degrees for the measure of angle BAC.

18. **9**

The area of a triangle is equal to one-half the base times the height. Here the base (along the x-axis) is 6 and the height (perpendicular to the base—i.e., parallel to the y-axis) is 3, so the area is $\frac{1}{2}bh = \frac{1}{2}(6)(3) = 9$

19. **140**

The key to solving this one is to draw OB:

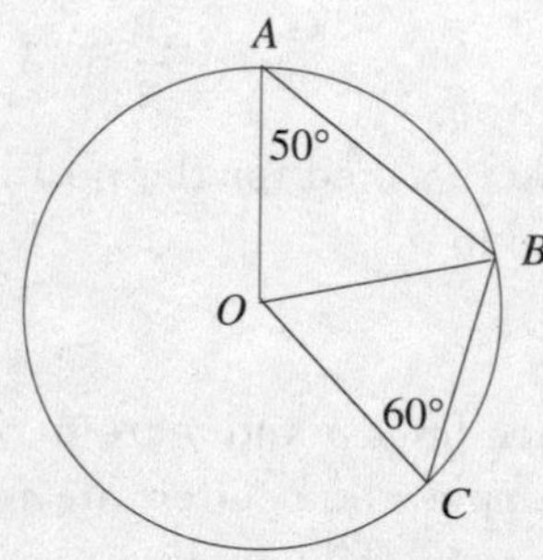

Because OA, OB, and OC are all radii of the same circle, ΔAOB and ΔBOC are both isosceles triangles, each therefore having equal base angles:

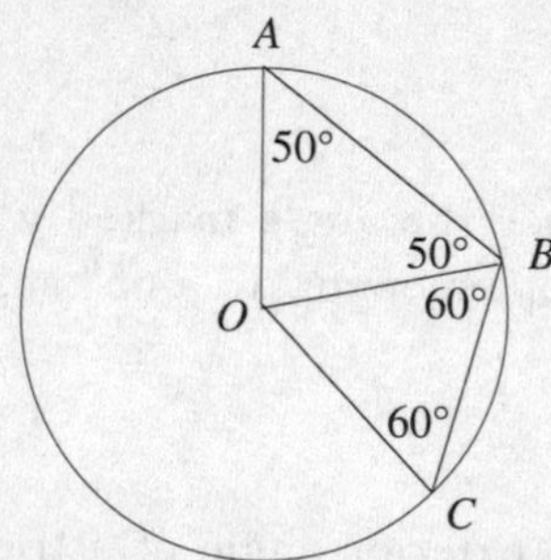

Using the fact that the three interior angles of a triangle add up to 180°, you can figure out that the vertex angles measure 80° and 60° as shown:

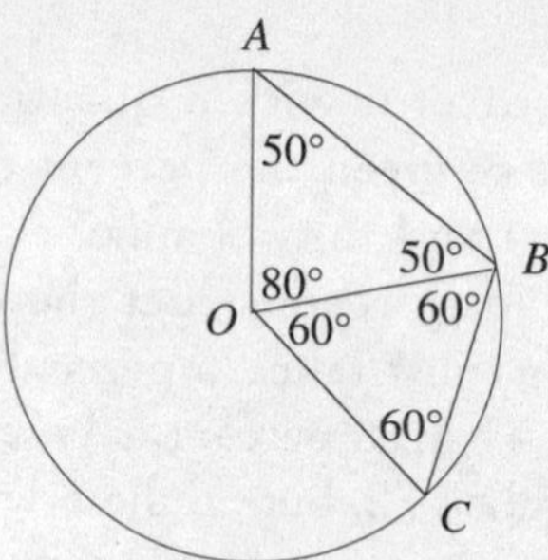

$\angle AOC$ measures 80° + 60° = 140°.

20. **24**

If the area of the right triangle is 24 and one leg is 6, then you can use the triangle area formula to find the other leg:

$$\frac{1}{2}(\text{leg}_1)(\text{leg}_2) = \text{Area}$$

$$\frac{1}{2}(6)(x) = 24$$

$$3x = 24$$

$$x = 8$$

If the legs are 6 and 8, you shouldn't have to use the Pythagorean theorem to find the hypotenuse. This is a 3-4-5 triangle with all side lengths doubled, so the hypotenuse is 10, and the perimeter is 6 + 8 + 10 = 24.

21. **8**

Because the exterior angle at C measures 150°, you know that the interior angle at C measures 180° – 150° = 30°. Now it's clear that ΔABC is a 30-60-90 triangle. You're given the length of the short leg AB and you're asked for the length of the hypotenuse AC. The ratio of the short leg to the hypotenuse of a 30-60-90 triangle is 1:2, so $AC = 2(AB) = 2(4) = 8$.

22. **12**

Although triangle XYZ isn't a right triangle, special right triangles is the key to this problem. $\angle XZY$ is 60°, so if you drop a perpendicular from Y to side XZ, you get a 45-45-90 right triangle and a 30-60-90 right triangle:

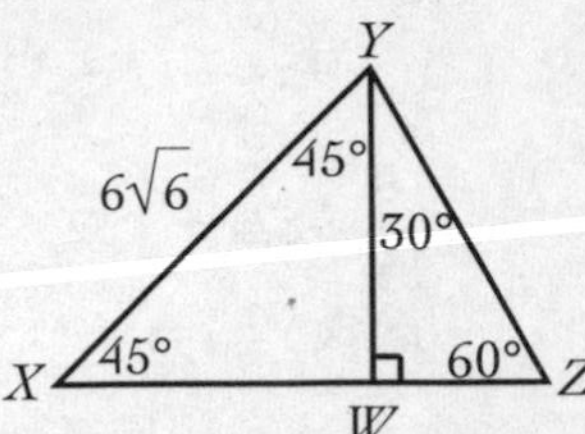

You have the length of XY, the hypotenuse of the 45-45-90 triangle, so start there. The ratio of sides in a 45-45-90 triangle is $1:1:\sqrt{2}$, so each leg has length $\frac{6\sqrt{6}}{\sqrt{2}} = 6\sqrt{3}$. Now that you know the length of YW you can work with the 30-60-90 triangle. The ratio of sides in a 30-60-90 triangle is $1:\sqrt{3}:2$, so WZ has length 6 and YZ has length 12.

23. **300**

Pick numbers. If the radius of circle B is 10, then the radius of circle A is 5. The radius of circle C is $1\frac{1}{2} \times 10$, or 15. So the radius of circle C is $\frac{15}{5} \times 100\% =$ 300% of the radius of circle A.

24. **16**

Sketch or visualize the problem as a right triangle. The length of the ladder is the hypotenuse. The distance from the foot of the ladder to the base of the wall is one leg. The height you're looking for is the other leg:

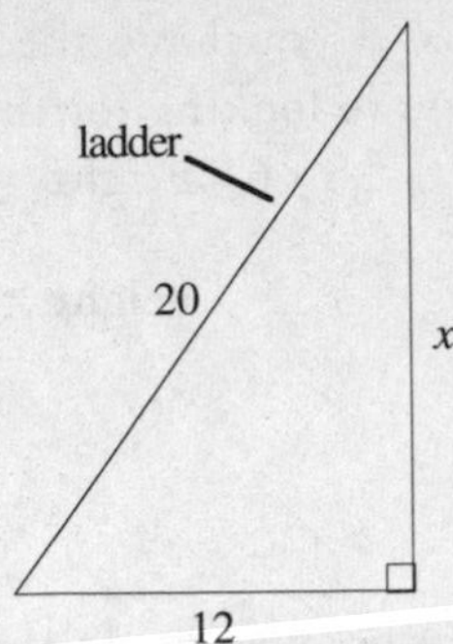

You could use the Pythagorean theorem, but it's easier and faster if you recognize the special right triangle. This is a 3-4-5 right triangle with all side lengths quadrupled, so $x = 16$.

25. **25**

You can use the legs of a right triangle as the base and height to calculate the area. A "right isosceles" triangle is the same thing as a 45-45-90 triangle. The ratio of the side lengths in such a triangle is $1:1:\sqrt{2}$. If you were given a leg and asked to find the hypotenuse, you would multiply by $\sqrt{2}$. Here, though, you're given the hypotenuse and you need to find the legs (to plug into the triangle area formula), so *divide* by $\sqrt{2}$:

$$\text{leg} = \frac{\text{hypotenuse}}{\sqrt{2}} = \frac{10}{\sqrt{2}}$$

You wouldn't leave the radical in the denominator if you were finished, but here finding this leg length is just an intermediary step toward finding the area:

$$\text{Area} = \frac{1}{2}(\text{leg}_1)(\text{leg}_2)$$

$$= \frac{1}{2}\left(\frac{10}{\sqrt{2}}\right)\left(\frac{10}{\sqrt{2}}\right) = \frac{100}{4} = 25$$

26. **12**

The shape of the water in each instance is a rectangular solid. The volume of the water does not change. The formula for the volume of a rectangular solid is "length times width times height." In Box A you have all three dimensions:

$$\text{Volume} = 4 \times 9 \times 10 = 360$$

In Box B you have the length and width, and you're looking for the height:

$$5 \times 6 \times \textbf{height} = 360$$

$$\textbf{height} = \frac{360}{30} = 12$$

27. **280**

The easiest way to do this problem is to set up a proportion. The first part of the proportion should be the ratio of milk cartons ordered to students enrolled, which is $\frac{240}{600}$. Reducing this ratio leaves $\frac{2}{5}$. The second half of the proportion is the new number of cartons ordered, which we'll call x, over the new number of students, 700. Set the two fractions equal and solve for x by cross-multiplying:

$$\frac{2}{5} = \frac{x}{700}$$

$$1400 = 5x$$

$$280 = x$$

28. **16**

This is an average rate problem, but don't just average the two rates. Instead, use total distance and total time to find the average rate. First pick a distance that is easy to use. In this instance, since the speed uphill is 12 miles per hour and the speed downhill is 24 miles per hour, 24 miles is convenient to work with. It took the cyclist two hours to climb the hill and one hour to descend it, so it took him three hours to ride a total of 48 miles. Now that you have a total distance and a total time, you can find the average rate:

$$\text{Average Rate} = \frac{48 \text{ miles}}{3 \text{ hours}} = 16 \text{ mph}$$

29. **203**

This looks like a physics question, but in fact it's just a "plug-in-the-number-and-see-what-you-get" question. Be sure you plug 95 in for C (not F):

$$C = \frac{5}{9}(F - 32)$$

$$95 = \frac{5}{9}(F - 32)$$

$$\frac{9}{5} \cdot 95 = F - 32$$

$$F - 32 = 171$$

$$F = 171 + 32 = 203$$

30. **$5 < n < 6$**

The way to handle this problem is to solve each inequality separately. Solving the first one for n gives us the following:

$$-5 - 4n < -25$$

$$-4n < -20$$

Don't forget to change the direction of the sign when dividing both sides by -4.

$$-4n < -20$$

$$n > 5$$

Now you know that n must be greater than 5, but is there an upper limit to the range of possible values for n ? The only way to know is to solve the second inequality:

$$-2n + 12 > 0$$

$$-2n > -12$$

$$n < 6$$

Now you also know that n must be less than 6, which means that it must be somewhere between 5 and 6.

11 ACT Practice Sets: Explanations

ACT Practice Set 1: English

Passage 1: The Acropolis

1. C At first glance, there may not seem to be anything wrong here. However, the dash after *Aegean Sea* alerts you that the writer has chosen to set off the parenthetical phrase describing the Acropolis with dashes instead of commas. This means that you have to replace the comma after *Acropolis* with a dash, in order to have a matching pair. If there were a comma after *Aegean Sea,* this underlined part of the sentence would not need to be changed. Knowing that you need to "make it all match" will help you score points on ACT English.

2. G This question tests your sense of parallelism. Your ear can often help you identify unparallel constructions. "To climb . . . is to have beheld" is unparallel. They should be in the same form: "to climb . . . is to behold. . . ."

3. D You have the option to omit the underlined portion, an option that you should definitely take. Athenian cuisine has nothing to do with the subject of the paragraph or the passage, which is the Parthenon.

4. F This verb is appropriately plural—the subject, *generations,* is plural—and in the present perfect tense. Choices G and H are singular verbs, while J is wrong because generations of architects can't all be proclaiming at the present time.

5. D Run-on sentences are common in the English section. There are a couple of ways to deal with this run-on sentence. You could put a semicolon after *subtle* to separate the clauses, or you could put a period after *subtle* and make the clauses into separate sentences. Since the choices offer you both options, there must be something more. And there is: you need a comma after *example* to set it off from the rest of the sentence. Choice D fixes both errors.

6. G This part of the sentence sounds strange; it seems that the fact is what is being viewed from a distance, not the straight columns. *Viewed from a distance* is a misplaced modifier that has to be moved to a position where it clearly modifies *columns.* Choice G accomplishes this.

7. D Read the sentence out loud and you'll hear that it has punctuation problems. There is no need for a semicolon or any other kind of punctuation mark between *of* and *uprightness.* Don't place a comma before the first element of a series (C), and don't place a colon between a preposition and its objects (B).

8. J The phrase *because of this* doesn't make sense here. The optical illusion the architects created is not the reason you'll get a different impression of the Parthenon from the one the ancient Athenians had; the reason is that the statue of Athena Parthenos isn't there anymore. The introductory phrase that makes sense is *Of course* (J).

9. **C** *Only by standing . . . Golden Age of Athens* is a sentence fragment that has to be hooked up somehow to the sentence after it. You can't just use a semicolon to join the two (B) because then the first clause of the new sentence will still be only a fragment. You have to reverse the subject and verb of the second sentence to attach the fragment to it, as C does.

10. **J** What was removed from the temple? The underlined part of the sentence is an introductory modifying phrase that you know describes the *statue,* but the word *statue* isn't anywhere in the sentence. As a result, the sentence doesn't make sense at all; it's impossible that "all that remains" in the temple was removed in the fifth century A.D. Choice J causes the sentence to make sense.

11. **D** Quite a few words come between the subject and the verb of this sentence. You shouldn't be fooled, though; *many* is the subject of the sentence, not *carvings, walls,* or *Acropolis.* Since *many* is plural, the verb of the sentence has to be plural as well. *Is* has to be changed to *are.*

12. **H** This sentence is really only a sentence fragment; it has a subject, *decision,* but no verb. Choice (H) rewords the underlined portion to make *Lord Elgin* the subject and *decided* the verb.

13. **C** *They* is an ambiguous pronoun because it's not immediately clear what group *they* refers to. You can figure out from the context that *they* refers to the Greeks; no other group could have won independence from the Turks and demanded the carvings back from the British. To make the first sentence clear, you have to replace *they* with *the Greeks.*

14. **J** What could have been destroyed by explosions in the Parthenon? Carvings. The fact that some of the carvings were destroyed during a war is another good reason that many of them can no longer be found in the Parthenon, as the fourth paragraph states. Therefore, the new material belongs in the fourth paragraph.

15. **C** Clearly, the writer did not fulfill the request, because only the second paragraph discusses techniques of construction at all. Even then, only one technique, the bulging of the columns, is described in any detail. The author covers several topics in the essay in addition to construction techniques, including the statue of Athena Parthenos and the fate of the carvings.

Passage 2: Robin Hood

16. **H** The previous sentence says, "Robin is the hero. . . ."; look for a verb form that matches the present tense *is,* since the sentence continues the discussion of the ballads. Choice H's *tell* is in the right tense. Choice F switches to another tense, the present progressive, which makes it sound as if the ballads were literally speaking. Choice G lacks a main verb, creating a sentence fragment. Choice J has the same tense problem as Choice F, and compounds it by adding an extra, unnecessary subject, *they.*

17. **C** Make it all match. You need a verb that is parallel to *robbing* and *killing,* so *giving* (C) is the correct choice.

18. **H** The adjective *frequent* is the correct choice to modify *enemy.* The underlined segment uses both the word *most* and the suffix *-est* to indicate the highest degree, or superlative form. Use one or the other, but not both. Likewise, choice G incorrectly uses *more* and the suffix *-er* together. Both of these express the comparative form—but again, you'd use one or the other, not both at once. In J, *frequently* is an adverb and so can't describe a noun.

19. **D** When you see the OMIT option, ask yourself if the underlined portion is really necessary. The use of parentheses was a clue that the underlined part wasn't really essential. It goes off on a tangent about modern adaptations of the King Arthur legend, whereas Robin Hood is the focus of the passage. Choices A, B, and C all reword the irrelevant sentence.

20. **F** This is correct as is. *Them* matches the plural noun it's standing in for: *writers*. Choice G *him* and choice H *it* are singular, so they don't.

21. **A** This is correct because we want the *possessive* apostrophe. Choices B and C are wrong because they are the plural, not the possessive, form of *Stukely*. And there obviously aren't a lot of Stukelys running around. Choice D is wrong because if you read it out loud you can tell that no pause—and so no comma—is called for.

22. **J** Since this passage is aimed at discussing the historical development of the Robin Hood legend, choice J would be most in keeping with the subject matter. Choice F goes way off track; you're asked to add more information on *Stukely*, not on English history. Choices G and H do relate their points to Stukely, but they pursue details. The main topic of the passage is Robin Hood, not antiquaries (G). (Remember, you want a choice that is most relevant to the passage *as a whole*.) As for choice H, King Arthur was mentioned earlier in the passage, but then only to make a point about Robin Hood. A discussion of Stukely's interest in King Arthur would stray from the topic of the passage.

23. **C** The shortest answer is the best choice. Choices A and D wrongly imply a comparison between Robin and a nobleman, when the claim was that Robin *was* a nobleman. Choice B is incoherent.

24. **G** The comparison with a puppy is silly in this context, since it jars with the matter-of-fact tone of this passage; all choices except choice G can be eliminated. The ACT will often try to fool you like this by sticking in a phrase that just doesn't go with the passage's tone.

25. **D** The only choice that will tie in both parts of the sentence is choice D. A dash in this context correctly makes an emphatic pause between *love interest* and its appositive, *Maid Marian*. All the rest of the choices have punctuation errors. Semicolons are used between independent clauses, and the part that would follow the semicolon in choice A isn't a clause. The plural form of the noun, *interests* (B), doesn't agree with the singular article. Choice C can be ruled out because there is no reason to pause in the middle of a name, and so the comma is incorrectly placed.

26. **H** All the choices, with the exception of choice H, have inappropriate connecting words. Since the passage moves to a discussion of a new time period, you *should* begin a new paragraph, ruling out choice G. In addition, *on the one hand* should be followed by *on the other hand*. *Consequently* (F) and *therefore* (J) wrongly imply that what follows is a result of something in the previous sentence.

27. **B** The correct verb tense, and the only choice that doesn't create a sentence fragment, is B. *Basing* (A) and *to base* (C) create sentence fragments. Of course, the omission of the verb would also result in a sentence fragment, so choice D is incorrect.

28. **G** Choice G is the only choice that fits the rest of the sentence both logically and grammatically. *And* doesn't make sense as a connecting word in the original. Choice H also uses a connecting word that doesn't logically fit; *therefore* inaccurately suggests a cause-and-effect relationship. Choice J is wrong because a semicolon should be used between independent clauses, and the first clause can't stand alone.

29. **D** Since we're told that the audience is unfamiliar with the story, it would make sense to include a summary of the Robin Hood legend (D), something the passage lacks. Choices A and C would do nothing for a reader curious about Robin Hood, since they go off on tangents about other issues. As the passage states that Robin Hood's existence is questionable ("legendary"), choice B doesn't fit in with the stance of the writer.

30. **J** Rarely are ACT English passages written for authorities or experts; they're usually written for the general public, as J correctly states in this question. If the passage were directed towards "experts" (F) or "authorities" (G), much of the basic information it presents would be unnecessary

and not included. Since the passage states that the existence of Robin Hood is legendary, the passage can't be aimed at readers craving confirmation that he "was an actual historical personage," so H is wrong.

ACT Practice Set 2: Reading

Passage 1: Philosophes

Passage 1 is a social studies passage about the *philosophes*, a group of mainly French intellectuals. Paragraph 1 defines the term *philosophes*—they were a group of thinkers who took the ideas of others and spread them through literary works. Paragraph 2 says that the *philosophes* developed and spread the philosophy of the Enlightenment throughout western Europe and the American colonies. Paragraphs 3, 4, and 5 discuss the influence of Newton, Locke, and English institutions on the *philosophes'* thinking. Paragraph 6, finally, describes the ideas and career of perhaps the most famous *philosophe*, Voltaire.

1. C This detail question asks for a description of the *philosophes*, so it's back to the first two paragraphs. Lines 13–16 say that they took the ideas of others and popularized them. The first sentence of the second paragraph goes on to state that they "developed the philosophy of the Enlightenment and spread it to much of the educated elite in Western Europe (and the American colonies)." Thus, choice C is correct. Choices B and D are contradicted by information in the first paragraph, which states that the *philosophes* were generally neither professors nor scientists. Choice A, on the other hand, is too narrow in scope. True, the *philosophes* were influenced by Locke, but they were also influenced by Newton and English institutions.

2. G This inference question asks about Voltaire, so your mental map of the passage should have sent you directly to the last paragraph. This paragraph says that Voltaire criticized both French society and religious institutions, so you can infer that he might have attacked French religious institutions, choice G. Choice H is contradicted by information in the paragraph, which states that Voltaire "came to admire" English government. It's unlikely that he would have criticized the Scientific Revolution (F) because the *philosophes* were disciples of this revolution. Finally, the passage says nothing about Voltaire's views of "courtly love" (J), so you can't infer what his position on this issue would have been.

3. D The answer to a question that contains a line reference is found in the lines around that reference. Locke's idea that "schools and social institutions could . . . play a great role in molding the individual" comes up right after his belief that humans are shaped by their experiences, choice D. Choice A is contradicted by lines 55–57, while choices B and C distort details in the fourth paragraph.

4. H Since this question asks about Newton's beliefs, your mental map should have pointed you to the third paragraph, where Newton is discussed. This paragraph says that Newton believed that the universe was "originally set in motion by God" (option I), and that the universe operates in a mechanical and orderly fashion (option III). But this paragraph doesn't say that Newton believed that human reason is insufficient to understand the laws of nature (option II). If anything, it implies just the opposite. Choice H, options I and III only, is correct.

5. D Lines 56–58 reveal that it was Locke who questioned the notion that "revelation was a reliable source of truth." Thus, you're looking for a work written by him, so you can immediately eliminate choices A, *Letters on the English*, and C, *Elements of the Philosophy of Newton*, both of which were authored by Voltaire. The remaining two works, *Second Treatise of Civil Government* (B) and *Essay Concerning Human Understanding* (D) were both written by Locke. But *Second Treatise of Civil Government* (B) is a political, not a philosophical, work, so it can be eliminated as well. That leaves choice D as the correct answer.

6. G The first sentence of the fourth paragraph states that Locke "agreed with Newton but went further." Specifically, Locke also thought that the human mind was subject to

"the mechanical laws of the material universe," choice G. The other choices distort details in the third and fourth paragraphs.

7. D The *philosophes*—as the fifth paragraph shows—were greatly influenced by an England that allowed more individual freedom, was more tolerant of religious differences, and was freer of traditional political institutions than other countries, particularly France. Indeed, the *philosophes* wanted other countries to adopt the English model. Thus, choice D, options I, II, and III, is correct.

8. G Since this question, like the last one, asks about England, it's right back to the fifth paragraph. In the second-to-last sentence of the paragraph, the author cites England's political stability and prosperity as evidence that England's system worked. The last sentence of the paragraph goes on to say that the *philosophes* "wanted to see in their own countries much of what England already seemed to have." Choice G, therefore, is correct. Choice F, on the other hand, flatly contradicts the gist of the fifth paragraph. Finally, choices H and J distort details from the wrong part of the passage.

9. A The French political and religious authorities during the time of Voltaire are discussed in the sixth paragraph. Voltaire got in hot water with the authorities over his outspoken views, so it's safe to assume that they weren't advocates of free speech, choice A. Since they first imprisoned and then exiled him, they clearly didn't regard the *philosophes* with indifference, choice C. The passage doesn't say *precisely* what Voltaire was imprisoned and exiled for, so you can't infer that the authorities "overreacted to Voltaire's mild satires" (B), which, in any case, weren't that mild. Finally, since Voltaire was an advocate of the English system of government, it's also safe to assume that the French hadn't accepted this model. So D's out as well.

10. J The notion that the *philosophes* were "more literary than scientific" appears in the middle of the first paragraph. A few lines further down, the paragraph furnishes a list of the types of literary works produced by the *philosophes*, so choice J is correct. The passage never mentions any political change (F). Nor does it compare the literary outputs of Newton and Voltaire (G). Finally, choice H is out because the *philosophes* were not scientists.

Passage 2: The Ozone Layer

Passage 2 in this section is a science passage about the ozone layer. Paragraph 1 introduces us to the problem of the ozone layer's depletion—the passage's big idea. Paragraph 2 describes the nature of the ozone layer. Paragraphs 3–5 discuss the study of the ozone layer, mentioning in particular that scientists have been carefully monitoring its depletion. Paragraphs 6–10 explain what is responsible for the depletion of the ozone layer—CFCs —and what is being done to stem their use around the world. Finally, the passage ends on a cautiously optimistic note in the eleventh paragraph, implying that a solution to the problem can be found if people work to find it. As is typical of ACT science passages, this one contains many, many details. Don't try to memorize them; instead, note their location (by paragraph), so that you can find them quickly when the questions demand it.

11. A The term *tenuous* is used twice in the passage—in the first sentences of the first two paragraphs. In the first instance, *tenuous* appears in the context of a discussion about the ozone layer's depletion. In the second instance, it appears in the context of a discussion about the tiny amount of ozone in the atmosphere. In this passage, then, *tenuous* means "thin" (A). "Substantial" (C) suggests just the opposite of what *tenuous* means in this passage. Finally, *dangerous* (B) and *fragile* (D) simply don't convey the correct idea.

12. J In passages that contain a lot of different dates, check back with the text to make sure that you know what each one represents. Lines 44–46 say that the public first took notice of the depletion of the ozone layer in 1985, choice J. 1930 (F) was the year that scientists first began to observe the ozone layer. 1958 (G) was the year that scientists first began to notice seasonal variations in the content of the ozone layer. And 1979 (H) was the year in which the October minimum in the ozone layer diminished.

13. A The last sentence of the fourth paragraph identifies temperature changes (C) and wind effects (D) as phenomena that *cause* fluctuations in the content of the ozone layer. Similarly, the sixth paragraph identifies CFCs (B) as a *cause* of fluctuations in content. That leaves choice (A), supersonic aircraft, as the correct answer. Indeed, the sixth paragraph relates that supersonic aircraft, originally thought to have contributed to fluctuations in the content of the ozone layer, have now been ruled out as a cause of these fluctuations.

14. H Paragraph 7 mentions such issues as market value, labor force, and production levels. In other words, it's all about economic matters related to CFCs. So (H) is correct. Choice F focuses on a detail in the paragraph, not its overall purpose. There's no criticism leveled at CFC producers (G). Finally, the Montreal Protocol (J) is dealt with in the eighth paragraph.

15. D Alternatives to CFCs are discussed in the last paragraph. Lines 100–104 say that it may be difficult to find alternatives to CFCs because substitute products may be toxic, option I; dangerous, option II; and contributors to global warming, option III. Choice D, therefore, is correct.

16. G The last two sentences of the third paragraph make it clear that it's Dobson network stations (G) that forecast the future of the ozone layer. The WMO (F) and the UNEP (J) entrusted this task to the Dobson network. The Montreal Protocol (H) concerns the preservation of the ozone layer by controlling the production of CFCs.

17. D There is no information in the passage to suggest either that scientists could replace lost ozone (A) or that they could destroy existing chlorine molecules (C). Choice B distorts a detail in the tenth paragraph, which states that CFCs have a lifespan of between 75 and 400 years. This doesn't mean that the ozone level in the atmosphere returns to "normal" after 75 years. But the last two sentences of this paragraph do say that it takes ten years for the effects of these CFCs to make themselves felt. You can infer from this information that the world would start to see benefits ten years from now if CFC production were banned *today*, choice D. If CFC production were banned today, ozone that still exists ten years from now would not be destroyed.

18. H The first sentence of the second paragraph states that the ozone layer itself is exactly 25 kilometers thick (H). Choice F refers to the compression of ozone gas at sea level, not the actual ozone layer itself. Choices G and J refer to the height of the ozone layer above the surface of the planet.

19. A The first sentence of the fourth paragraph brings up the issue of seasonal variations in the ozone layer. The rest of the paragraph then goes on to describe these variations in more detail. Choice A, therefore, is correct. Choice B flatly contradicts information in the fourth paragraph. Choice C distorts a detail in the fifth paragraph. And choice D introduces an idea that the passage doesn't support.

20. G In the last sentence of the passage, the author ends on a somewhat optimistic note, saying that a solution to the ozone problem might be found if people "lend a hand." He says this even though he acknowledges that today's substitute products present problems of their own. Choice G reflects this partially optimistic assessment. The other choices are either too pessimistic or distort the author's point of view.

ACT Practice Set 3: Math

1. A Do what's in parentheses first:

$$\left(\frac{1}{2}+\frac{1}{6}\right)-\left(\frac{1}{12}+\frac{1}{3}\right)=\left(\frac{3}{6}+\frac{1}{6}\right)-\left(\frac{1}{12}+\frac{4}{12}\right)$$
$$=\frac{4}{6}-\frac{5}{12}$$
$$=\frac{8}{12}-\frac{5}{12}$$
$$=\frac{3}{12}$$
$$=\frac{1}{4}$$

The numerator of $\frac{1}{4}$ is 1.

2. H Probability equals the number of favorable outcomes divided by the total number of possible outcomes. In this problem, a favorable outcome is choosing a green marble—that's 4. The total number of possible outcomes is the total number of marbles, or 20:

$$\text{Probability} = \frac{\text{Favorable outcomes}}{\text{Total outcomes}} = \frac{4}{20} = \frac{1}{5}$$

3. B Be careful. The question is not asking, "What is $\frac{1}{4}$ of 16?" It's asking, "What is $\frac{1}{4}$ *percent* of 16?" One-fourth of 1 percent is 0.25 percent, or 0.0025:

$$\tfrac{1}{4}\% \text{ of } 16 = 0.0025 \cdot 16 = 0.04$$

4. H Be careful with the decimal points and exponents:

$$\frac{(3.0\times10^4)(8.0\times10^9)}{1.2\times10^6}$$
$$= \frac{(3.0\times8.0)\times(10^4\times10^9)}{1.2\times10^6} = \frac{24.0\times10^{13}}{1.2\times10^6}$$
$$= \frac{24.0}{1.2}\times\frac{10^{13}}{10^6} = 20\times10^{(13-6)}$$
$$= 20\times10^7$$
$$= 2.0\times10^8$$

5. C Set up a proportion:

$$\frac{12\text{ pages}}{1\text{ hour}} = \frac{100\text{ pages}}{x\text{ hours}}$$
$$12x = 100$$
$$x = 8\tfrac{1}{3}$$

One-third of an hour is 20 minutes, so $8\frac{1}{3}$ hours is 8 hours and 20 minutes.

6. K Just multiply the exponents:

$$\left[\left(5^{-2}\right)^2\right]^{-1} = 5^{[(-2)\times2\times(-1)]} = 5^4$$

7. C To rationalize the denominator, multiply both the top and bottom by the same quantity, one that will cancel the radical from the bottom. The number to use here is $2+\sqrt{2}$:

$$\frac{1}{2-\sqrt{2}} = \frac{1}{2-\sqrt{2}}\cdot\frac{2+\sqrt{2}}{2+\sqrt{2}}$$
$$= \frac{2+\sqrt{2}}{2^2-\left(\sqrt{2}\right)^2}$$
$$= \frac{2+\sqrt{2}}{4-2}$$
$$= \frac{2+\sqrt{2}}{2}$$

8. H This looks like a solid geometry question, but in fact it's just a "plug-in-the-number-and-see-what-you-get" question.

$$S = \pi r\sqrt{r^2+h^2}$$
$$= \pi(3)\sqrt{3^2+4^2}$$
$$= 3\pi\sqrt{9+16}$$
$$= 3\pi\sqrt{25}$$
$$= 3\pi\cdot5$$
$$= 15\pi$$

9. E Raise both sides of the equation to the sixth power:

$$\sqrt[6]{x} = 5^{\frac{1}{3}}$$
$$\left(\sqrt[6]{x}\right)^6 = \left(5^{\frac{1}{3}}\right)^6$$
$$x = 5^{\frac{6}{3}}$$
$$x = 5^2$$
$$x = 25$$

10. J You can see from a peek at the answer choices that this is an equation that calls for the quadratic formula. Plug $a=1$, $b=6$, and $c=7$ into the formula:

$$x = \frac{-b\pm\sqrt{b^2-4ac}}{2a}$$
$$= \frac{-6\pm\sqrt{6^2-4(1)(7)}}{2(1)} = \frac{-6\pm\sqrt{36-28}}{2}$$
$$= \frac{-6\pm\sqrt{8}}{2} = \frac{-6\pm2\sqrt{2}}{2}$$
$$= -3\pm\sqrt{2}$$

11. B The four fractions on the left side of the equation are all ready to be added, because they already have a common denominator: a.

$$\frac{1}{a}+\frac{2}{a}+\frac{3}{a}+\frac{4}{a}=5$$

$$\frac{1+2+3+4}{a}=5$$

$$\frac{10}{a}=5$$

$$10=5a$$

$$a=2$$

12. F You solve an inequality much the way you solve an equation: do the same things to both sides until you've isolated what you're solving for. (Just remember to flip the sign if you ever multiply or divide both sides by a negative number.)

$$-3(x-2)\le 15$$

$$x-2\ge \frac{15}{-3}$$

$$x-2\ge -5$$

$$x\ge -3$$

The greater-than-or-equal-to symbol is graphed as a solid circle.

13. A Read carefully. This question's a lot easier than you might think at first. It's asking for the total *number* of coins, not the total value. q quarters, d dimes, and n nickels add up to a total of $q + d + n$ coins.

14. J Use the points where the line crosses the axes—(1,0) and (0,2)—to find the slope of the borderline:

$$\text{Slope} = \frac{y_2-y_1}{x_2-x_1}=\frac{2-0}{0-1}=-2$$

The y-intercept of the borderline is 2, so the equation of the borderline is $y = -2x + 2$. Now you can see that the answer will be either J or K—the only difference between them is the direction of the sign. Pick some point in the shaded region—say, (2, 0)—to see which direction is correct. Plug $x = 2$ into $-2x + 2$ and you get -2, which is *less* than 0, so y is *greater than or equal to* $-2x + 2$ and the correct answer is J.

15. C This looks at first like a coordinate geometry question, but once you understand what it's asking, you realize it's a system-of-equations question. The point of intersection is the point whose coordinates satisfy both equations. So it's just a matter of solving two equations in two variables.

Solve for one variable at a time. You can use the substitution method on this one. Rewrite the second equation as $y = x - 3$, and plug that into the first equation:

$$5x+2y=29$$

$$5x+2(x-3)=29$$

$$5x+2x-6=29$$

$$7x=35$$

$$x=5$$

Normally you would then plug the $x = 5$ back into either of the original equations to solve for y—but that's not necessary this time because there's only one answer choice with 5 for an x-coordinate. Choice C, (5, 2), has to be the correct answer.

16. F The easiest way to find the equation of a given parabola is to take a point or two from the graph and plug the coordinates into the answer choices, eliminating the choices that don't work. Start with a point with coordinates that are easy to work with. Here you could start with (3, 0). Plug $x = 3$ and $y = 0$ into each answer choice and you'll find that only choice F works.

17. C Use the distance formula:

$$d=\sqrt{\left(x_2-x_1\right)^2+\left(y_2-y_1\right)^2}$$

$$=\sqrt{(5-3)^2+(12-4)^2}=\sqrt{2^2+8^2}$$

$$=\sqrt{4+64}=\sqrt{68}=\sqrt{4\cdot 17}$$

$$=2\sqrt{17}$$

18. J When a transversal crosses parallel lines, all the resulting acute angles are equal and all the resulting obtuse angles are equal. You can generally tell just by looking which angles are equal. In this problem's figure, $a = c = e = g$, and $b = d = f = h$. Only choice J is true: c and g are both obtuse. In all the other choices you'll find an obtuse and an acute.

19. B First find the slope of the line that contains the given points:

$$\text{Slope} = \frac{y_2 - y_1}{x_2 - x_1} = \frac{10-6}{6-5} = 4$$

Line m is perpendicular to the above line, so the slope of m is the negative reciprocal of 4, or $-\frac{1}{4}$.

20. K Altitude $\overline{FH}$ divides the big triangle into two smaller triangles such that all three triangles are similar—they're all right triangles. And either of the two small triangles has an acute angle in common with the large triangle, which means that either small triangle is similar to the large triangle. Since the two small triangles are each similar to the large triangle, the two small triangles are similar. So all three triangles have the same angle measures all around. Because the triangles are similar you can set up a proportion of corresponding sides:

$$\frac{EG}{EF} = \frac{EF}{EH}$$

$$\frac{25}{10} = \frac{10}{EH}$$

$$25 \times EH = 100$$

$$EH = 4$$

If $EH = 4$, then $HG = 25 - 4 = 21$.

21. E If you find the distance from the center to the given point on the circle, you'll have the radius. The difference between the x's is 8, and the difference between the y's is 6. If 8 and 6 are the lengths of the legs of a right triangle, then the hypotenuse is 10. The radius, then, is 10. Now you can plug the radius and the coordinates of the center point into the general form of the equation of a circle:

$$(x-h)^2 + (y-k)^2 = r^2$$

$$(x+1)^2 + (y+1)^2 = 10^2$$

$$(x+1)^2 + (y+1)^2 = 100$$

22. J It *is* a square because it has four right angles and four equal sides. It *is* a rectangle because it has four right angles. (Equal sides do not disqualify it as a rectangle.) It *is* a parallelogram because opposite sides are parallel. It is *not* a trapezoid because, by definition, a trapezoid has *exactly one* pair of parallel side—this figure has *two* pairs of parallel sides.

23. D Because $\overline{BD}$ bisects $\angle ABC$, the measure of $\angle ABD$ is 50°. Now you know two of the three angles of ΔABD, so the third angle measures 180° – 60° – 50° = 70°.

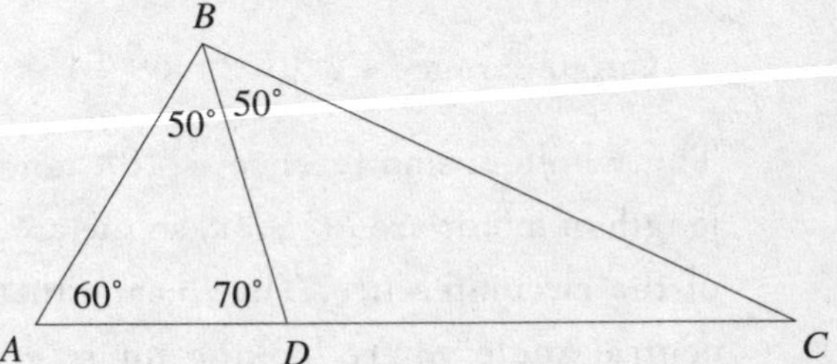

$\angle BDC$, the angle you're looking for, is supplementary to the 70° angle, so $\angle BDC$ measures 180° – 70° = 110°.

24. J Use the circumference formula to find the radius, then double that to get the diameter:

$$2\pi r = \text{Circumference}$$

$$2\pi r = 36\pi$$

$$2r = 36$$

$$r = 18$$

If the radius is 18, the diameter is 36.

25. C Since $\sin \alpha = \frac{4}{5}$, you could think of this as a 3-4-5 triangle:

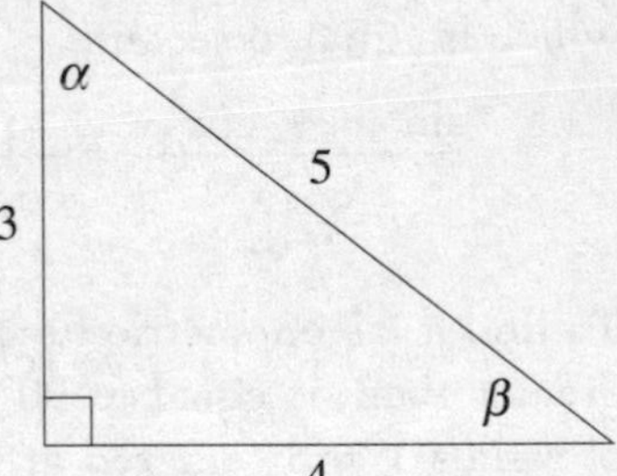

Cosine is "adjacent over hypotenuse." Here the leg adjacent to β is 4, and the hypotenuse is 5, so $\cos \beta = \frac{4}{5}$. (Notice that the sine of one acute angle in a right triangle is equal to the cosine of the other acute angle.)

26. **K** Think of the arc as a piece of the circumference. You can use the given radius of 9 to find the whole circumference, then use the given arc length of 2π to figure out what fraction of the circumference constitutes the arc:

$$\text{Circumference} = 2\pi r = 2\pi \times 9 = 18\pi$$

The whole circumference is 18π, and the length of minor arc *PQ* is 2π, so the arc is $\frac{1}{9}$ of the circumference. That means that the central angle you're looking for is $\frac{1}{9}$ of a complete 360° rotation:

$$\text{measure of } \angle POQ = \tfrac{1}{9}(360^\circ) = 40^\circ$$

27. **B** The 4-foot length you're given is the leg adjacent to the 70° angle, and the ladder length you're looking for is the hypotenuse. "Adjacent over hypotenuse" is cosine, so it's cos 70° that you'll use:

$$\cos 70^\circ = \frac{\text{adjacent}}{\text{hypotenuse}} = \frac{4}{x}$$

$$.342 \approx \frac{4}{x}$$

$$x \approx \frac{4}{.342} \approx 11.7$$

28. **H** The numerator is equal to 1, so the whole expression is really just "1 over cosine," which is equal to secant:

$$\frac{\sin^2 x + \cos^2 x}{\cos x} = \frac{1}{\cos x} = \sec x$$

29. **C** To find a trigonometric function of an angle greater than or equal to 90°, sketch a circle of radius 1 and centered at the origin of the coordinate grid. Start from the point (1,0) and rotate the appropriate number of degrees counterclockwise. When you rotate 240°, you end up 60° into the third quadrant:

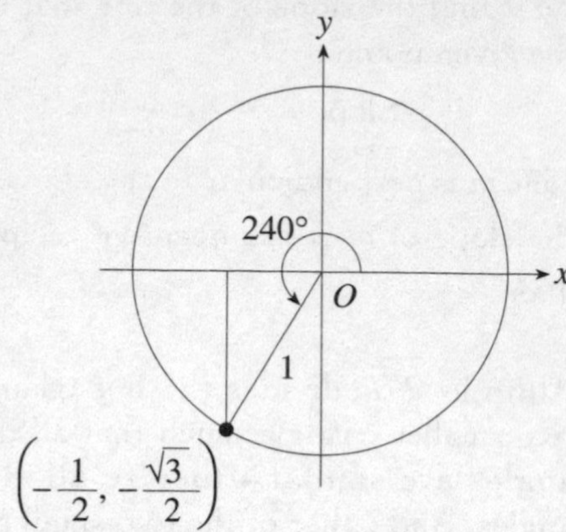

In this "unit circle" setup, the basic trigonometric functions are defined in terms of the coordinates of the endpoint of the terminal side. The cosine is simply the x-coordinate, $-\frac{1}{2}$.

30. **H** To match the equation to the graph, pick a point or two from the graph and try them out in the answer choices, eliminating the choices that don't work. The point (0, 0) works in all five choices—it's no help. Try the point $(\frac{\pi}{2}, -2)$. Remembering that the sine of $\frac{\pi}{2}$ is 1, and the sine of π is 0, you can test the answer choices and you'll find that only choice H works:

$$-2\sin\tfrac{\pi}{2} = -2(1) = -2$$

ACT Practice Set 4: Science Reasoning

Passage 1

Passage 1 is a Data Representation passage with practically no text and one diagram that illustrates the carbon cycle. Each box of the diagram is a state in which naturally occurring carbon can be found (for example, in carbon dioxide in air or in animals) and the arrows show how carbon can move from one state to another. For example, the carbon found in carbon dioxide can, through the process of photosynthesis, be taken up by green plants and incorporated into various carbon compounds (in fact, according to the diagram, this is the only way that the carbon in carbon dioxide can enter the carbon cycle). Pay attention to the direction of the arrows.

1. C Decay bacteria, according to the diagram, get carbon from the carbon compounds of dead plants and animals and add to the supply of carbon dioxide in air and water through fermentation and putrefaction. Since there is no other way to get carbon from dead plants and animals back to carbon dioxide, you know that a drop in decay bacteria will reduce the amount of carbon available for forming carbon dioxide. The carbon dioxide level will not be greatly affected, though, because there are three other sources of carbon for carbon dioxide. Choice C is correct.

2. G Let's take each of the statements one-by-one. Statement I is false because the diagram shows that the carbon in "animals" can move to "other animals" through the process of "animal digestion." An animal that eats only other animals is participating in the carbon cycle when it digests its prey. Statement II is clearly true; there are arrows labeled "respiration" going from the "green plants," the "animals," and the "other animals" stages back to the carbon dioxide stage. Statement III, however, is not true, because some carbon dioxide is released into the air by fermentation and putrefaction. Since only Statement II is true, choice G is correct.

3. D There are four direct sources of atmospheric carbon dioxide, according to the diagram: fermentation by decay bacteria and respiration by green plants, by animals, and by "other animals or animal parasites." Choice D correctly cites the respiration of animal parasites. If you were tempted by choice B, note the direction of the arrow for photosynthesis. Photosynthesis removes atmospheric carbon dioxide, using it as a source for carbon.

4. G The arrow signifying animal respiration and the arrow signifying photosynthesis are linked in the diagram by the "carbon dioxide in air or dissolved in water" box. Animal respiration is one of the sources of carbon for carbon dioxide, and the carbon dioxide in turn provides carbon for the process of photosynthesis. In this sense, "animal respiration provides vital gases for green plants" (choice G).

5. A Look closely at the diagram. The only way that carbon dioxide can enter the carbon cycle is through the process of photosynthesis in which it is taken up by green plants. Note that green plants also emit carbon dioxide back into the air via the process of respiration. Therefore, if green plants were eliminated, the carbon cycle would come to a complete stop, making choice A correct.

Passage 2

The purpose of the three experiments described in this Research Summary was to investigate the effect of glucose on lens proteins in the eye. You should expect, after reading the first paragraph, that glucose would be found to react adversely with the lens proteins and damage them.

Experiment 1 showed that when human tissue protein is dissolved in glucose, an Amadori product forms that causes one protein to bind with another in a brown pigmented cross-link called an Advanced Glycosylation End product (AGE). Experiment 2 demonstrated that the lens proteins in older subjects are often bound to each other by cross-links; the cross-links are either di-sulfide bonds or "an indeterminate formation with brownish pigmentation" (you can guess from the color that it is the same type of cross-link as was found in Experiment 1). In Experiment 3, it was found that the lens proteins of cow lenses form brown cross-links when dissolved in glucose—the same type of brown cross-links found in Experiment 2 (and, you can infer, in Experiment 1).

6. J The researcher who designed the experiments was interested in the effect of dietary glucose on lens proteins in the human eye, not the cow eye. There would be no reason to use cow lens proteins in Experiment 3 if cow lens proteins were expected to react any differently from human lens proteins, especially when human lens proteins were readily available for use—they were used, after all, for Experiment 1. Therefore, you know that the researcher assumed that cow lens proteins would react the same as human lens proteins, (choice J).

7. C Make sure that you stick to the results of Experiment 1 only when you answer this question. All you know from Experiment 1 is that when a human tissue protein was dissolved in a glucose and water solution, the proteins formed Amadori products that combined with other proteins to make brown cross-links. You can conclude from this that the glucose reacted with the proteins to form cross-links (choice C). Based on Experiment 1, though, you know nothing about disulfide cross-links (choice A) or glucose metabolism (choice D). Choice B contradicts the results of Experiment 1 because it is protein, not glucose, that forms AGE.

8. G Take another look at the results of Experiment 2. It was found that in the samples from older subjects, the lens proteins often formed cross-linked bonds, some of which were brown. The senile cataracts in the lenses of older people are also brown. The conclusion suggested by the identical colors of the cataracts and the cross-linked bonds is that the senile cataracts are made up of, or caused by, cross-linked bonds (choice G).

9. C You don't know from the results of Experiment 2 how the brown pigmented cross-links developed among the lens proteins of older humans. Experiments 1 and 3 indicate, however, that glucose reacts with lens proteins in such a way that brown pigmented cross-links form among the proteins. And remember the main purpose of the experiments: the researcher is investigating the effects of glucose on lens proteins in order to see whether dietary sugar (glucose) damages proteins. The hypothesis that dietary sugar reacted with lens proteins to cause the brown pigmented cross-links found in older subjects would seem to be supported by the results of the three experiments (choice C).

10. J The relevant results are those from Experiment 2: the lens proteins of younger subjects were found to have formed cross-linked aggregates much less frequently than were the lens proteins of older subjects. So you would expect that the lens proteins of a 32-year-old man would have fewer cross-links than the lens proteins of an 80-year-old man (choice J).

11. C String together the hypotheses that were the correct answers from Questions 8 and 9, and you have the following overall hypothesis: dietary glucose causes brown pigmented (AGE) cross-links to form among lens proteins, and these brown cross-links in turn cause the formation of brown senile cataracts. According to this hypothesis, the excess glucose in an uncontrolled diabetic's blood should cause the formation of AGE cross-links among lens proteins and subsequently the development of senile cataracts (C).

Passage 3

This passage contains a lot of scientific information and terms that you probably have never seen before. Mesons, baryons, deep inelastic scattering experiments, the Millikan oil drop experiment—all of this is pretty intimidating until you remember that you are not expected to recognize or understand everything in the passage. Your job is to answer questions, not to learn particle physics, so don't worry about the stuff that looks alien.

Scientist 1 explains the Quark Model—the structure of protons, mesons, and baryons in general—and then proceeds to give the reasons she thinks the Quark Model is correct. It explains the existence of the many different types of mesons, and it predicted the properties of at least one meson. Although individual quarks have not been observed, the deep inelastic scattering experiments indicated that the proton did indeed have a substructure of "three distinct lumps," which agrees with the Quark Model.

Scientist 2 asserts, however, that the Quark Model is flawed. He argues that if quarks really existed, they would have been found already; since they haven't been found, they don't exist. In addition, he says, the Quark Model violates the Pauli exclusion principle, the rule that no two particles of half-integer spin can occupy the same state. The Δ^{++} baryon is cited as an example of a particle predicted by the Quark Model that violates the Pauli exclusion principle.

12. **G** Scientist 1 is a proponent of the Quark Model, which says that baryons (including the proton) and mesons are made up of quarks, which have fractional charge. Quarks have never been observed, however. You find out from Scientist 2 that quarks should be easy to distinguish from other particles because they would be the only ones with fractional charge. If a particle with fractional charge was detected, then, it would most likely be a quark, and this would strengthen Scientist 1's hypothesis that the Quark Model is correct. Mesons, baryons, and the Δ^{++} baryon have all been detected, but mere detection of them does not tell us anything about their substructure, so it cannot be used to support the Quark Model.

13. **C** Scientist 2 says that it should be easy to split the proton into quarks; that the quarks should be easy to distinguish because of their unique charge (Statement I); and that they should be stable, because they can't decay into lighter particles (Statement III). Statement II is wrong because it is Scientist 1's explanation of why quarks cannot be detected. Therefore, choice C is correct.

14. **F** Scientist 2 says that the Quark Model is wrong because it violates the Pauli exclusion principle, which states that no two particles of half-integer spin can occupy the same state. He says that in the Δ^{++} baryon, for example, the presence of two up quarks in the same state would violate the principle, so the model must be incorrect. If Scientist 1 were able to show, however, that quarks do not have half-integer spin (choice F), she could argue that the Pauli exclusion principle does not apply to quarks and thus counter Scientist 2's objections. Evidence that the D^{++} baryon exists (choice G) or that quarks have fractional charge (choice H) isn't going to help Scientist 1, because neither has anything to do with the Pauli exclusion principle. Evidence that quarks have the same spin as electrons (choice J) would only support Scientist 2's position.

15. **D** According to Scientist 2, the Δ^{++} baryon has three up quarks. Each up quark has a charge of +2/3 each, so the three quarks together have a total charge of 2 (D).

16. **G** Scientist 2 thinks that the Quark Model is flawed for two reasons: (1) quarks have not been detected experimentally, and they would have been if they existed, and (2) the Quark Model violates the Pauli exclusion principle. The first reason is paraphrased in choice G, the correct answer. Choice F is wrong because the existence of individual baryons, including protons, has been verified experimentally. Scientist 2 never says that he thinks particles cannot have fractional charge, nor does he complain that the Quark Model doesn't include electrons as elementary particles, so choices H and J are wrong as well.

17. **A** The deep inelastic scattering experiments, according to Scientist 1, showed that the proton has a substructure. The three distinct lumps that were found to bounce high-energy electrons back and scatter them through large angles were the three quarks that make up the proton (at least in Scientist 1's view), so choice A is correct.

18. H This question is a follow-up of the last one. If the three lumps were indeed quarks, then this supports the Quark Model because in the Quark Model the proton consists of three quarks. "Protons supposedly consist of three quarks" is not one of the choices, though, so you have to look for a paraphrase of this idea. Protons are baryons and not mesons, so choices F and G are out. Baryons, like the proton, are all supposed to consist of three quarks, so this rules out choice J and makes choice H the correct answer.

SAT or ACT? Score Comparison Chart

In the chart below, enter your results from the SAT and ACT practice quizzes and practice sets, and then compare your performance on equivalent sections. Convert each total score below to a percentage (using your calculator) to arrive at your % correct on each section. Then use this information to determine whether you're currently stronger on SAT or ACT questions.

Example: Todd Eisemann scores 3/4 (three out of four) on SAT Analogies, and 2/4 on SAT Sentence Completions. This would give him a score of 5/8 on SAT Short Verbal, or 62.5 %.

SAT	Score	ACT	Score
Short Verbal		**English**	
Practice Quizzes		*Practice Quizzes*	___/15
Analogies	___/4	**Total as a %**	=___%
Sentence Completions	+___/4		
Total	=___/8	*Practice Sets*	___/30
Total as a %	=___%	**Total as a %**	=___%
Practice Sets			
Analogies	___/30		
Sentence Completions	+___/30		
Total	=___/60		
Total as a %	=___%		
Critical Reading		**Reading Comp.**	
Practice Quizzes	___/8	*Practice Quizzes*	___/10
Total as a %	=___%	**Total as a %**	=___%
Practice Sets	___/21	*Practice Sets*	___/20
Total as a %	=___%	**Total as a %**	=___%
Math		**Math and Science**	
Practice Quizzes		*Practice Quizzes*	
Regular Math	___/7	Math	___/8
QCs	+___/4	Science	+___/8
Grid-ins	+___/4	**Total**	=___/16
Total	=___/15	**Total as a %**	=___%
Total as a %	=___%		
Practice Sets		*Practice Sets*	
Regular Math	___/30	Math	___/30
QCs	+___/30	Science	+___/18
Grid-ins	+___/30	**Total**	=___/48
Total	=___/90	**Total as a %**	=___%
Total as a %	=___%		